THE ARMY OF JAMES II, 1685–1688

The Birth of the British Army

Stephen Ede-Borrett

'This is the Century of the Soldier', Falvio Testir, Poet, 1641

Helion & Company

Helion & Company Limited
26 Willow Road
Solihull
West Midlands
B91 1UE
England
Tel. 0121 705 3393
Fax 0121 711 4075
Email: info@helion.co.uk
Website: www.helion.co.uk
Twitter: @helionbooks
Visit our blog http://blog.helion.co.uk/

Published by Helion & Company 2017
Designed and typeset by Serena Jones
Cover designed by Paul Hewitt, Battlefield Design (www.battlefield-design.co.uk)
Printed by Henry Ling Limited, Dorchester, Dorset

Cover: King James II in the Uniform of a General Officer *c*.1686. Godfrey Kneller, Oil on Canvas, National Army Museum London Collection, ©NAM, Reproduced With Permission.

ISBN 978-1-911512-36-3

British Library Cataloguing-in-Publication Data.
A catalogue record for this book is available from the British Library.

For details of other military history titles published by Helion & Company Limited contact the above address, or visit our website: http://www.helion.co.uk.

We always welcome receiving book proposals from prospective authors.

Contents

Foreword

My immediate reaction to learning that Stephen Ede-Borrett was writing a book on the army of James II was to admire the bravery of following in the footsteps of John Childs and his seminal work of 1980. However, nearly forty years have passed and it is time for another and indeed a fresh view. Unlike Childs, Ede-Borrett narrowly focuses upon James' army and whilst it may seem to some that he does so at the expense of contextualising decisions, in doing so he allows the reader to concentrate upon the finer organisational and operational details of the regiments. My recent book explored how and why James increased the size of his royal regular forces, literally at the expense of the militia, and this one completes that story, by describing the army he created, often giving new information not already in the general domain. Having worked at the Royal Armouries I particularly enjoyed the revelation concerning their 'silk armour'!

Ede-Borrett packs his book with pertinent information, for example not only does he give the areas from where the various new regiments of Horse were raised but also gives the locations and establishments of England's various garrisons. Other new topics explored include the colours and cornets carried, information not made available to general readers since Milne published his limited edition of just 400 copies in 1889. The great majority of the book's content has been researched from the original primary or contemporary sources, and I am particularly envious of his access to the Royal Archives at Windsor; never the easiest of places to visit. However, he does not make the work a compendium of tables, and alongside a first class piece of scholarship full of close reference to original sources with perceptive conclusions, he also delivers a rattling good read which holds the attention and maintains the narrative flow.

In his military aspirations James II was by all accounts a fastidious planner who tended to micro-manage. In order to keep him abreast of progress and developments and to ensure they did not get anything wrong, his military staff wrote things down in great detail. These documents are a boon to historians and many of them have been meticulously searched by Ede-Borrett, gleaned for their telling gems and are now presented for our edification. Not only does this work delight those interested in military history with its plethora of facts and wealth of information but in appreciating the scale of James' undertaking we are encouraged to have a greater understanding of just what a fine administrator this king was, even if he later proved a flawed monarch. Despite Charles II being credited with its 1660 foundation, Ede-Borrett shows us that it was James II who, by hard work and application in less than three years, took his brother's 'guards and garrisons' and augmented and moulded them to create the modern regular British Army.

Christopher L. Scott,
Swindon, July 2016.

Preface

I have long been fascinated by the early British Army but the more I studied the subject the greater was my impression that James II's place in the Army's creation has been, and often still is, deliberately suppressed. In extreme cases some recent regimental histories of James' Regiments manage to cover the entire early years of the regiment without even mentioning the King who authorised their raising!

In 1935 C. T. Atkinson wrote that it was perhaps time to redress the balance of historians' writing that had studiously chosen to exclude James II or at the very least play down his part in the creation of the British Army.[1] Since then – now coming up to a century ago – the work of a few historians, particularly of John Childs, has moved that situation along somewhat although it still has a long way to go before James' true part in the creation of the British Army is fully recognised. I hope that this work will go a little bit further in correcting that and shed some light upon this first real English Army since the fall of Cromwell.

I have deliberately tried to avoid covering the same ground as John Childs' seminal trilogy of books although there are certainly some unavoidable crossovers with the first two of these. For details of the internal 'bureaucracy' of the Carolean and Jacobean Armies and much of the military politics of the period I make no excuses in referring the reader to Childs' books. Most of what is below, however, is I hope new to many.

As far as possible, I have used either primary sources or those secondary sources where the primary source has been cited. There are, sadly, many assertions made about the armies of the 17th century that are based on 'tradition', guesswork or just plain 'wishful thinking' and I have tried to correct these where I can but I have no doubt that I may still have fallen into this trap on occasion, and if this has happened I apologise in advance.

I would like to take this opportunity to thank the staff of the many libraries and archives whose help has been invaluable in my research for this work. My particular thanks go to the staffs of the British Library Rare Books Department, the National Army Museum Library, the Royal Library at Windsor and the Royal Archives at Windsor (thanks for the coffee). My thanks also to Mary who has often been a 'manuscript widow' but whose

---

1   C. T. Atkinson, 'Two Hundred and Fifty Years Ago', *Journal of the Society for Army Historical Research*, Vol. XIV (1935).

encouragement has been constant, and to Charles Singleton, the Century of the Soldier series editor, and to Duncan Rogers, both of Helion, who have similarly encouraged this work and been patient when the manuscript deadline has shifted again.

Without the groundbreaking work of Clifford Walton, Cecil Lawson and John Childs much of this book would not have been possible and I fully acknowledge the debt I owe them. I would additionally like to acknowledge the help of some of the others who have worked in this field but particularly Chris Scott, John Tincey, Keith Roberts and my friend the late Bill Braham, all of whom have given freely of their time, often in somewhat relaxed conversations and when I am sure that they would have preferred to be at the bar; truly 'If I have seen further it is because I have stood on the shoulders of giants' and, as always, any errors that remain in the text are my own.

Notes on the text

In order to keep a consistency within the text regiments have not been listed within an arm by the modern order of precedence, since many regiments have not survived and the recent amalgamations have destroyed any semblance of seniority and heritage anyway; nor are they listed by their contemporary order of precedence, which of course often varied with each change of colonel. The compromise that I have chosen is to list regiments simply by the date of the commission of their first colonel, which I hope enables the reader to follow the details of a particular regiment more easily.

It should be noted that the English and Scots military establishments were not united until the Act of Union of 1707, which is the true date of birth of the British Army as opposed to that of the English Army or the Scots Army. The Irish Army remained separate from the Anglo-Scots / British Army until 1803 (which, it has to be said, proved of very great convenience to various 18th century governments!) However throughout this whole period the English Crown paid for the bulk of the army, as its army establishment was considerably larger than that of the other kingdoms, and is thus always considered as the senior force (thus the precedence and rank of a regiment was taken from its first placing on the English establishment). It should, I hope, always be obvious when the term 'army' refers to the force of one kingdom or to the total armed forces of the Three Kingdoms.

The rank and file of the army's foot appear in the various warrants of the period as 'souldier', 'centinell', 'private centinell', and even 'standing centinell' each with numerous variations of spelling as might be expected. All are simply terms for the individual private soldier and there would appear to be no consistent reason why one term is chosen over another.

In addition to the 'marching regiments' there were a number of 'Guards and Garrisons' scattered throughout both England and Scotland (the majority of those in Ireland disappeared into the new regiments formed in 1672 and 1684). These units varied in strength from a few men to complete companies but as the permanent establishments grew larger so most of these independent companies were absorbed or disbanded. This was particularly so during the summer and late autumn of 1685. Where these units existed as complete companies they are covered in as much depth as possible below. In addition, Scotland boasted a small number of 'independent Highland companies' (raised in 1662 by order of Charles II), but these served as more of a 'local police force' than as a part of the army and I have made no attempt to cover them here.

Similarly the Yeomen of the Guard, The Yeomen Warders of the Tower, The Gentlemen Pensioners in England and the Battle-Axe Guards in Ireland are omitted, as although these were all officially part of the armies in the widest sense, by the 1660s they were all purely ceremonial bodies.

The traditional 'red coat' of the British soldier was prominent (although not universal) in James' army (or more correctly armies, but I have usually used army in a generic rather than a specific sense) but the exact shade of red is a matter of much contention. It was certainly *not* 'British Scarlet', except perhaps for some officers – although even these often preferred their coats to be of crimson cloth – but was a much darker brick red colour. However, with the vagaries of the natural dyes available to our 17th century ancestors the actual hue of red must have varied almost from man to man and certainly from issue to issue. Modern experiments with early dyes show that even the usual pillar box or brick reds rapidly fade to a red-brown, which is probably how much of the army looked quite soon after the coats were issued.

In all examples where a standard, guidon or colour is illustrated this is shown as the obverse. The reverse was always, or at least as far as any records show, identical.

Where there are omissions in the tables of uniform colours, the reason is simply that I have been unable to find that information and rather than make a so-called 'intelligent guess' I have chosen to leave the blanks in the hope that future research may fill them in.

Currency

To many readers of this work the joyous eccentricity of the pre-decimal English currency system that was in use until 1971 will be a mystery, so this may help.

12 pence (d) = 1 shilling (s)
20 shillings (s) = 1 pound (£ or sometimes l)

It was usual to write currency as pound / shilling / pence, or if the amount was less than a pound, simply shilling / pence. Thus one pound, ten shilling and eight pence would appear simply as:

1 / 10 / 8 (or sometimes as 1 / 10 / 08)

The abbreviations themselves incidentally do not refer to 'pounds, shillings, pence' but come from the Latin 'Libra, Sestercii, Denarrii' – hence l / s / d.

The 'New Pence', introduced in 1971 was at the rate of 100p = £1, thus:

1s = 5p
2s 6d = 12.5p

and so on.

Introduction

The creation of the British Army is traditionally dated to the Restoration of Charles II in May 1660, and whilst there may certainly be a strong argument for this, in February 1685 when Charles died and his brother James ascended the throne as James II, the total establishment of the combined English and Scots armies was only 9,215 men, all ranks (Childs gives the English Army at the beginning of June 1685 as 7,472 men in the marching regiments and 1,393 in the independent companies[1]). By 1 November 1688 on the eve of the 'Glorious Revolution', James II had raised the strength of the English Army alone to a comparatively massive total of 34,592 all ranks, made up of:

> 6,002 horse
> 1,994 dragoons
> 26,596 foot.[2]

This was an almost fourfold increase over three and a half years – the largest pro rata peacetime expansion of the British Army in its history. In 1659 the Cromwellian army had mustered barely 40,000 men,[3] James had built an army as large as Cromwell's!

In the same period the Scots Army had barely changed its strength; it added only a single regiment of foot from the recalled Anglo-Scots Brigade in 1688 and a few additional companies to its existing regiments to its tiny establishment.

Similarly the Irish Army hardly changed its establishment during James' reign, but as John Childs comments it was not a field army in the true sense but more of a 'territorial force', although even so it sent a brigade to England in 1688. By November 1688 the Irish Army had added only a single regiment of dragoons, raised in England in 1685, of 590 men plus officers, and a single regiment of foot, raised in England from returnees of the Anglo-Scots Brigade from Dutch service. On James II's accession the army's total strength

---

1   John Childs, *General Percy Kirke and the Later Stuart Army* (London: Bloomsbury, 2014), p. 71.

2   All figures from Clifford Walton, *History of the British Standing Army, A.D. 1660 to 1700* (London: Harrison, 1894) p. 496.

3   Corelli Barnett, *Britain And Her Army: A Military, Political and Social History of the British Army, 1509–1970* (London: Allen Lane, 1970), p. 115.

is calculated, by J. C. Beckett, at strength of 8,000 men,[4] or more precisely by John Childs at 8,238 men and 406 commissioned officers;[5] either way it was not much over 9,000 when James fled in December 1688. Unfortunately the majority of the contemporary documents relating to the Kingdom of Ireland at this period were destroyed in the early 20th century, and we are therefore reliant on such small pieces of information as remain, so there is much about this army that we may never know.

The army of James II was, for the first time since the Restoration, and in strong contrast to the force of 'Guards and Garrisons' that he had inherited, a true army with strength in all arms and it had gained much of that command and control, logistics and training that was required for it to function as an effective army. The annual Hounslow 'Camp of Instruction' allowed for battalions to be exercised as brigades and even, as at the 1687 camp, to work together in mock battlefield conditions. The King was justifiably proud of his army when he wrote that he 'had formed a very complete body of men tho' not numerous, with the reputation of being the best paid, the best equipped and the most sightly troops of any in Europe.'[6]

It is, as Correlli Barnet noted, contentious as to the date of the actual creation of the English Army as distinct from the Guards and Garrisons but 'it might well be said that if the British royal standing army was in fact founded at one given time, it was between 1685 and 1688, and that James II was the army's creator.'[7]

King James II of England and Ireland, VII of Scotland. (Public domain) Second son of Charles I, born at St James's Palace on 14 October 1633. James succeeded his elder brother Charles II at the latter's death on 24 February 1685 and was crowned at Westminster Abbey on 23 April of the same year. His reign is often taken as ending when he first fled England on 11 December 1685 (he returned and finally fled on 11 December 1688) but legally he remained King until Parliament declared he had abdicated on 28 January 1689 (and on 11 April 1689 by the Scottish Parliament). James died in exile in France on 16 September 1701.

It is also worth noting that in 1685 Sir Winston Churchill, a Burgess of Lyme, moved that a supply be granted 'for the Army'. This despite the fact that, constitutionally, a standing army was considered illegal until at least as late as the early 18th century. Nonetheless Churchill's words were an acknowledgment that England was gaining (regaining if you take into account the Cromwellian Military Government's army) an army rather than a few disparate regiments officially termed the Guards and Garrisons which were, in truth, very little more than that. John Tincey perhaps summed it up

---

4   J. C. Beckett, 'The Irish Armed Forces, 1660–1685', in John Bossy, *Essays Presented to Michael Roberts* (Belfast: Blackstaff Press, 1976), p. 53.
5   Childs, *General Percy Kirke and the Later Stuart Army*, p. 121.
6   Cecil C. P. Lawson, *A History of the Uniforms of the British Army, Vol. 1 – the Beginnings to 1760* (London: Norman Military Communications, 1940), p. 38.
7   Barnett, p. 120.

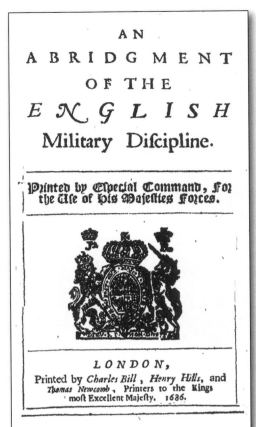

AN
ABRIDGMENT
OF THE
ENGLISH
Military Discipline.

Printed by Especial Command, For the Use of his Majesties Forces.

LONDON,
Printed by *Charles Bill*, *Henry Hills*, and *Thomas Newcomb*, Printers to the Kings most Excellent Majesty. 1686.

Title page of the 1686 edition of *An Abridgement of English Military Discipline*, the English Army's first official army-wide drill book. (Author's collection)

Printed by the Charles Hill, Henry Hills and Thomas Newcomb 'Printers to the Kings most Excellent Majesty', and 'Printed by Especiall Command, for the Use of his Majesties Forces'. John Bill, who printed the first edition in 1678 and after whom the book is usually called, died c.1680.

succinctly: that the reign of James II saw 'a transformation of the English army from a collection of disparate units into a large and well-organised military force.'[8]

In law however the army continued to be officially termed, and indeed considered, as 'Guards and Garrisons'; a fiction which continued until well after James fell from power. It was this 'consideration' that was highly influential in the 'great disbandment' of 1697–1699 which reduced the army (albeit very temporarily) back to the establishment of Charles II's reign.[9]

Under James II for the first time the army gained an official, army-wide drill book, *An Abridgement of English Military Discipline* (usually known simply, although perhaps somewhat inaccurately, as 'Bill') 'printed by special command for the use of His Majesty's Forces' and officially authorised by the King.[10] Similar drill books had, of course, already existed for well over a century and even Bill in its earliest form had first been published many years earlier.[11] But what was new, was that James decreed that this was an official drill to be used throughout the army thus ensuring that disparate companies and regiments could operate together. The appointment in early 1687 of an Inspector General of the Exercise and Garrisons, who was responsible for ensuring the standardisation of drill throughout the army, served to further enforce this uniformity. Alan Guy commented that 'In one sector William of Orange [after the Revolution of 1688] found his newly acquired British army to be as fit for service as any armed force in Europe – its drill and tactics.[12] This says much about not just the army's drill but also the success of the annual Hounslow 'Camp of Instruction', itself another innovation which had not previously existed even under the Protectorate.

---

8   John Tincey, *Sedgemoor 1685: Marlborough's First Victory* (Barnsley: Pen & Sword Military, 2005), p. 25.

9   See John Childs, *The British Army of William III, 1689–1702* (Manchester: Manchester University Press, 1987).

10 London, 1685. The drill book was printed by Henry Hills and Thomas Newcomb, 'printers to the King's Most Excellent Majesty'. Hills and Newcomb were also responsible for the printing of the twice-weekly *London Gazette*.

11 'Bill' probably first appeared in 1678, a new printing/edition appeared in 1682, another in 1684, and further editions in 1685 and 1686 (both of these latter editions were 'officially authorised'). The early editions varied little from their predecessor but the 1685 edition was significantly different and the number of copies of the 1685 and 1686 editions that survive are indicative of its proliferation at the time. John Tincey's *Monmouth's Drill Book* (Leigh on Sea: Partizan Press, 1986), contains an excellent account of the development of *An Abridgement...*

12 Alan Guy, 'The Fall and Rise of the British Army 1660–1704' in Alan Guy and Jenny Spencer-Smith (eds.), *1688 Glorious Revolution? The Fall and Rise of the British Army 1660–1704* (London: National Army Museum, 1988), p. 11.

(132)

First Rank of Musketiers, Kneel.

Which they are to do by Falling back with the Right Legs, and not stepping forward with their Left, and keeping their Muskets so low, that the Two other Ranks may Fire easily over them.

At the same time that the Command is given for the First Rank to Kneel, The whole Rank of Officers at the Head of the Battalion, retire at one time into the Intervals, just behind them of the first Rank of Soldiers, but are to take care that the Soldiers perform their Duties. The Officers (as is said before) are to have their Pikes in the posture conform-

conformable to the Pikemen. And those with the Musketiers are to Kneel as they do.

When the first Rank is Commanded to Kneel, the Two other Ranks of Musketiers are to Close forward, as also the Five Ranks of Pikes as close as they can with conveniency to use their Arms, without any other Word of Command.

Two last Ranks present.

Which they are always to do Breast high, and the First of the Two is always to stoop without any word of Command. And the Pikes at the same Word of Command are to Charge their Pikes, and to continue so Charged.

I 3   Fire

James, unlike Charles, had a very positive attitude towards his army; whereas the latter seems to have looked at his Guards and Garrisons as a 'necessary evil' James was actually proud of the army and genuinely appears to have enjoyed the company of the military – perhaps something that went back to his service under Turenne in the 1650s.

Perhaps the most visible and obvious outward appearance of this pride are the portraits of the King in the dress of a general officer. For many years the aristocracy had evoked a military appearance by having their portraits painted wearing 'studio' three-quarter armour;[13] James had similar portraits made but also went beyond this convention and chose to be painted in a military coat, for which there was no precedent in England (except perhaps for a few non-aristocratic officers and, of course, the well-known painting of the Duke of Monmouth which celebrated his time commanding the English Army in France in the 1670s). James had, of course, served under Turenne with distinction in the 1650s and, from his memoirs, apparently both enjoyed his time on campaign and had a genuine aptitude as a staff officer. Conversely there are no paintings of Charles in military uniform – although it might be

Pages 132 and 133 of *An Abridgement of English Military Discipline*: instructions for how to fire by one rank and two ranks in battle. (Author's collection)

---

13   The armour in such portraits was rarely, if ever, the property of the sitter, it usually belonged to the studio. The same suit can sometimes be identified on different sitters.

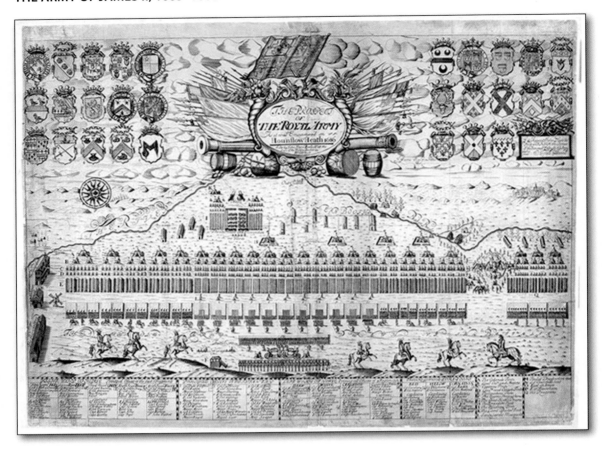

The Prospect of the Royal Army …. on Hounslow Heath 1686. (Private collection)

Such broadsheets must have served almost as propaganda pieces for the army. The number of examples that survive speaks for large numbers being printed and sold at the time.

argued that this was because Charles was more sensitive to public opinion and its view of the army (too many remembered the military dictatorship of Oliver Cromwell). If at the time the paintings of James in uniform did receive any negative comments, they must have been fairly private as none have survived to be recorded by history. At the 1686 camp in Hounslow, James, wearing military uniform, perhaps that in the portrait now in the collection of the National Army Museum, rode at the head of his army as he led it in review past the multitude of Londoners who had come to the Heath to view the spectacle and received some acclaim for the 'show'.

The annual mustering of the army on Hounslow Heath is usually portrayed by later 'Whig' historians as an attempt to 'overawe' the City and bully it into being more amenable to the King and his policies, but despite assertions otherwise the camp was not a permanent garrison on the Heath[14] – it was only of around eight to ten weeks' duration – and in reality any such implied threat would have quickly disappeared as the army dispersed when the camp broke up. It is difficult to assess whether, in the long term James really intended the Army to be seen as a threat – he reigned for barely four years – but Charles

---

14 As asserted by Michael Barthorp, *The Armies of Britain, 1485–1980* (London: National Army Museum, 1981), p. 35, who states that 'The camp remained in being for three years'. This claim is not an unusual one from James' detractors despite the facts to the contrary.

had similarly mustered his small forces during the Dutch War and again with the return of the Tangier Garrison in 1684. It is much more likely that James' intention was more prosaic and he simply wanted to train his regiments as an Army, something that was impossible without such musters, and that any other effect was by way of a 'bonus' neither looked for nor planned.

From 1686 this annual camp was officially termed a 'Camp of Instruction', which lends some credence that it was indeed James' primary intention to train his forces to operate as an army. As a choice of location, Hounslow was chosen to be convenient for the King's summer residence at Windsor – certainly a great many Londoners visited the camp to witness the parades and mock battles without any apparent feeling of being threatened. Quoting from contemporary accounts John Childs says that the influx of civilians turned the heath 'into more of a funfair than an encampment.'[15] In February 1686 Commissary General Shales erected a semi-permanent market on the Heath for 'the tyme that the forces are encamped' and it was proposed that this would continue 'on thursdays weekly forever for the benefit of the neighbouring towns'.[16]

Top: James II 3d coin, 1686. Bottom: James II 4d coin, 1686. (Both author's collection)

As part of the increased professionalism of the army, under James regiments gained some medical staff – the King added a regimental chirurgeon as well as a chirurgeon's mate to a regiment's staff. During the annual musters on Hounslow Heath the King even had a temporary hospital built there and a nursing staff provided to look after the sick, and no doubt also some injured, soldiery. This nursing provision continued for soldiers already in the hospital even after the camp had broken up, and Margarett Harris and Mary Hopkins were each paid £18 per annum as matrons there.[17]

But there were other examples of the evolution of the force into a professional, and effective, army. When James ascended the throne in 1685 many 'unfit men had been retained in service … [and] large numbers … were incapable of fulfilling their role.'[18] Partly, of course, this was because any discharged veteran had no place to go and little chance of civilian employment. Building on the foresight of his brother Charles gave James the opportunity to correct this fault through the use of Chelsea Hospital to take in the infirm veterans,[19] but to

---

15   Childs, *General Percy Kirke and the Later Stuart Army*, p. 118.

16   *Calendar of State Papers, Domestic Series*; James II, Volume II, January 1686–May 1687 (London: HMSO, 1964), under the date of 3 February 1686.

17   V. A. Roseweare, 'Notes on the Hospital on Hounslow Heath', Unpublished typescript, undated, in the Local Collection of Richmond Town Library.

18   Eric Gruber von Arni, *Hospital Care and the British Standing Army, 1660–1714* (Aldershot: Ashgate, 2006), p. 39.

19   Although, the creation of the Hospitals of Chelsea in England and Kilmainham in Ireland may owe more than a little to Charles' consistent imitation of his cousin Louis XIV – in this case the

further care for his troops after their service, ensuring that they were not on the streets begging, James instituted a formal level of army pensions. These were available to any who qualified for the hospitals but could not yet gain admission due to a lack of vacancies, but were also to be automatically given to any soldier who had completed 20 years of service.

These pension rates were:[20]

Rank	Pension, per day
Corporal of a regiment of horse	1s 6d
Trooper of the regiments of Horse Guards	1s 6d
Trooper of a regiment of horse	1s 0d
Corporal of a regiment of dragoons	9d
Private soldier of a regiment of dragoons	6d
Sergeant of a regiment of foot	11d
Corporall of a regiment of foot	7d
Drummer of a regiment of foot	7d
Private soldier of a regiment of foot	4d
plus	1d for clothing
Master gunner	1s 2d
Gunner	7d

If a soldier was killed in service then his widow received a lump sum equivalent to 11 months' pay, or, if there was no widow, the same sum was payable to his mother providing she was over 50 and herself a widow. There were further orders for allowances for unmarried children.

James recognised that as well as care for his rank and file there needed to be some change in the army's officer corps to change it from 'an army of courtiers to a modern army'.[21] However this could not be done immediately, nor was it universally popular with many of those courtiers who had seen their army rank as a sinecure; John Childs cites a number of examples of officers who left the army 'rather than endure the fatigue and inconvenience of the Hounslow Camp.' Even by 1688 the process of professionalisation was not complete, but at least it can be said that James improved the army's officer corps and the army was 'treated as a serious career.'[22]

As has already been said, in February 1685 the army was less than 10,000 of all ranks, it had no formal general staff, little logistical support and could have barely functioned as an army in the Continental sense if it had been called on to fight a war, so it really was genuinely little more than the 'Guards and Garrisons' of its name. James II changed the disparate regiments that he inherited into what was truly the first 'British Army' and therefore can rightly claim be considered as the true creator of the army; unfortunately his

---

latter's creation of the French Army Hospital at Les Invalides.

20   Arni, p. 40.
21   John Childs, *The Army, James II and the Glorious Revolution* (Manchester: Manchester University Press, 1980), p. 40.
22   *Ibid*.

reputation (and here I am making no comment on the political side of his reign, purely the military) is still suffering from generations of Whig historians, and it is still not unusual to see regimental histories of James' regiments which manage to avoid even mentioning the king that ordered their raising!

On 10 December 1688, the day before he left Whitehall in his first attempt at flight, James wrote to his commander-in-chief, the Earl of Feversham; the letter was effectively an order to disband the army.[23] William went to great efforts to reverse this order and keep the British Army in being, which perhaps reflects on how the new king saw the quality, or potential quality, of the army he had inherited.

Whilst many in Parliament and the country had genuinely feared James' army and were vociferous in their opposition to it (Cromwell's rule as a military dictator backed by a regular army had ended barely three decades earlier, within the living memory of many) and indeed backed 'The Glorious Revolution' out of a fear of a new military dictatorship, it is worth noting that William III, the 'Protestant Saviour' did not disband the army and resisted the forced disbandments of the late 1690s, a fact conveniently ignored by those same Whig historians who berate James for its creation.

James II finally left England for France on 23 December, and the army he left behind was disorganised, demoralised and its morale had collapsed – as evidenced by the massive increase in desertions during the months following. Nonetheless it was rebuilt fairly quickly by William and within a few years was again, as James had called it, amongst the best in Europe and within two decades it would destroy the so-called 'Finest Army in Europe' at Blenheim.

At its highest number just before William's invasion in 1688 only some 11 percent of the army's officers had been Catholics, but barely a third of the Army's officers overall continued their career under William. Of the other two thirds roughly half had been cashiered because of their overt loyalty to James and the rest had simply refused to serve under the new king, including every senior officer except John Churchill and Percy Kirke.[24] It is a testament to the discipline and professionalism of James' Army that it could recover from this chaos within a year.

---

23 National Archives SP28/2 f. 79.; cf. also John Callow, *James II: The Triumph and the Tragedy* (Kew: National Archives, 2005), pp. 82–85.

24 Childs, *General Percy Kirke and the Later Stuart Army*, pp. 115–116.

1

The General Officers and Staff

In the course of his reign James issued commissions to a number of general officers as well as those for the necessary army staff. As at all periods a commission as a general officer did not mean that the officer gave up command of his regiment or troop, as a comparison of the list below with Appendix I will show; neither did a staff command alter the officer's Army rank as this list demonstrates.

The generals and staff who received commissions and appointments from James were:[1]

Officer	Rank	Date of Commission
James Pearce	Chirugeon Generall of Our Land Forces	15 February 1685
Sir Bernard de Gomme	Surveyor of the Ordnance	23 February 1685
Sir Christopher Musgrave	Lieutenant-General of the Ordnance	23 March 1685
Henry Sheere	Comptroller of the Artillery, 'for this present expedition'	15 June 1685[2]
Nicholas Sandford	Commissary of the Train, 'for this present expedition'	15 June 1685[3]
William Craven, Earl Craven	Lieutenant-General over all Our Forces	18 June 1685
Louis de Duras, Earl of Feversham	Lieutenant-General over all Our Forces	19 June 1685
Robert Werden	Brigadier over all Our Forces	19 June 1685
Sir John Fenwick	Brigadier over all Our Forces	19 June 1685
Captain John Shales	Commissary General for the Army	23 June 1685
Dr Thomas Lawrence	Physician-General to the Army	24 June 1685
John, Lord Churchill	Major General over all Our Forces as well Horse and Foot	3 July 1685

1   Mainly extracted from Charles Dalton's *English Army Lists and Commission Registers, 1661–1714*, Volume 2 (London: Francis Edwards, 1894), pp. 40–64 and 67–68. Hereafter referred to as Dalton, *English*.
2   National Archives, Kew, SP 44/164, f. 189.
3   National Archives, Kew, SP 44/164, f. 188.

Officer	Rank	Date of Commission
Hugh Mackaye	Major General over all Our Forces as well Horse and Foot	3 July 1685
Piercy Kirke	Brigadier over all Our Forces as well Horse and Foot	3 July 1685[4]
Edward Sackville	Brigadier over all Our Forces as well Horse and Foot	3 July 1685
Robert Ramsay	Adjutant-General of our Foot Forces	13 July 1685
George Douglas, Earl of Dumbarton	Lt-Gen over all Our Forces as well Horse and Foot	31 July 1685
Robert Werden	Maj-Gen in same form as his comm as Brig	31 July 1685
Major Charles Orby	Adjutant-Gen of our Horse Forces	1 August 1685
Gilbert Thomas	Provost Marshal Gen of Our Forces	1 August 1685
Major Martin Beckman	Chief Engineer[5]	30 November 1685
Lt. Col. Thomas Maxwell	Quartermaster General of all Our Forces	1 January 1686
Richard Whittle	Apothecary-General of Our Army	1 January 1686[6]
John Maugridge[7]	'Our Drum Major-Genl of Our Forces'	1 May 1688[8]
Ferdinando Watkins	'Chirugeon of Our Hospitall to Attend Our Army'	9 October 1688
John Churchill	Lieutenant-Generall of our Forces	7 November 1688
Edward Sackville	Major-Generall of our Forces	7 November 1688
Robert Werden	Lieutenant-Generall over all HM's Forces	7 November 1688
Percy Kirke	Major-Generall of our Forces	8 November 1688[9]

4   In August 1685 Kirke was also being referred to as 'Comander in Chief of Our Forces in the West'; National Archives, Kew, WO55/1, f. 222, warrant dated 6th August 1685.

5   'in place of Sr Bernard de Gomme deceased', National Archives, Kew, WO44/164, f. 282.

6   'Richard Whittle Gent.' was already being referred to as 'Apothecary to the Army' during the Sedgemoor campaign. National Archives, Kew, WO55/2, ff. 133–4.

7   In 1684 on Nathan Brooks' army list, a Robert Maugridge is given as kettledrummer to the 1st Troop of Horse Guards. If he is a relation, which seems likely, then this was apparently a musically talented family.

8   Dalton, *English*, p. 159 refers to this being the sole commission for the rank during the reigns of both Charles II and James II. Maugridge however is referred to by this rank in June 1685 (National Archives, Kew, WO5/1, f. 83 et seq.) Maugridge died in office in 1705 (NS) and was succeeded by his brother: 'Whereas John Mawgridge Esq; deceased, late Drum-Major-General, is succeeded in that Employment by his Brother Mr. Robert Mawgridge; He does hereby give Notice, That all Deputations heretofore granted by his said Brother (for Impressing, Drums, Fifes, Houtboys, &c.) are void, and of no effect: And if any Officers, have occasion to impress Drums, Fifes, Hautboys, &c. as aforesaid, for Her Majesty's Service, they are desired to give Notice thereof to the said Mr Robert Mawgridge, now Her majesty's Drum-Major-General, within two Doors of the Queen's-Head in Cartwright-street, Westminster.' *London Gazette Numb 4099, From Monday February 19 to Thursday February 22 1704*, London 1705.

9   This commission is not listed in Dalton, *English*, but is in the *Calendar of State Papers, Domestic Series*.

Officer	Rank	Date of Commission
Earl of Arran	Brigadier-Generall over all the Horse	9 November 1688
Edmund Main	Brigadier-Generall over all the Horse	9 November 1688
Sir Theophilus Oglethorpe	Brigadier-Generall over all the Foot	11 November 1685
Thomas Buchan	Brigadier-Generall over all the Foot	12 November 1688
Richard Hamilton	Major-Generall over all HM's Forces	12 November 1688
Israel Fielding	Comptroller-Generall of the Provisions of the Army	15 November 1688

Additionally lieutenants in the various troops of horse guards were commissioned as 'Brigadier and Eldest Lieutenant in…' which gave them 'general officer' rank within the army.

Officers for the Scots Establishment[10]

Officer	Rank	Date of Commission
Andrew Middleton	Muster-Master General of all Our Forces in Scotland	30 March 1685
Matthew Hamilton	Adjutant-General of all Our Forces in Scotland	30 March 1685
George Douglas, Earl of Dumbarton	Commander-in-Chief of all Our Forces in Scotland	2 May 1685
Captain George Barclay	'to be employed in Our Service for the inspecting, reviewing, and exercising Our Forces throughout Scotland'	2 May 1685
James Douglas	Brigadier of the Horse and Foot in Scotland	16 May 1685
John Graham	Brigadier of the Horse and Foot in Scotland	18 May 1685
Thomas Dalzell	Lieut-General 'of all his Majesty's Forces in Scotland'	30 May 1685
Hugh Mackay	Major-General of his Majesty's Forces in Scotland	4 June 1685
William Drummond	Lieut-General of all his Majesty's Forces in Scotland[11]	7 October 1685
James Douglas	'to be Master-General of the Ordnance in Scotland'	26 October 1685
William Borthwick	Surgeon-Major of His Majesty's Forces in Scotland	24 March 1686
John Graham	Major-General of all his Majesty's [Horse] Forces in Scotland	20 September 1686

---

10 Mainly extracted from Charles Dalton, *The Scots Army, 1661–1688* (London: Eyre & Spottiswoode, 1909), pp. 165–166. Hereafter referred to as 'Dalton, Scots'.

11 'in place of Lieut-General Thomas Dalyell of Binns deceased'.

Officer	Rank	Date of Commission
Sir Charles Carney	'for inspecting and exercising his Majesty's Forces in Scotland excepting Our Royal Reg^t of Horse Guards and Our Royal Regt of Horse.'	31 December 1686
John Douglas	His Majesty's Secretary at War to all his Forces in Scotland during his Majesty's pleasure only'	4 May 1688
James Cathcart	'first and Chief Commissary of all Musters'	1 October 1688
Sir George Munro	Major-General of all his Majesty's [Militia] Forces in Scotland	24 October 1688
Captain James Campbell	Commissary of Our Train of Artillery in Scotland	22 October 1686
Colonel James Douglas	Master-General of His Majesty's Ordnance in Scotland	26 October 1686
Thomas Buchan	Brigadier over all the Foot	12 November 1688
Sergeant John Stitt	Commissary of the Trains [of Artillery] in Scotland	12 November 1688
John Sleazer	Captain of Our Artillery Train[12]	12 November 1688

Note: Barclay's (1685) and Carney's (1686) commissions were by Royal Warrant and appear to be intended to bring the Scots regiments into line with the ways of doing things in the English Army, since there is no equivalent warrant for an English officer.

Officers for the Irish Establishment:

Officer	Rank	Date of Commission
Sir Abraham Yarner, Bt	Muster Master General of Ireland	pre-17 August 1684[13]
Earl of Granard	Lieutenant-General of the Army in Ireland	31 July 1684[14]
Captain Frederick Fieffe	Engineer and Fire-Master of Ireland	1 January 1685[15]
Richard Talbot, Earl of Tyrconnell	Lieutenant-Generall of the Army in Ireland	April 1686
Justin MacCarthy[16]	Major General	1 March 1686
Richard Hamilton	Brigadier	April 1686

---

12 This is the Scots artillery train that marched into England in October, to support the King against William of Orange's invasion.

13 *Calendar of State Papers, Domestic Series*, James II, May 1 1684–February 5 1685 (London: HMSO, 1938), p. 121.

14 *Ibid.*, pp. 108–109.

15 *Ibid.*, p. 238; Charles Dalton, Irish Army Lists, 1660–1685 (London: private circulation, 1907), p. 146. gives the date of Fieffe's commission as 6 December 1684.

16 In 1688, when James summoned a brigade of the Irish Army to England to assist in resisting William of Orange's invasion, it was commanded by MacCarthy as a Lieutenant-General, although the commission for this promotion cannot be traced. National Archives, Kew, WO5/3, f. 284.

Officer	Rank	Date of Commission
The Lord Primate of all Ireland	Chaplain General of the Army in Ireland	31 January 1687
Sir William Stewart, Viscount Mountjoy	Brigadier	2 March 1687
Henry Brenne	Quartermaster General of the Horse of Our Army in Ireland	1684
Sir Charles Murray	Quartermaster General of the Army in Ireland	28 April 1684
William, Viscount Mountjoy	Master-General of Our Ordnance in Ireland	28 April 1684

Organisation

The staff of James' army was, by modern standards, tiny in the extreme but few armies of the late 17th century had a formal staff structure and staffs were often extemporised as and when the need arose. Perhaps the best, although by no means only, example of this latter is the complete lack of any *formal* appointment of an aide-de-camp and yet aides and couriers were vitally necessary to carry information and messages enabling the army to move and manoeuvre both on and off the battlefield and so we have records of officers, and uncommissioned individuals, being simply seconded as needed. Thus the army would have had an effective and fully functioning staff capability even if this had no formal establishment.

One officer, however would have been familiar to armies in the following centuries – the provost marshall who, with his staff, was responsible for keeping order in the army. He was also one the few general officers of the staff to have had a formal establishment.

The provost marshall's staff was expanded early in James's reign as the army itself was expanded to counter Monmouth's rebellion, but as the new regiments brought their own regimental provosts onto strength these additional officers were deemed unnecessary and on 24 July 1685 Provost Marshall Generall Thomas was ordered to reduce his staff to two men with horses, and the Provost's supernumeraries were to be discharged.[17]

These regimental provosts were either found to be insufficient for their tasks or James simply wanted a more army-wide solution, and in 1686 the provost marshall generall's staff was again expanded:

> His Matty is pleased to Order that Gilbert Thomas Esqr Provost Marshall Generall of his fforces do forthwth list Eight Men more than are at present allowed him upon the Establishment, with good And able Horses, and to have them ready to be mustered by the First of May next, from wch time they are to be entertained in his Mat's Pay untill further order. Dated this 23. of April 1686.[18]

---

17 National Archives, Kew, WO4/1, f. 20.
18 National Archives, Kew, WO5/2, f. 177.

Officers, *c*.1688. (After C. C. P. Lawson)

Note the fashionable affectation of knotting the scarf at, or almost at, the front rather than to the left, as was the practice later. Many officers were still wearing their own hair during James' reign; wigs did not become de rigeur until some years later. Note, as mentioned in the text, that these company officers are wearing stockings and shoes and armed with half-pikes, along with the ubiquitous sword.

There are no records of any further change in the strength of this staff until the reign of William and Mary.

Uniform

The late 17th century is far too early to envisage a true 'uniform' for general officers, however some idea of the appearance of the Army's senior officers can be reconstructed from the numerous portraits of the King and of many of his general officers in army 'uniform' that survive from these years.

The most well known of these portraits is that by Godfrey Kneller of the King himself, now in the collection of the National Army Museum in London; it should be noted that other copies or versions of this portrait also exist in various private collections, although the general appearance of the King is the same throughout. James was proud to be portrayed in uniform and we can be fairly certain that the portrait showed an actual uniform and not some fantasy of the artist's.

The King's coat is scarlet red with bright blue cuffs and lining – this blue is the same as that shown in the portrait of Captain Hawley of the Guards, a blue a little lighter than that used on the sash of the Order of the Garter. The multitude of buttons down the front are gilt (unusually they are square), as are the eight buttons close together on the front of the cuff and the two vertical rows on the front, which appear to be for two pockets on each side. The coat is richly laced with a gold lave along all seams and either side of the pocket openings. A light gold 'spotting' effect appears over the whole of the cuffs. The waistcoat is white with small gold buttons and the heavy black jackboots hide any view of the breeches. The military scarf is worn low on the waist and knotted at the left hip, it is gold coloured and heavily fringed with gold wire at the ends with a short gold fringe along the edges. The King's black hat is not turned up but does curl upwards at the outer edge and has a white feather pluming around the brim. He wears grey gloves and carries a plain brown staff of command. This latter, of course, strongly suggesting that all general officers' batons were similarly of plain brown wood appearance. It should perhaps be noted that a cuirassier's cuirass and close helm are shown on the floor but these are purely decorative and serve only to accentuate the 'military appearance' of the painting, as they are not even of a late 17th century style or pattern.

Of course, if this is James' choice of 'uniform' it would have been a very courageous general officer that chose to depart far from it, and we may thus be fairly safe in suggesting that most general officers and staff officers would have appeared broadly similar, although perhaps with a little less gold lace.

Interestingly the painting of Monmouth in France in 1674 by Jan van Wyck shows him wearing a coat very similar to that in which his uncle was portrayed a decade later. The only real noticeable differences between these two uniforms are that Monmouth's coat has white facings (unusually with a gold fringe along the top edge) in place of James's royal blue, his gloves are buff (perhaps more practical buff leather for use in the field) and the hat feathers are a mixture of red and white. Monmouth's horse furniture is hidden by the fullness of his coat, but the holster caps are so heavily embroidered in gold that no ground can be seen.

Armour

Although it was still fashionable for officers to have their portraits painted wearing the full three-quarter 'cuirassier armour' of a half century or more earlier, it is highly unlikely that this was ever worn in the field or, indeed, if in most cases the sitters even possessed such a suit! However, that armour was worn by general officers in the field is confirmed by several issues from the Tower, but this was of a more practical and fashionable form.

For the Earl of Feversham for the Sedgemoor campaign:

To Henry Griffith for the service of the R[t] Hon[ble] the Earle of Feversham dd order 20th June 1685

Back	1
Breast	1
Skull in a hatt	1
Quilted Capp	1

These items were issued and signed for on the same day that the warrant is dated.[19]

This warrant from February 27 1689 is interesting, as though very slightly later it still indicates the overall habits:

To Sir Henry Shere L[t] Gen[ll] of y[e] late Traine of Artillery

	Backs	1
Arquebuss Armour	Breast	1
Carbine Proofe	Pott	1'
	Elbow Gauntlet	1[20]

---

19 National Archives, Kew, WO55/1656, f. 17.
20 Ibid, f. 41.

Officer's gorget, *c*.1685. Probably for a lieutenant. (Collection of the Royal Armouries. Author's photograph)

The 'studs' are still distinctly gold as are the rolled edges even though the main body of the gorget is now a dark brown colour. This pattern would conform exactly to the order laid down by Charles II on 1 September 1684.

The gorget fastens with a stud and 'keyhole', which can be distinctly seen at each side of the piece.

Noteworthy here are both the 'pott', the English 'triple-bar' lobster style so beloved of the English Civil Wars, and the 'elbow gauntlet' designed to protect the left lower arm while it held the reins of the horse.

This penchant for armour and a true martial appearance was undoubtedly led by the King and one of the warrants that survives records:

To Mo[r] DeLasze The Suite of Armour hereafter mentioned being for his Ma[ts] Owne use by order of the Board dated 30th off Aprill 1687

	Breast Carbine proofe	1
	Back	1
Harquebuss Armour	Pott	1
plain & Samguin'd Lynd	Gauntlett	1
wth Crimson Sattin	Gorgett of Crimson Sattin	1[21]

No doubt a very attractive suit, and whilst obviously only issued for a military spectacle (probably the annual camp on Hounslow Heath), since the Kingdoms were not at war, it again serves to indicate how James felt a general officer should appear. An indication confirmed by the fact that throughout the autumn of 1688 there are a large number of issues of armour to the officers and staff of the army.[22] These issues always comprise back and breast plates *and* pott, plus, more often than not, a 'gauntlett' for the left or bridle arm. This latter piece seems to have been a usual part of an officer's armour during the English Civil Wars,[23] but had fallen into disuse by the army as

---

21 *Ibid.*, f. 25.

22 *Ibid.*, ff. 35–39.

23 Numerous examples survive in the collection of the Royal Armouries as well as in other collections, both public and private. There are no records, however, to suggest that it was ever general issue to troopers either during the English Civil Wars or later, and to date no document

a whole by the 1680s, although apparently not by senior officers. Without exception suits issued to staff and individuals are specified as 'carbine proofe'.

Out all of these warrants, however, two stand out as exceptionally worth recording. The first appears as part of a warrant for the issue of armour to the Royal Regiment of Horse Guards but includes:

	Armour consisting of	
For the Earle of Feversham	Breast Back Pott and Long	1 suite
	Gauntlett made for king	
	Charles ye 2d'[24]	

The second unusual issue in the 1688 warrants is:

To Mr Robert Harrison for his owne use in attending his Ma^t in this present Expedition; By order of the Board and proporton 14th of Novemb 1689

	Breast wth Plaquett	
harquebuss Armo^r	Musqtt proof	.1
	Back and pott of carbin	
	Proof	.1 each[25]

The 'plaquett' was a last vestige of the old 'cuirassier armour' of the 1640s and was a secondary breastplate to give the additional protection – hence 'Musqtt proof'. There is no record of any similar issues of this heavier armour nor any explanation as to why Mr Harrison was issued it.

Pay

The pay of the 'staff' during James' reign may seem extraordinarily high when compared to that of the rank and file (8d in the foot) or to the civilian farm labourer (around 1s in 1685) but it is well in line with the pay during the English Civil War (indeed many rates are the same) and proportionately to that in later periods.

It is also worth noting that pay as a general officer or staff officer was in addition to any pay received for army rank. Thus Robert Werden, major general from July 31st 1685 and colonel of horse from 24 October 1685 would have drawn three separate pays.

Major General	£2 0s 0d per day
Colonel of horse	12s 0d per day
Captain of horse	10s 0d per day
plus allowances for	
2 horses at 2s each	4s 0d per day (as colonel of horse)

---

has come to light indicating its issue to any troopers albeit that many modern illustrations show it in use by the rank and file.

24 National Archives, Kew, WO55/1656, f. 32.

25 National Archives, Kew, WO55/1656, f. 32.

6 servants at 2s 6d each   15s 0d per day (as colonel of horse)

Obviously the same multiple pays held true for all officers who held multiple posts (all rates are per day):

General, Commanding in Chief	£10 0s 0d
General	£ 6 0s 0d
Lieutenant General	£ 4 0s 0d
Major General	£ 2 0s 0d
Brigadier General	£ 1 10s 0d
Paymaster General	£ 3 0s 0d
Commissary General of Musters	17s 6d
Chief Deputy Commissary General of Musters	13s 0d
Deputy Commissary General of Musters	5s 0d
Clerk to Commissary General of Musters	2s 6d
Commissary General of Provisions	£ 1 10s 0d
Secretary to the Forces	£ 2 0s 0d
Quartermaster General	£ 1 0s 0d
Adjutant General	£ 1 0s 0d
Scoutmaster General	£ 1 0s 0d
Judge Advocate	12s 6d
Clerk to Judge Advocate	2s 6d
Deputy Judge Advocate	2s 6d to 10s[26]
Provost Marshal General	8s 0d
Inspector General of the Exercise & Garrisons	16s 5¾d
Marshal of the Horse	7s 0d
Aide-de-Camp	10s 0d
Physician General	10s 0d
Chirurgeon General	10s 0d[27]

---

26 There is no explanation as to why the deputy should be on one or the other of these extremes.
27 Walton, pp. 649, 651.

2

The Horse Guards

The Royal Regiment of Horse Guards, the Scots Troop of Horse Guards, and the Irish Troop of Horse Guards

Organisation

In February 1685 the Royal Regiment of Horse Guards comprised three troops, additionally the Scots Horse Guards and the Irish Horse Guards were each a single troop on their own national military establishments. The three English troops and the Irish troop each had an attached company of horse grenadiers in addition to the 'gentlemen' of the troop proper (The Scots Troop later added a company of horse grenadiers in 1702 but this was disbanded in 1746). Gentlemen, the troops' equivalent of an ordinary trooper, were nominally to be of a higher social standing than the ordinary soldier and were to able to provide their own uniform, horse, etc. whilst the King undertook the supply of their armour and weapons. Horse grenadiers (who seem to have been considered as equivalent to dragoons) were recruited in the usual way and totally equipped by the Crown. That this distinction between 'gentlemen' and others was by 1685 nominal may be seen in the method of the raising of Lord Dover's 4th Troop of Horse Guards, see below.

In 1686 a fourth troop of horse guards was raised under the command of Henry Jermyn, Lord Dover, its manpower recruited by disbanding Dover's Regiment of Horse, raised the previous year. This latter troop was, in turn, disbanded in late 1688 after James' flight and abdication, although many of its personnel fled to Ireland and were used to strengthen James' Horse Guards in exile. That an entire regiment of horse should be used to raise a single troop of horse guards may seem excessive, until it is considered that in 1686 the total establishment of NCOs and rank and file of a regiment of horse was only 258 men,[1] and it required 264 men to raise a full troop of horse guards with attached horse grenadiers.

In 1685 the English and Irish troops of horse guards comprised:

---

1   Six troops, each containing 40 troopers and 3 corporals. See Chapter 3 below.

1 Captain and colonel[2]	4 Lieutenants and lieutenant colonels

1 Cornet and major	1 Guidon and major
1 Quartermaster and captain	
4 Brigadiers and lieutenants	4 Sub brigadiers 'as Assistants'
4 Trumpeters	1 Kettledrummer
200 Gentlemen	

Each troop had an attached troop of Horse Grenadiers composed of:

2 Lieutenants and Lieutenant Colonels	
2 Sergeants	2 Corporals
2 Drummers	4 Hautboys
64 Horse grenadiers	

Modern writers have sometimes considered the Irish troop of horse grenadiers as a separate unit, but when Charles II commissioned the troop in 1684 he intended it to be attached to the Irish Horse Guards in the same way as the English troops of horse grenadiers were attached to the English troops of horse guards.

Each *troop* also maintained a small staff, equivalent to that of a regiment of horse, which comprised a quartermaster and captain, a chirurgeon, and a chaplain.

The Scots Troop of Horse Guards remained independent of the Regiment of Horse Guards throughout this period and had an establishment of:

1 Captain	2 Lieutenants
1 Cornet	1 Guidon
1 Quartermaster	4 Brigadiers
4 Trumpeters	1 Kettledrummer[3]
1 Surgeon and his Mate	
1 Clerk	1 Farrier
118 Guardsmen	

The troop was quartered in Edinburgh throughout the reign of Charles II and for most of James' reign, even when the King that they had been raised to protect was in London, although it did march south with the Scots Army in 1688. Similarly the Irish troop was quartered in Dublin throughout both reigns.

---

2 In the troops of horse guards officers held a 'double-rank': their rank in the troop and then their rank in the army. Thus the 'Captain and Colonel' was captain of the troop but a full colonel in army rank.

3 *Calendar of State Papers*, 1684–1685, p. 279. Warrant for the provision of new liveries and new kettledrums to the troop.

Uniforms

Sandford's description of the coronation of James II, reprinted as Appendix I, gives an extremely detailed analysis of the appearance of the first three troops, but the uniform is set out more succinctly below. Particularly noteworthy is the use of differing 'troop colours' (what Sandford calls 'facings') for carbine belts, holster caps, etc.; something that seems to have been copied from, or by, the various companies of the French Garde du Corps of the Maison du Roi. There has sometimes been some confusion that the 'troop colour' was used for facings as well as the troop accoutrements – this is almost certainly a misreading of the sources, and all warrants for coats under Charles II and later give the linings and facings as blue,[4] almost certainly the 'bright blue' in use by the Foot Guards (see 'The Royal Regiments of Foot Guards', below).

1st Troop
Gentlemen: scarlet coats and cloaks, lined and faced in blue, 'laced about' with silver galoon two inches wide and edged in gold. This scarlet coat was worn over a buff coat, which served as a waistcoat. Buff gauntlets. Black hat turned up at the side with blue hatbands and bunches of ribbons. Blue velvet carbine belts edged with silver galoon so wide that 'not above an inch of velvet appeared'. this in turn was edged with narrow gold lace. Silver plate buttons. Black over-knee 'Jackboots'. The troop's horses had blue ribbons tied into their manes (presumably only for formal parades). The housings and holster caps were of scarlet cloth embroidered with the King's cypher and a border of foliage, all in gold. Armament consisted of a sword, carried from a buff leather shoulder baldric, a pair of pistols and a carbine, slung from the carbine belt worn over the left shoulder.
Grenadiers: dressed similarly to the Gentlemen except that their coats, cloaks and holster caps were red. Buttons were white metal. Lace was silver only. They also replaced the gentlemen's hats with caps, 'the crowns … raised to a high point falling back at the top in the form of a capouch which were turned up before and behind triangular and faced with blue plush and on the back of the crowns was a roundel or grenado ball of the same.' The coats had 'large loops of blue worsted edged and tufted with black and white' on buttonholes at the front, tails and cuffs. Armament consisted of a sword, a pair of pistols, 'a long carbine strapt', a bayonet and a grenade pouch, presumably containing the usual issue of four grenades. The sword was worn from a buff waist belt.

2nd Troop
Gentlemen: Dressed the same as the 1st Troop except that the ribbons (both in hats and horses' manes) and carbine belts were green; the housings and holster caps were green with the King's cypher in gold; and all lace was gold edged with silver.
Grenadiers: Armed and equipped like their namesakes in the 1st Troop but

---

4   Anon, *Travels of Cosmo the Third, Grand Duke of Tuscany … etc.*, translated, London 1821, p. 334, makes it clear that all troops wore red coats lined and faced light blue.

like the Gentlemen of the 2nd Troop using green for the 'troop colour' and also as the colour of the loops on their coats (though still 'edged and tufted' in black and white) and turn-up on their caps. Gilt buttons. Gold lace.

3rd Troop
Gentlemen: uniformed like the other two troops but using yellow for ribbons, housings, etc. Holster caps motif the same as the 1st Troop. Lacing on coats, hats, etc. silver only.
Grenadiers: uniformed as the Gentlemen of the 3rd Troop but with yellow buttonhole loops, edged and tufted in black and white. Silver buttons and lace. Yellow turn-up to cap.

4th Troop
Gentlemen: lacking the detailed description of Sandford, information on this troop is scarce but the uniform seems to have been the same as the other three troops, though using white as the 'troop colour' and gold only lace.
Grenadiers: As for the other troops but with white for the turn-ups, loops, etc.

Grenadier caps, *c*.1685. (After C. C. P. Lawson)

The cap at left was cloth and the front and lower edge could be 'furred' or alternately red or regimental facing colour cloth. The cap at right is that shown in the portrait of Captain Hawley (see text) as being in use by the regiments of foot guards, but this pattern may not have been exclusive to them.

Armour

Whether armour was issued to the composite troop of the Royal Regiment of Horse Guards that accompanied their colonel, the Earl of Feversham, at Sedgemoor is not recorded (cf. 'Armour' in Chapter 3 below), although as has already been recorded, Feversham himself was issued a suit. The likelihood, however, is that an issue was made in 1685 simply by inference from the fact that it was in 1688 when a warrant records:[5]

To the Four Troops of Horse Guard and The Earl of Feversham Lt Gen[ll] of his ma[ts]
Forces by Order and Proporton, 25[h] September 88
Grounded on his Ma[ts] warr[t] of the same date

	Breasts	800
Harquebuss armor	Backs	800
carbine proofe	Potts	800

The second part of this warrant covers the issue to the Earl himself and has already been discussed in Chapter 1. Noteworthy, however, on this document is the fact that there is no issue of armour to either officers or to trumpeters, although officers must have been issued theirs under a separate warrant as in the regiments of horse (see below), which has simply not survived. It is however apparent that trumpeters were not to have been issued with armour.

---

5   National Archives, Kew, WO55/1656, f. 32. The warrant of authority for this issue was also issued and dated 24 September 1688, SP 44/165, f. 68.

As in the regiments of horse, the Horse Guards appear to have worn the 'English triple-bar lobster' 'potte helmet' on campaign in place of their beaver hats. See Chapter 3 for a more in-depth discussion on the subject of armour.

Officers

Officers of all troops wore crimson coats with crimson linings and facings, gold and silver lace upon cuffs, buttonholes, edges, etc. Gold buttons. Black hats with white tours of feathers and edged in gold lace. Waist sashes were of crimson, gold or silver net and edged and fringed in gold and/or silver. No carbine or carbine belt was carried and the sword was carried from a waist belt. Housings, holster-caps and ribbons were of the troop colour.

The officers of the Royal Regiment of Horse (see below) by a warrant from the Colonel in 1686 used silver and gold lace in various styles and combinations to denote an officer's rank. Major N. P. Dawnay speculates, very logically, that a similar system may have existed in other mounted regiments,[6] but I would venture to suggest that the troops of horse guards would, as later, have disdained such a system and officers' coats would have been broadly similar. This is, I would stress, purely my own opinion and unless other information is discovered it must remain so.

Trumpeters and Kettledrummers

All troops: crimson velvet coats lined and faced in sky blue, heavily laced all over with gold and silver lace, including buttonhole loops, cuffs, seams, etc., gold buttons. Crimson 'hanging sleeves' (actually no more than wide strips of cloth attached at the shoulder) were worn and these too were decorated in gold and silver. The crowned royal cypher was worn on the front and back of the coat in the same manner as musicians of the Household Cavalry still do today; indeed, the whole appearance of the coat was remarkably similar to that worn today on full State occasions. The trumpet and kettledrum banners were crimson, embroidered with the Royal Coat of Arms, including supporters, in gold and fringed gold and silver.

Cornets and Guidons

The illustration below (page 52) shows the basic design of the cornet and guidons of the horse guards. Unusually, and uniquely, each troop carried both a cornet and a guidon, both identical in design and colouring but, obviously, varying in shape. It has been suggested that the guidon was for use by the horse grenadiers and the cornet by the main troop. However, as the guidon was authorised in 1673 and the horse grenadiers not until 1674, and whereas the latter were disbanded in 1788 the regiment continued to carry both guidon and standard until c.1823, the suggestion appears unlikely;

---

6   Major N. P. Dawnay, *The Distinction of Rank of Regimental Officers 1684 to 1855*, Society for Army Historical Research Special Publication No. 7, London 1960, pp. 8–9.

although, of course, not impossible.

The 1st Troop's cornet was two feet six inches by two feet three inches; the other troops' cornets were two feet six inches square. The guidons were all two feet three inches on the pole by three feet three inches flying and, of course, had the split rounded ends that their name implies. The illustration shows the guidons' shape, which is completely different to that of the dragoons.

1st Troop
Crimson damask with gold embroidery, fringes, cords and tassels; the motto black on a silver scroll. These seem to be the only new standard and guidons initially supplied to the regiment, since the bill for the new standards, colours and guidons survives but only includes the making of a standard and guidon for the 1st Troop:

> made and provided against H.M.'s … Coronation by Thos Holford, Portcullis Pursuivant of Arms. For a Standard and Guidon for the First Troop of Horse Guards, by agreement with Chas. Fox. Esqr., Paymaster-General, at £24 each 48 0 0[7]

2nd Troop
White damask with gold embroidery and gold fringes, cords and tassels; black on gold motto and scroll. Uniquely, the 2nd Troop's cornet and guidon bore angels or cupids supporting the large central crown; the significance of this addition is, unfortunately, unknown.

3rd Troop
Identical to the 1st Troop but in yellow damask with all embroidery in silver, fringes etc. mixed silver and gold.

4th Troop
Blue damask of the same design as the 1st Troop with all embroidery, fringes, etc. in gold, except the scroll, which was of silver.

The standards and guidons for the 2nd, 3rd and 4th Troops must have been made and supplied later in 1685 since they are shown with the 'JR' monogram in *The James II Colour Book* in Windsor Castle, although no warrants or bills have yet come to light. Since at least 1674 the troops had been supplied with leather cases for their standards and guidons, an indication of the need to protect these highly costly flags.

The Scots Troop

This was, in all respects, uniformed identically to its English counterparts but with white linings, facings etc. Blue waistcoat and carbine sling. Gold lace on hats and coats, gold buttons.

The regiment marched south during the crisis of the Prince of Orange's invasion in 1688 and a warrant of 10th November records the issue of 380

---

7   War Office State Papers quoted in Walton , pp. 460–461.

The Scots Troop of Horse Guards, 1685. (After C. C. P. Lawson)

Sketch by C. C. P. Lawson after a contemporary illustration. Trumpeter, kettledrummer, officer and (in the background) two gentlemen of the troop. The uniform follows that described in the text but the musicians' coats are somewhat simpler than those shown in use by the English troops suggesting either that the Scots preferred a simpler style or this is a simpler coat, perhaps for everyday use.

suits of armour to 'His Mats Horse Guards lately come from Scotland'.[8] However at this strength it seems more likely that this issue is for the Royal Regiment of Scots Horse as on 11th October only 120 troopers of the Scots Troop of Horse Guards had entered York,[9] exactly its known establishment. Thus whilst the issue of armour to this troop must remain speculative it would seem highly likely that back, breast and pott were issued in accordance with practice within the whole of the rest of the army.

The trumpeters of the Scots Troop again followed the lead of their English counterparts in wearing coats of royal livery. However it is worth noting that in the case of the Scots Troop the royal cypher would have been for 'James VII', which was James' title in Scotland, as opposed to the 'James II' that he was in England. The arms on the trumpet banners would likewise have been the Royal Stuart arms as carried in Scotland, which were significantly different from those in use in England.

The troop cornet (they carried no guidon) was identical to the English 4th Troop but embroidered in gold throughout. The Scottish United Services Museum in Edinburgh Castle has the standard of the Scots Troop carried from c.1661 to at least 1685 but, to date, no bills or warrants have come to light for its replacement with a standard carrying James' monogram in place of that of Charles II.

The Irish Troop

Again this troop was uniformed in the same manner as the four English troops but with blue linings, facings, etc., and presumably a blue waistcoat and carbine sling. Coat and hat was gold as were the buttons. Housings and holster caps were in blue, edged in gold and embroidered with the crowned royal cypher.

---

8   National Archives, Kew, WO55/1656, f. 38.
9   National Archives, Kew, WO4/1, f. 102.

Whilst there is no direct evidence for the dress of the troop's trumpeters and kettledrummers it seems fairly safe to speculate that they also wore royal livery although the cypher would have been for 'James II', as in the English troops.

In 1689 the troop cornet was a crimson version of the English 2nd Troop's, including the two angels or cupids. All embroidery was in gold, except for the angels, which were silver. The fringe was in gold as were the cords and the lance head. This *may* have been the form of the cornet carried during the earlier period as well.

No information survives regarding the guidon of the troop of horse grenadiers, assuming that they had one, but it may well have simply been a guidon version of the horse guards' cornet. Unlike the English troops the Irish Troop of Horse Grenadiers had a semi-separate existence so probably carried its own guidon.

Pay

The pay scales of the Horse Guards were, as might be expected, substantially higher than in the regiments of horse (see below), all rates are per day:

Captain of the 1st Troop	£ 1 10s 0d
Captains of the 2nd & 3rd Troop	£ 1 0s 0d
Lieutenant	15s 0d
Cornet of the 1st Troop	14s 0d
Cornets of the 2nd & 3rd Troops	13s 0d
Guidons	12s 0d
Quartermaster	9s 0d
Chaplain	6s 8d
Chirugeon	6s 0d*
Corporal of the 1st Troop	7s 0d
Corporals of the 2nd & 3rd Troops	6s 0d
Trumpeter	5s 0d
Kettledrummer	5s 0d
Gentleman Trooper	4s 0d
Lieutenant of Horse Grenadiers	8s 0d
Sergeant of Horse Grenadiers	4s 0d
Corporal of Horse Grenadiers	3s 0d
Drummer or Hautboy of Horse Grenadiers	2s 6d
Horse Grenadier	2s 6d

*Plus an allowance of 2s per day for a horse for his chest

From this pay all except officers had 'off reckonings' deducted of 6d per man per day.[10]

---

10 For more details on how pay was distributed and what constituted the 'off reckonings', see John Childs, *The Army of Charles II* (London: Routledge, 1970).

3

The Regiments of Horse

Organisation

At James' accession in February 1685, apart from the troops of horse guards, the mounted strength of the armies of the two kingdoms comprised only the two Royal Regiments of Horse[1] (Graham of Claverhouse's Regiment of Horse on the Scots establishment did not actually become the Royal Regiment until 21 December 1685,[2] but for the sake of clarity I have considered it under its later title throughout). The English Regiment comprised eight troops and the Scots Regiment six troops. Noteworthy is the fact that in the Royal Regiment of Horse there was no colonel's troop in the commission list of 10 February 1685, although one of the eight had been a colonel's troop in 1684.[3]

By comparison the Irish Establishment boasted three full regiments of horse, each of eight full troops,[4] and from early 1684 the Irish regiments of horse had each also boasted an attached troop of dragoons (at the same strength as the troops of horse). These latter continued in being until shortly after Colonel Richard Hamilton's Regiment of Dragoons arrived from England in the autumn of 1685 when they were absorbed into that regiment (see below).

The establishment of the individual troops in all regiments was identical at:

1 Captain	1 Lieutenant
1 Cornet	1 Quartermaster
3 Corporals	2 Trumpeters
50 Troopers (one of whom was designated as a farrier)	

---

1 There were, of course, the two regiments of Royal Dragoons (one English, one Scots) but at this period dragoons were not yet truly considered as mounted regiments.

2 Lawson, p. 92.

3 Dalton, *English*, vol. 1, p. 313 and vol. 2, p. 4. cf. National Archives, Kew, WO5/1, f. 109, order dated 1 October 1684.

4 *Calendar of State Papers*, 1686–1687, p. 215. SP 63/351, ff. 269–274.

In addition the senior troop carried on its strength the regimental staff of an adjutant, chaplain,[5] chirurgeon,[6] quartermaster and a single kettledrummer. On 3 November 1688 this staff was augmented slightly by the addition when a surgeon's mate was added to each regiment of horse and dragoons.[7] Noticeably there is no allowance for a provost marshal on the staff of the regiments of horse or dragoons. The colonels of the Irish Army complained of this omission in January 1686,[8] saying that 'they cannot correct their regiments for want of such an officer', but there is no evidence that this omission was corrected either in Ireland or in the other kingdoms.

In Ireland the troops of horse had only 45 troopers and a single trumpeter, but otherwise the regiments were identically organised.

On 13 June 1685 with the threat of imminent invasion by Charles II's illegitimate son, the Duke of Monmouth, James II authorised the establishment of all troops of horse of the English Army to be increased to 60 men. At the same time he ordered the raising of two further regiments of horse, The Queen Consort's with an establishment of nine troops (Major Boade was without a Troop),[9] and the Earl of Peterborough's with an establishment of four.[10]

The warrants to the individual captains of the Queen Consort's (termed then and often afterwards as Lanier's) are all dated 13th June and give the captains authority 'to raise volunteers with able Horses for one Troop of Horse … consisting of Threescore Soldiers, Three Corporalls and Two Trumpetts',[11] 'besides Commission Officers.' Officers' and other ranks' pay and muster to commence when twenty men 'besides officers' were recruited.[12] All of the other warrants are similarly worded and specify where the troops are to be mustered, and were thus sent to:[13]

The Colonel at Kensington & Hammersmith
Major William Legge at Kingston upon Thames[14]
Captain Charles Nedby at Colebrooke in Bucks
Captain George Hastings at Uxbridge
Captain George Hamilton at Egham
Captain John Staples at Staines
Captain Lewis Billingsley at Fritham
Captain James Fortsey at Chertsey

5   A position not recorded in the Royal Regiment of Scots Horse.
6   A 'chryurgeon and his mate' were added to the Royal Regiment of Scots Horse by a letter of 21 December 1685.
7   National Archives, Kew, WO4/1, ff. 108–109.
8   *Calendar of State Papers*, 1686–1687, p. 10; National Archives, Kew, SP 63/351, ff. 129–130.
9   Sir John Lanier's colonel's troop commissions were signed at Whitehall on 6 June, the other troops were commissioned between 6 and 13 June. Dalton, *English*, vol. 2, p. 5.
10 Peterborough's own troop's commissions were signed at Whitehall on 20 June, as were the commissions for Major John Chetham's Troop. The other two troops' commissions are dated 24 July. Dalton, English, vol. 2, p. 6.
11 National Archives, Kew, WO5/1, f. 45 and f. 48.
12 Warrant to recruit Captain Henry Lumley's Troop of the Queen Consort's Regt., National Archives, Kew, WO5/1, f. 45.
13 National Archives, Kew, WO5/1, f. 46.
14 In fact Legge had been commissioned lieutenant colonel on 6 June 1685. Dalton, English, vol. 2, p. 5.

Plate VII / 20 from *Grosse Uniformenkunde* by Richard Knötel, published in Germany *c*.1895. (Author's collection)

The original plate is titled as 'France: Cavalry 1684' but the appearance of these two troopers is little different from how those of James II's army would have looked. The low positioning of the military scarf was a fashionable affectation and is common in period illustrations although by 1684 this was already on its way out.

As well as these two regiments, on 18 June Captain David Lloyd was authorised to raise an additional troop for the Royal Regiment of Horse to bring its establishment to nine troops. Authority was also given to raise a large number of independent troops of horse; twenty-one were commissioned at Whitehall on 18 June, two more on the 19th, no less than 29 on 20 June, and a further eight between the 22nd and 27th, a total of 60 troops in all. The troop captains are listed in Appendix 4. All of these new troops were to be at the increased establishment of 60 troopers besides the officers, as above.[15] Again recruits were to be 'volunties with able horses.' Recruitment and training of these new units was remarkably fast by modern standards, the Queen Consort's Regiment was already available to Feversham during the Sedgemoor campaign.[16] This would have been aided, however, by the fact that the new troopers brought with them their own horses and thus also the ability to ride. Whether uniforms would be available this fast is somewhat doubtful but no doubt the troopers looked the part in their issued armour and armed from the Tower's massive stores.

---

15   National Archives, Kew, WO5/1, f. 40.

16   The battle was fought on 6 July and some part at least of the Queen Consort's was in support of the army at that time. The first commissions for this regiment were signed on 6 June – exactly one month earlier.

During the reign of Charles II, units raised for similar emergencies were disbanded after the crisis had passed. James II, however, although disbanding some (see Appendix 4) used the majority of these new troops to raise seven further regiments of horse for the permanent establishment. From notes and references in the 'Orders for the Marching and Moving of Forces',[17] the origins of the new regiments, and the troops that comprised them can be identified as:

The Queen Consort's Regiment of Horse

Charles Somerset, Marquis of Worcester. Mustered at Bristol.

Dalton English gives Worcester's as being incorporated into this regiment on 26 October 1685 and this troop must therefore have been a replacement for Charles Nedby's, which had been transferred into the Earl of Arran's Regiment of Horse, in which its captain had been commissioned as lieutenant colonel (see below).

Earl of Peterborough's Regiment of Horse

Lieutenant Colonel Sir John Talbot. Mustered at Hounslow.

Richard Bertie. Mustered at Oxford.

Charles Montague, 4th Earl of Manchester. Mustered at Kimbolton.

Thomas Bruce, Lord Bruce. Raised 'near London.'

Jonathon Lloyd. Mustered at Edgware.

Sir Michael Wentworth.[18] Mustered at Wakefield and Pontefract.

Earl of Plymouth's Regiment of Horse

Thomas Windsor, 1st Earl of Plymouth. Mustered at Worcester and Droitwich. Plymouth was commissioned as colonel on 15 July 1685.

Henry Savile, Lord Eland. Mustered at St Albans.

Ambrose Browne. Mustered at Dorking.

Claudius Hamilton, 4th Earl of Abercorn. Mustered at Oxford.

D'Oyley Michell. Mustered at Dorchester.[19]

Henry Yelverton, Lord de Grey of Ruthyn. Mustered at Dunstable.

Lord Dover's Regiment of Horse

Henry Jermyn, 1st Baron Dover. Mustered at Waltham Abbey 'and places adjacent.'

Dover's commission as Colonel is dated 26 July 1685.

Hugh, 2nd Viscount Cholmondeley. Mustered at Nantwich.

Henry Bertie. Mustered at Oxford.

Bryan, Lord Viscount Cullen. Mustered at Rowell.[20]

---

17 'Orders for the Marching and Moving of Forces', National Archives, Kew, WO5/1 and WO5/2. Particularly WO5/1 ff. 208–213, which are dated 1 August 1685.

18 The allocation of Wentworth's Troop into the Earl of Peterborough's Regiment of Horse is somewhat tentative.

19 This became Lieutenant Colonel Hugh Sutherland's Troop, and Michell was appointed its lieutenant.

20 This is first mentioned as being commanded by 'Lord Cullen's Son', although the original commission was issued to Cullen.

Lyonel Walden. Mustered at Huntingdon.

James Griffin.

Earl of Thanet's Regiment of Horse

Thomas Tufton, 6th Earl of Thanet. Mustered at Gravesend.

Thanet's commission as Colonel is dated 27 July 1685.

Lieutenant Colonel Bernard Howard.

Robert Bertie, Lord Willoughby de Eresby. Mustered at Spilsby.

Sir Thomas Mauleverer. Mustered at Burroughbridge.

Sir Charles Tufton. Mustered at Rochester.

Sir Thomas Fairfax Bt. Mustered at Leeds.

Earl of Arran's Regiment of Horse

Sir Edward Carterett. Mustered at Croydon.[21]

William Baggot. Mustered at Lichfield.

Thomas Harrington. Mustered at Grantham.

William Ogle. Mustered at Morpeth.

Jonathon Fetherstonhalgh. Mustered at Durham.

Arran's 6th troop was commanded by Captain Charles Nedby, transferred from the Queen Consort's Regiment of Horse as lieutenant colonel. The evidence suggests that he transferred with his troop.

The Earl of Shrewsbury's Regiment of Horse

Charles Talbot, 12th Earl of Shrewsbury. Raised at Lichfield. Shrewsbury's commission as colonel was dated 29 July 1685.

Francis Brudenell, Lord Brudenell. Mustered at Kingston upon Thames.

Roger Pope. Mustered at Bridgnorth.

Francis Spalding. Mustered at Bristol.

Sir Thomas Grosvenor, 3rd Bt. Mustered at Chester.

The 6th troop of this regiment was that of Lieutenant Colonel Jonathon Darcy who was commissioned directly into it on 29 July 1685, and who raised his troop in London.[22] This troop was, however, complete by 1 August,[23] and Darcy must therefore have begun its raising somewhat earlier, or alternatively have taken in some of the personnel of the disbanded independent troops (see Appendix 4).

Princess Anne of Denmark's Regiment of Horse

Robert Leke, 3rd Earl of Scarsdale. Mustered at Ware.

The Earl of Scarsdale was commissioned Colonel on 30 July 1685.

Sir Edmund Andros.

Edmund Chafin. Mustered at Bromley.

---

21 Carterett's Troop became the Earl of Arran's own, Carterett was commissioned as its captain lieutenant.

22 Richard Cannon, *Historical Records of the Fifth, or Princess Charlotte of Wales's Regiment of Dragoon Guards* (London: Longman, Orme, 1831), pp. 2–3.

23 National Archives, Kew, WO5/1 f. 206.

William Paston, 2nd Earl of Yarmouth.[24] Mustered at Norwich.
Robert Smith. Mustered at Dartford.
Archibald Clincard. Mustered at Maidstone.

The Queen Dowager's Regiment of Horse

Richard Lumley, Viscount Lumley. Raised in Hampshire.[25] Lumley was commissioned colonel of this regiment on 31 July 1685.
Richard Lumley, Viscount Lumley.[26]
Robert Sutton, Lord Lexington. Mustered at Newark.
Sir William Villiers, Bt. Mustered at Hoddesdon.
Robert Byerley. Mustered at Doncaster.
Henry Hevingham. Mustered at Ipswich.
Robert Cornwall.[27] Raised in Hertfordshire.

The captains do not appear to have been recommisioned, and almost all had resigned from their places within the year;[28] perhaps leading a troop in a short-term emergency was an entirely different matter to continued service in a regular army. The locations given as 'mustered at' both above and in Appendix 4 are those directed in the original warrants, it must logically be that the troops were therefore raised in that area.

On July 16 1685,[29] James ordered that the strength of each troop of horse, except those of the Royal Regiment of Horse, was to be reduced back to 50 troopers. The regimental establishment was also simplified and generally unified across the regiments: except for the Royal Regiment of Horse and the Queen Consort's Regiment of Horse each regiment was to consist of six troops, with a strength as above, plus a major without a troop.[30] The Royal Regiment of Horse and the Queen Consort's Regiment of Horse both retained their nine troop establishments. The former was still without a colonel's troop but the latter was in line with the rest of the regiments of horse in that it was its major who was without a troop. The small regimental staff of four remained on the colonel's troop strength, or the lieutenant colonel's in the Royal Regiment of Horse.

On 23 July 1685 Secretary at War William Blaythwayt sent a circular letter to the Earl of Peterborough, the Earl of Plymouth, the Earl of Shrewsbury, the Earl of Arran, the Earl of Thanet, the Baron Dover, the Earl of Scarsdale and Viscount Lumley requesting a return of the condition and readiness of their

---

24 National Archives, Kew, WO5/2, f. 91.
25 Richard Cannon, *Historical Records of the Sixth Dragoon Guards* (London: Longman, 1839), pp. 2–3.
26 Lumley was commissioned to raise two independent troops of horse – see Appendix 4.
27 Cornwall was commissioned captain lieutenant of this regiment. His troop apparently became that of Lieutenant-Colonel Sir John Clobury.
28 Dalton, *English*, vol. 2.
29 National Archives, Kew, WO5/1, f. 167.
30 Initially in Peterborough's Horse the lieutenant colonel was without a troop in place of the major, but Major Chitham's troop was disbanded on 25 July (National Archives, Kew, WO5/1 f. 182/3) and his men presumably used to raise the lieutenant colonel's troop.

regiments.[31] Sadly, if the colonels responded to this letter none of the replies have survived. More remarkable is the fact that all but two of these officers had yet to be formally commissioned to the rank of colonel, cf. Appendix 2.

Nine days later, on 25 July 1685,[32] the order for a reduction in troop establishment was amended in that a troop was to be reduced further still to only 40 Troopers, or 50 in the Royal Regiment of Horse. The establishment of officers, NCOs, etc. still remained unchanged, however, and thus a troop now comprised:

1 Captain	1 Lieutenant
1 Cornet	1 Quartermaster
3 Corporals	2 Trumpeters
40 Privates (50 in the Royal Regiments of Horse)	

One private in each troop of the two Royal Regiments of Horse was designated as 'a farrier', although paid at the same rate as an ordinary trooper, whether this was repeated throughout the other regiments of horse is not known although there is no record that it was.

Trumpeters appear to have been recruited from men who could already play the instrument rather than, as was the case in the 18th century recruited and then trained. Thus a 1688 warrant, undated but either March or April, to Matthias Shore 'Serjeant Trumpetter', allowed him 'to impress trumpetts for any Troops of horse which need them, new or existing.'[33]

Noticeable here is, as with the drummers of foot (see below) that the term used is 'impress' and not 'recruit'.

In the Irish Army a restructure in the autumn of 1685 gave all three regiments of horse eight troops, still with a troop strength of 45 troopers and a single trumpeter. The Duke of Ormonde's own troop (the colonel's troop of his own regiment) was allowed the 50 men and three trumpeters of the Royal Regiments. The same restructure appears to have removed the troops of dragoons and incorporated them into Colonel Richard Hamilton's Regiment of Dragoons, newly arrived from England.[34]

These troop establishments remained unchanged throughout the majority of the rest of James II's reign except and until in September 1688, as the relationship with the Netherlands deteriorated further, each troop's strength was augmented by an additional 10 troopers,[35] thus bringing the strength back to 50 troopers plus officers, NCOs, etc., as above.

The speed with which a regiment of horse could be raised is, to the modern mind, truly astonishing, although this rapidity is perhaps indicative of the prevalence of the horse-riding society of the 17th century. Whereas it is usually

---

31 National Archives, Kew, WO4/1, f. 11. This is the order in which the colonels appear in the document in the National Archives.

32 National Archives, Kew, WO5/1, ff. 184–185.

33 National Archives, Kew, SP 44/165, f. 92.

34 National Archives, Kew, SP 8/1, Part 2, ff. 97–104.

35 Warrant 24 Sept 1688, to arm an augmentation of 10 men in each company of 'Horse, Grenadeers, Dragoons, and Foot', National Archives, Kew, SP 44/165 f. 66.

stated the new regiments of horse that James commissioned in September and October 1688 in preparation for the obviously forthcoming confrontation with the Netherlands were 'incomplete' or 'partly formed', when they were disbanded on 31 December of the same year the pay warrants for this disbandment actually show that the troops were already at full strength.[36] Of course, although these regiments may have been at full strength this does not mean that they were fully trained or disciplined but even this aspect of raising a regiment is somewhat easier if the recruits are already competent riders.

Both tactically and non-tactically three troops formed a squadron, which remained the case for some decades afterwards. The 1st Squadron was usually 'led' by the colonel's troop and the 2nd Squadron by the lieutenant colonel's troop, and this squadron organisation seems to have been at least semi-permanent. Thus movement orders etc. are often given to 'First Squadron of E of Scarsdale's',[37] or to 'one troop of the second squadron of the Queen Dowager's Regiment', and suchlike. From about August 1685 orders are rarely sent to troops as such but to regiments or squadrons, or as mentioned, to a troop from a specified squadron. Needless to say the Royal Regiment of Horse and the Queen Consort's obviously each comprised three squadrons, the third of which was comprised only of captains' troops. As early as June 1685, during the Sedgemoor Rebellion, in letters to his son-in-law the Prince of Orange, James was already counting his mounted troops, interestingly both horse *and* dragoons, by squadrons.[38]

Uniform

The uniform of the regiments of horse was essentially the same as that of the Royal Regiment of Horse Guards as covered above but with none of the latter's finery of lace and galoon, except for the officers. Where known the facings, linings, buttons, etc. of the various regiments are given in Table 1. According to Walton, until *c.*1686 the regiments of horse wore buff-coats under their coats as waistcoats,[39] but all research has so far failed to confirm this point; certainly from early 1686 cloth waistcoats of grey, red, white

English three bar pott of post-Restoration manufacture. (Collection of the Royal Armouries. Author's photograph)

Note the lack of a comb across the bowl (a manufacturing style unknown before 1660), and typical of the form of helmet that would have been issued to the horse in 1685 and 1688. The downward slope of the peak indicates that this is a late 1670s production piece. Given the surviving number of helmets in the Royal Armouries collection that date to before 1660 (that is, with a comb along the bowl) it is likely that many of these must have seen just as much service with the army.

36 Montagu Army Accounts, British Library Add MS 10123, f. 3.
37 National Archives, Kew, WO5/1 f. 256. Movement order dated 28 August 1685. Apart from James' own correspondence this is the earliest mention of aquadrons in a non-tactical sense that I have found in James' Army. The troop captains are specified as 'You', i.e. the earl to whom the order was directed, 'Captain Edmund Chaffin' and 'Captain Robert Smith'. Folio 257 of the same piece gives orders to the earl for his '2d Squadron' and again specified its composition.
38 'Next weeke they [the Army] are to chang their Camp, and twenty Squadrons of horse, and ten of Dragoones, are to joyne them, and a smale traine of Artillery also', National Archives, Kew, SP 8/4.
39 Walton, p. 370.

or buff were definitely issued. Whatever form waistcoats took they were normally obscured by the fullness of the coat.

All ranks wore the hat of black felt or beaver with a hatband of the regimental 'facing' colour and with the edge bound in white or yellow tape. Traditionally this is said to have been worn over an iron skullcap or 'secrete' but there is no evidence for the issue of this item to other ranks, and as demonstrated below under 'armour', helmets were still being issued for service. Given the issue of helmets it would be highly unlikely that a secrete would be issued as well, although, of course, officers may have worn them by private purchase.

Regrettably, because the colonel contracted for uniform at a regimental level it is not possible to track when the new regiments actually received their uniforms.

On active service brown gauntlets were worn by all ranks.

Housings and holster-caps were of the colour of the regiment's coat linings.

Armour

In Charles II's 'Regulations' of 5 May 1663 it was ordered that 'Each Horseman to have for his defensive armes, back, breast, and pot.'[40]

Armour was certainly being sent to Tangier in 1682 for the regiment of horse garrisoned there,[41] but it has long been believed that, except in the Royal Regiment of Scots Horse, where blackened triple-bar 'lobster-tailed' helmets were still worn, the regiments of horse at home had abandoned their armour by 1685 and in place of pots wore iron skull caps over hats. The evidence, however, suggests otherwise.

Sadly for the military historian and researcher the bulk of the Tower issue warrants for 1685 are missing, but there are two that survive in the National Archives at Kew.[42]

May 1685 'to be transported to Barwick for his Mats service', '56 Backs, 60 Breasts, 60 Potts'

15 June 1685 to be transported to Carlisle for arming Regim^t of horse to be lodged there'

	Backs	360
Harquebuss armor	Breaste	360
	Potts	360

Both of these units have so far defied identification and the Berwick armour may, indeed, never have been issued, since no regiment of horse appears to have been sent there. However the inference is quite clear that

---

40 Richard Cannon, *Historical Records of the Seventh Dragoon Guards* (London: Longman, Orme, 1839), p. iii.

41 This Regiment became the Royal Regiment of Dragoons after its return to England, see Chapter 4.

42 National Archives, Kew, WO55/1656, f. 16.

back, breast, and 'pott', the contemporary term for the famous 'English triple-bar lobster pot helmet', were issued to the horse in 1685.[43] The 360 sets equates to six troops each of 60 men, which includes the augmentation of 13 June, but makes no allowance for armour for officers – although this could have been by a separate warrant as in the 1688 issues, and may simply be that this has not survived.

The issues for 1688, for which year the majority of the Tower issues warrants luckily do survive, strongly reinforce this evidence. Thus on 29 September 1689 the following issue is recorded:[44]

To the severall Regiments hereafter mentioned By Order and proporton of this 29ʰ September 1689			
	Harquebuss Armoʳ Pistoll Proof		
	Breasts	Backs	Potte
To the Duke of Barwick Regim	486	486	486
To Sr John ffenwicks	324	324	324
To R hamiltons	324	324	324
To Majʳ Genˡˡ Wardens	324	324	324
To the Lᵈ Peterburroughs	324	324	324
To Sʳ John Lanyers	414	414	414
To Sr John Talbotts	324	324	324
To the Duke of St Albans	324	324	324
To the Earle of Arrans	324	324	324
	3,168	3,168	

Five days earlier, on 24 September, armour had been issued to the officers of these regiments, see below.

Similar issues, but of 318 suits each, were made to:

Henry Slingsby's Regiment of Horse	5 October 1688[45]
Marquis of Miremont's Regiment of Horse	6 October 1688[46]
George Holman's Regiment of Horse	6 October 1688[47]
Lord Brandon's Regiment of Horse	6 October 1688[48]
The Earl of Salisbury's Regiment of Horse	17 November 1688[49]

---

43 A warrant for the repair of armour in the Tower dated March 1687 lists nearly 1000 'potts' in the armour for horse but specifies, for a single example, a 'Pott with one Barr'. National Archives, Kew, WO55/1656, f. 28. It is worth noting that this number of approximately 1,000 refers only to those items in need of repair.
44 National Archives, Kew, WO55/1656, f. 33.
45 *Ibid.*, f. 37.
46 *Ibid.*, f. 33.
47 *Ibid.*, f. 34.
48 *Ibid.*, f. 38.
49 *Ibid.*

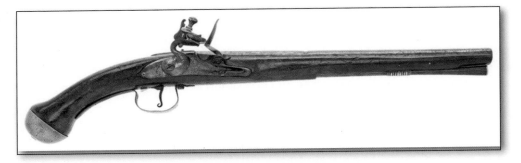

Military pattern pistol for use by the Horse, late 17th century.

A military issue pistol, sold at auction by Military Heritage in 2012, and has a traditional flintlock mechanism. It is 21½ inches overall and is marked 'J2R'. forward of the hammer. The butt cap is brass but all other metalwork is iron. The ramrod is original wood with a brass end. It is of approx 60 calibre bore, making a ball a little over a half inch in diameter. Photograph courtesy of Heritage Auctions and reproduced with kind permission.

Again all issues are to be 'pistoll proofe'. The issues of this armour to the newly raised regiments may be indicative of their readiness for muster, but given the dates of the commissions of the colonels given in Appendix 2 this is by no means certain.

Noticeable about these warrants, however, is the fact that all issues again include 'potte' and it would therefore seem an extremely high probability that the regiments of horse *were* still wearing these. Although no potts had been ordered and manufactured for a number of years the Tower inventories for 1687 show 8,449 breasts, 8,274 backs, and 6,834 potts in store.[50] The inventory also lists numerous other items that fall into this category, but the above is what might be termed the 'ammunition quality' armour, excluding those items in need of repair. Additionally there were, of course, other smaller stores elsewhere in England.

Quartermasters again seem to have fallen into the no-man's land between officers and were not included in the issue of armour to officers. Thus 324 suits or 56 per troop must have been required for 50 troopers, 3 corporals, 2 trumpeters and 1 quartermaster. For the new-raised regiments, Dalton, *English*, lists no quartermasters to the troops and this would appear to be confirmed here.

The issue to the Queen Consort's Regiment of Horse only equals 46 suits per troop and one must assume here that a clerk has made a mistake and omitted the September increase of ten men per troop. The 486 suits to the Royal Regiment of Horse however is equal to 54 suits for each of its nine troops, a number which makes absolutely no sense at all, unless we make the logical assumption that in this regiment, as apparently in the Royal Regiment of Horse Guards, the trumpeters did not wear armour.

The Royal Regiment of Scots Horse was included in these 1688 issues:

To His Mats Horse Guards lately come from Scotland
By Order of the Board and Proportn 10th of Novemb 1688

	Breasts	380
Harquebuss armo^r. Pistoll	Backs	380
	Potts	380'[51]

---

50 British Library Add MS 9458-7463. The number of potts excludes 289 'with one bar' and 482 'without bars'.

51 National Archives, Kew, WO55/1656 f. 38.

This in turn suggests that armour was *not* in general issue in this regiment. Although given in the warrant as the 'Royal Regiment of Horse *Guards*' (author's italics), given the size of this issue it must have been for the Royal Regiment of Horse, a hypothesis confirmed by the issue of armour to its officers six days later (see below).[52]

The back and breast plates, when worn on active service, were apparently usually worn over the coat but may occasionally have been worn under it, as was the later practice during the War of the Spanish Succession. However this latter would have required the coat to have been very loose fitting at all other times since any tightness over a breast and back plates will otherwise preclude and hamper movement and manoeuvrability, a highly dangerous situation in hand to hand combat.

On 6 November as the campaign closed and James' resolve to fight failed him (his first flight from London and the famous incident of the throwing of the Great Seal into the River Thames took place on 11 November), an order was sent out to all of the regiments of horse to the effect that they were to leave their armour 'at the places from whence they are next to march.'[53]

The Ordnance Office was then to send 'persons to receive the Armour so left … and bring it away thence to the Tower of London.'[54] The bureaucrats of the Ordnance Office wanted their armour back!

Armament

Charles II's 'Regulations' of 5 May 1663 referred to above ordered 'Each Horseman to have … for his offensive armes, a sword, and a case of pistolls, the barrells whereof are not be und^r fourteen inches in length; and each Trooper of Our Guards to have a carbine.'[55]

Essentially this order was still in force 22 years later when James became king. The sword was a straight-bladed heavy sword, the pistols were of flintlock pattern, but what had changed is that troopers of all regiments of horse, in all three kingdoms, now carried a carbine.[56] This latter was carried from a sling worn over the left shoulder whilst the sword was suspended from a baldric slung over the right. The characteristic 'cross-belts' thus formed by these two belts were considered to be the distinctive mark of the horse over the dragoons. The pistols were carried in holsters either side of the saddlebow, the relevant ball bags and powder box were also carried at the saddlebow.

---

52 Dalton, *English*, vol. 2, p. 210 gives the strength of these two units as 132 and 352 respectively on 1 November 1688.

53 Although an order dated 22 November gives special instructions to one unit: 'the Second Squadron of Sr John Talbott's Regiment to March forthwith to Farnham, and that they bring their Armour with them', National Archives, Kew, WO5/4, f. 22. This is the only such order that has so far come to light.

54 National Archives, Kew, WO4/1, f. 109.

55 Cannon, *Historical Records of the Seventh Dragoon Guards*, p. iii.

56 The first recorded issue of carbines to the regiments of horse appears in 1678.

All leatherwork was buff coloured except the sword scabbard, which was traditionally always black.[57]

Officers

As in the Regiment of Horse Guards, the officers of horse wore coats of a finer material than their men, in either crimson or scarlet as the mood took them. Often officers' coats were lined and faced with in the same colour (i.e. either crimson or red) but coloured facings may just have been beginning to come into use in the regiments of horse.[58] In this latter respect it may have been that a regiment's officers either all used facings colours or none did, at the discretion of the colonel – it would seem unlikely that the two variations existed side by side amongst brother officers. There is, nonetheless, some evidence that at least one regiment's officers were equipped by contract under direction by their colonel, presumably to ensure uniformity amongst them. Lace, either gold or silver as the colonel decreed, was added in some profusion to seams, edges, buttonholes, etc. Hats were of black beaver,[59] braided with gold and/or silver galoon and additionally sported tours of white feathers. Officers of all ranks wore crimson sashes, edged and fringed in gold. Officers carried swords of a similar style to their men, although usually of private purchase, sometimes from a waist belt as they carried no carbine (although they did carry pistols, with the cartridge boxes attached to the holsters).

At an army level, there was no set arrangement of rank badges or distinctions for the Horse, even for the company officers. However in 1686 the Earl of Oxford, the then colonel of the Royal Regiment of Horse, issued orders to his regiment which were exceptional in setting out the earliest known form of rank distinctions in a regiment of horse (distinctions for company officers in the regiments of foot had been issued by Charles II in September 1684 – see Chapter 5 below).

All Captains' coats are to be of blue cloth faced with the same, the lace of the said coats to be gold laid double upon every Seam and slits with gold foot between the two laces, the buttons of gold thread with a gold thread round the sleeves, under which must be laid the same gold lace as down the sleeves.

All Lieutenants and Cornets must be the made as the captains only a single gold lace on each seam, slits, and sleeves, the fringe excepted.

---

57 This peculiarity goes back to at least the mid 16th century.

58 In 1697 a 'red coat Lined with yellow silk' was stolen from a quartermaster of the Queen Consort's Regiment, National Army Museum manuscript 6807/125. Although it should perhaps be noted that quartermasters appear to have existed in a strange limbo somewhere between 'proper' officers and NCOs.

59 Imported from the New World. Beaver had already been extinct in England and Scotland for the best part of a century.

The Quartermaster – coats must be the same cloth as the rest of the officers with a gold edging down before, at the pockets, slits and round the sleeves as the Lieutenants and Cornets, and gold buttons as the rest of the officers.

The pockets must be of the same fashion. viz. two long slits on each side.

Every officer must have a black hat edged with gold lace and with a white feather. The trimming of the hats must be yellow as also the cravat strings.

Whether any other regiment of horse either followed this system or used a variation of the idea is unknown although N. P. Dawnay makes some speculation that it may have done,[60] and in which case we might expect it to broadly echo or copy that of the Royal Regiment of Horse.

Armour was worn by officers including those of field rank and amongst the Tower issues for the Sedgemoor campaign, of which it has to be said very few survive, is one such:

To the Rt Honble the Earle of Arran and to the Lord Ferrers ... 4th July 1685[61]

    Silke Armoure consisting
    Of Back Breast Skirts
    Gauntletts Quilted Capps 2 Suite
    with Sculls

These items were actually issued on 12 July. Other entries make it clear that a suit comprised only one gauntlet, presumably the bridle gauntlet for the left arm. Silk armour is very rare but one suit does appear in the inventories of the Tower,[62] and a 'breastplate' and 'helmet' do survive in the collection of the Royal Armouries. The breastplate is the same size and shape as that of a contemporary iron piece but is made of perhaps fifteen or sixteen layers of silk that are held together by a broad cross-stitching over the whole surface (creating 'squares' of silk approximately ½ inch between). A second layer of the same has then been put below and the two joined along the edge. The whole then appears to have been covered with white silk, which would have given a smooth appearance and hidden the quilting. The helmet is a period skull from a 'pott' which has been simply covered in white silk but the tail has been removed and silk, of the same construction as the 'breastplate' although only simplex, made into a new combined earpieces and tail.[63] The armour, when new, must have looked exceedingly impressive and would also have been cooler and easier to move in than iron armour without too much, if any, overall loss of protection – it would, however, have been very expensive

---

60 Dawnay, pp. 8–9.
61 National Archives, Kew, WO55/1656, f. 17.
62 British Library Add MS 7458-7463 f. 16r: 'Armor taken fr Disaffected Persons Silk Armour 1 suite'.
63 My thanks to Thom Richardson of the Royal Armouries for the opportunity to examine this unique piece.

to make,[64] and would have required a greater level of care and maintenance. 'Quilted Capps with Sculls' are the armoured 'secretes' worn beneath the hat.

By contrast, in 1688 the warrants for the issue of armour are almost complete and thus on 24 September armour was issued to the officers of the eight 'old' regiments listed above in the proportion of 20 suits to each 'line' regiment,[65] and 30 suits to each of the Royal Regiment of Horse and the Queen Consort's Regiment of Horse.[66] This number makes sense as three officers in each troop, less the colonel who, as we have seen, received a separate issue when required, plus three of the four Regimental staff – it seems a safe assumption that the fourth staff member, the chaplain, did not wear armour.

With regards to the strength of the new raised regiments of 1688 whose troopers were issued with armour between 5 October and 17 November 1688, see above; it may be a better guide to the strength of these regiments at this time to note the issues to their officers that were as follows:

Marquis of Miremont's Regiment of Horse	20 suits	19 October[67]
Lord Brandon's Regiment of Horse	18 suits	19 October[68]
Henry Slingsby's Regiment of Horse	15 suits	6 & 8 November[69]
George Holman's Regiment of Horse	No recorded issue	
The Earl of Salisbury's Regiment of Horse	No recorded issue	

All of the above suits are specified as 'carbine proofe'.

There are no separate recorded issues to the colonels of these new regiments.

The officers of the Royal Regiment of Scots Horse received an issue of armour on 16 November 1688, specified as 'musquett proofe' although the regiment received only 19 suits for its six troops.

Trumpeters

In most regiments the trumpeters, and the regimental kettledrummer, wore coats of either in the regimental facing colour lined in crimson and laced with gold or silver like the officers or simply in the same colours as the rank and file with the addition of gold and or silver lace (usually along all seams and along all edges of the coat). However the Royal Regiment of Horse and the Queen's Regiment of Horse were granted the privilege of musicians dressed in the royal livery exactly the same as the Horse Guards (see Chapter 2). In December 1685, when he made Graham of Claverhouse's Regiment into the Royal Regiment of Scots Horse, the King sent a letter to the Treasury (who

---

64 British Library Add MS 28082 values an iron back, breast and pott at 50s. In Add MS 7458-7463, the silk armour is valued at £5, exactly twice as much.

65 A suit of armour comprised back, breast and pott, unless specifically given as otherwise.

66 National Archives, Kew, SP 44/165, f. 67.

67 National Archives, Kew, WO55/1656, f. 35.

68 Ibid.

69 Ibid., f. 37.

would have to pay for such things) extending this privilege to them: 'in future [Claverhouse's Regiment is] to be Our Own Regiment of Horse and to have rank and precedence accordingly and the Trumpeters of the several Troops and the Kettle Drummers of that regiment to be in future in Our own livery.'[70]

On campaign, as has already been mentioned above, it would appear that the trumpeters wore armour of back, breast and pott in the same way that all other members of the regiments did.

Cornets

During the reign of James II each troop of horse still carried its own cornet, of a design that was left almost entirely to the regimental colonel's personal whim. Usually colonels took the opportunity to use some form of personal or family armorial device, which would, of course, alter, with any change of colonel.

Cornets were around two to two and a half feet square with roughly a two-inch fringe around all 'flying' edges. Cords were between two and three feet long. The cornet was carried on a lance-like pole of about eight feet that was topped by a steel or gilt lance point.

The following are drawn from *The James II Colour Book* in Windsor Castle Library. This manuscript seems, from internal evidence, to have been compiled between approximately mid-March and 29 July 1685.

The Royal Regiment of Horse

All cornets were crimson with gold fringes, cords and tassels, the lances had gilt finials.

The King's Troop carried a cornet similar in design to that of the 1st Troop of the Horse Guards, except that it had a silver scroll lettered in black above the central crown and cypher, these latter and all other embroidery were in gold.

The remaining troops all used royal badges on their cornets, viz.: Colonel's troop: the royal crest in gold; lieutenant colonel's troop: a gold rose crowned gold; the captains' cornets bore, in order of seniority: a gold thistle leaved green, a gold fleur-de-lys, a gold harp, the Royal Oak in gold, a gold portcullis and the Cross of St. George within a garter, proper; all devices surmounted by the royal crown.

These cornets were made almost immediately after James' accession to the throne and were supplied 'against H.M.'s ... Coronation by Thos Holford, Portcullis Pursuivant of Arms':

> For a Standard for H.M.'s Troop in the Royal Regt. of Horse, commanded by the Earl of Oxford, Sir John Parsons, Captain, by agreement as above[71]   24 0 0

> For the other 8 troops of the Royal Regt. of Horse, a standard for each, at £20, by agreement as above   160 0 0[72]

---

70 Lawson, p. 92.
71 'By agreement with Chas Fox Esqr., Paymaster-General.'
72 War Office State Papers quoted in Walton, pp. 460–461.

Above & left:

Standard and cornet of the 2nd Troop of the Royal Regiment of Horse Guards.

See plate W2 and text for colouring.

Note that the design of the two flags is identical, as it was in all troops.

The standard pole and odd pattern on the leaf-point is exactly as shown in *The James II Colour Book* for all standards and guidons, both guards and 'line'. The tassels on the horse guards flags are shown as somewhat heavier than those in use in the line.
(after C. C. P. Lawson)

Below, left:

Standard of the colonel's troop of the Earl of Thanet's Regiment of Horse, 1686 (after C. C. P. Lawson).

Below, right:

Standard of the colonel's troop of the Earl of Arran's Regiment of Horse, 1686 (after C. C. P. Lawson).

The Queen Consort's Regiment of Horse

All troops bore identical cornets of yellow silk damask, fringed and tasselled in gold, bearing the Queen's cypher of MBER in gold surmounted by a crown.

Earl of Peterborough's Regiment of Horse

The cornets were all of plain white damask without any device; fringing and tassels were yellow and silver.

Earl of Plymouth's Regiment of Horse

All cornets of plain green silk damask, fringed gold and silver, tassels green and silver.

Lord Dover's Regiment of Horse

No information has come to light concerning the cornets of this short-lived regiment.

Earl of Thanet's Regiment of Horse

The colonel's cornet was of blue damask with blue and silver fringes and tassels, in the centre a silver lion on a wreath of silver and black, the whole surmounted by a silver earl's coronet.

The lieutenant colonel's troop bore a cornet of plain blue, fringed and tasselled like the Colonel's. The captains' cornets were as for the Lieutenant Colonel's, except that they bore silver numerals ('I' 'II' etc.) in the upper corner next to the pole to indicate their seniority.

Earl of Arran's Regiment of Horse

The colonel's troop cornet was of white silk damask with gold fringes, in the centre was an oak tree proper on a green ground and penetrated by a silver saw; the whole on a wreath of red and silver and surmounted by a silver scroll bearing the motto THROVGH in black. All other troops' cornets were plain white, without any device, fringed and tasselled gold.

Earl of Shrewsbury's Regiment of Horse

The colonel's troop cornet was of yellow damask bearing a lion rampant in silver, within a narrow silver engrailed line, the fringe and tassels being mixed yellow and silver.

The cornets of the remaining troops were plain yellow with mixed yellow and silver fringes and tassels.

Princess Anne of Denmark's Regiment of Horse

This regiment's cornets were all crimson, fringed and tasselled gold, bearing in the centre the Princess' cypher PAD surmounted by her coronet.

The Queen Dowager's Regiment of Horse

All of the regiment's cornets were identical and of sea green silk damask with green and gold fringes and tassels. In the centre was the Queen Dowager's cypher of two Cs interlaced and crowned, all in gold. The same device, incidentally, was borne on the colours of her regiment of foot.

The Marquis de Miremont's Regiment of Horse; Lord Brandon's Regiment of Horse; Henry Slingsby's Regiment of Horse; George Holman's Regiment of Horse; Earl of Salisbury's Regiment of Horse

These five regiments do not appear in the Windsor Colour Book as they were raised in 1688, and to date no information is known about their cornets.

Regiments on The Scottish Establishment:

The Royal (Scots) Regiment of Horse

Aside from the fact that the regiment's cornets were crimson and bore Royal badges, no details have yet been discovered.

Regiments on The Irish Establishment:

The Duke of Ormonde's Regiment of Horse; the Earl of Tyrconnell's Regiment of Horse; the Earl of Ossery's Regiment of Horse

No information has yet come to light regarding the cornets of these three regiments during James' reign.

Pay

The following rates are per day. The colonel and lieutenant colonel were also captains of a troop and drew separate pay and allowances for each:

Colonel (as Colonel)	12s 0d
Lieutenant Colonel (as Lieutenant Colonel)	8s 0d
Major	£ 1 0s 0d
Captain	14s 0d*
Lieutenant	10s 0d*
Cornet	9s 0d*
Adjutant	5s 0d
Quartermaster	6s 0d**
Chirugeon	6s 0d
Chaplain	6s 8d
Corporal	3s 0d
Trumpeter	2s 8d
Trooper	2s 6d

* Includes an allowance for 2 horses at 2s each.
** Includes an allowance for 1 horse at 2s.

As in the Horse Guards there was a 6d deduction for 'off reckonings' from all except officers.[73]

---

73 For further details on 'off reckonings' see John Childs, *The Army of Charles II.*

The pay of a major was comparably high because, except in the Royal Regiment of Horse, he was not a troop captain and therefore did not draw the extra pay for that rank.

In the Royal Regiment of Horse, where the major was a troop captain, his pay was only 5s 6d per day as major but then, of course, his pay as captain in addition. Captains in the Royal Regiment of Horse were paid 15s per day, and when the regiment was quartered in Southwark or London the pay of troopers (and presumably others below the rank of quartermaster) was raised by 8d per day.

Additional to the above rates of pay and allowances all officers were given an allowance for servants: the colonel received an additional daily allowance for six servants at 2s 6d each; the lieutenant colonel, the major and captains for three servants at the same rate; the lieutenants and cornets were allowed two servants each, again at 2s 6d per head.

'The colonel's clerk', who was responsible for keeping the regiment's accounts, was not one of these six servants but an allowance for his pay was made only in the two senior regiments of foot guards. In other regiments, according to Clifford Walton, an unauthorised deduction of two pence in the pound of the whole pay of the regiment was used for his salary.[74] During James II's reign this individual came to be known as 'the colonel's agent', a position that would soon become 'the regimental agent' of the 18th century. It is worth noting that many of the men who are contacts for the rewards offered for deserters (see Deserters' Notices below) are 'the colonel's agent' and not the company's officer. As in the 18th century some agents worked for multiple regiments, making the post quite a lucrative one.

There was one further 'stoppage' from the pay of all ranks except officers: from 1684 one day's pay (two days in a leap year) was taken for the support of the new Chelsea Hospital.

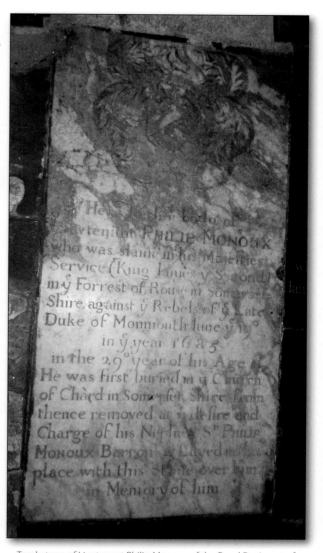

Tombstone of Lieutenant Philip Monoux of the Royal Regiment of Horse. Monoux was killed in a minor skirmish at Ashill in Somersetshire on 19 June 1685 in an obscure skirmish during the Sedgemoor campaign. He was the first officer of the Household Cavalry regiments to be killed in action. The tombstone in St Mary's Church, Wootton, Bedfordshire. Author's photograph, with thanks to Alan Larsen and the Revd. Peter Ackroyd of St Mary's.

---

74 Walton, pp. 644–645.

4

The Regiments of Dragoons

Organisation

On James' accession there were only two full regiments of dragoons on the three armies' strengths, plus the three troops in Ireland that were on the strength of the regiments of horse. On the English establishment was the Royal Regiment of Dragoons, raised in 1679 as the Earl of Ossory's Regiment of Horse for service in Tangier. When Tangier was abandoned and the garrison came home in 1683, the four remaining troops of horse of this regiment were converted into the Royal Regiment of Dragoons. On the Scottish establishment was an older regiment, the Royal Regiment of (Scots) Dragoons raised in 1679 from previously existing independent troops.

The establishment of the two regiments was basically identical, each was of six troops with each troop having an establishment of:

1 Captain[1]	1 Lieutenant
1 Cornet	1 Quartermaster (not in the Scots regiment)
2 Sergeants	3 Corporals
2 Drummers	2 Hautboys
50 Dragoons (55 in the Scots Regiment)	

In addition the colonel's troop carried on its strength the small regimental staff of adjutant, quartermaster and provost,[2] chaplain,[3] chirurgeon and gunsmith,[4] augmented on 3 November 1688 by the addition of a surgeon's mate.[5] The three troops of the Irish Army were of the same strength and establishment as the troops in the English and Scots Regiments. Like the regiments of horse the major of the regiments was not a troop commander.

---

1 In the two senior troops the 'captain' was the colonel and lieutenant colonel.
2 Both positions combined in one office holder.
3 This position is, oddly, missing from the establishment pay warrant for the Royal Regiment of Scots Dragoons. National Archives, Kew, SP 8/1, part 2, ff. 257–259.
4 This man may have been either a civilian or a trooper detached from the ranks, he does not appear as a separate rank on the pay warrants.
5 National Archives, Kew, WO4/1, ff. 108–109.

The strength of the dragoon arm was augmented slightly when, on 27 February 1685, James commissioned the raising of an independent troop of dragoons under Captain William Strother, to be quartered near Berwick-upon-Tweed. On 8 June this troop was ordered to be incorporated into the Royal Regiment of Dragoons. Then between 9 and 15 June James issued five more commissions to raise additional troops for the Royal Regiment of Dragoons,[6] all were raised in or around London, thus bringing the regiment to a total strength of twelve troops.

Dragoons, *c.*1688. (After C. C. P. Lawson)
Although based on an illustration of French dragoons skirmishing *c.*1689 this shows the general appearance of the dragoons of the period. Note the mixture of 'furred caps' and the ubiquitous felt hat and, in the background, a drummer still mounted.

On 13 June 1685, with Monmouth's invasion and rebellion looming, James gave authority for each troop of dragoons to be increased to 60 men. But barely a month later with the imminent crisis past, after the utter defeat of the rebellion at Sedgemoor, on July 16 1685 James ordered that the strength of each dragoon troop was to be reduced back to 50 troopers.[7]

On 17 July James further expanded his dragoon arm by commissioning Colonel John Berkeley, Viscount Fitzhardinge, to raise and command a new regiment of eight troops, with an internal organisation identical to that of the Royal Regiments, and Colonel John Berkeley, Baron Berkeley, to command a new regiment of six troops. Troop captains were commissioned between 17 and 22 July (although in Fitzhardinge's case they were all named on the original warrant[8]); the field officers and regimental staff all received their commissions at the same time as the colonels. Remarkably in light of the recent crisis, in both cases the troops all appear to have been raised in the western counties. The former of these two regiments adopted the title of the Princess Anne of Denmark's Regiment of Dragoons sometime around early August of 1685, perhaps on the 2nd when the other new dragoon regiment was titled the Queen Consort's Regiment of Dragoons (see below.)

---

6   According to Dalton, *English*, commissions were to Francis Russell (10 June), George Churchill (9 June), Richard Leveson (11 June), Thomas Hussey (12 June), John Williams (13 June), Edward Leigh (15 June), although one of these captains was as a replacement for Charles Nedby who had transferred to the Queen Consort's Regiment of Horse on 6 June. This is confirmed by National Archives, Kew, WO5/1, ff. 48–49 which specifically refers to 'the five Troops added to the Royall Regiment of Dragoons.'

7   National Archives, Kew, WO5/1, f. 167.

8   *Ibid.*, f. 186.

Two troops of the latter regiment, Lieutenant Colonel Butler's and Captain Conner's were ordered to embark for Ireland on 31 July,[9] and the regiment in full was ordered to Ireland on 29 September 1685,[10] and then transferred onto the Irish Army establishment.

The only independent troop of dragoons which appears to have actually been raised in 1685 was that of Captain Walker, but the order for the disbandment of this troop was given as early as 8 July 1685.[11]

On 25 July 1685[12] the same warrant which ordered a reduction in the strength of a troop of horse ordered likewise for the dragoons and thus a troop was reduced further still to only 40 troopers. The establishment of officers, NCOs, etc. still remained unchanged and the troop establishment was now:

1 Captain	1 Lieutenant
1 Cornet	1 Quartermaster
2 Sergeants	3 Corporals
2 Drummers	2 Hautboys
40 Dragoons	

The Royal Regiment of Scots Dragoons varied slightly from this establishment and its troops had a strength of:

1 Captain	1 Lieutenant
1 Cornet	
2 Sergeants	2 Corporals
2 Drummers	
55 Dragoons	

This same streamlining of the army's establishments that affected the horse also reduced the strength of Fitzhardinge's Regiment to the 'standard' six troops and on 2 August caused Charles, Duke of Somerset to be commissioned as colonel of another dragoon regiment to be titled The Queen Consort's Regiment of Dragoons. This regiment was created by taking Leveson's, Hussy's, and Williams' from the Royal Regiment of Dragoons and Philpot's and St George's from Fitzhardinge's, although as Philpot transferred with the rank of major his troop must have gone either to the Colonel the Duke of Somerset or to Lieutenant Colonel Alexander Canon. The Royal

---

9   *Ibid.*, f. 193.

10 National Archives, Kew, WO5/2, f. 60. It is worth noting that the orders infer that this is simply the transfer of a regiment from one establishment to the other. There is no implication that the regiment had been specifically raised for Ireland.

11 National Archives, Kew, WO5/1, f. 172. WO4/1, f. 10 contains a warrant dated 21 July 1685 to disband an independent troop of dragoons but gives no captain's name, it may merely be a repeat of the warrant of 8 July.

12 *Ibid.*, ff. 184–5.

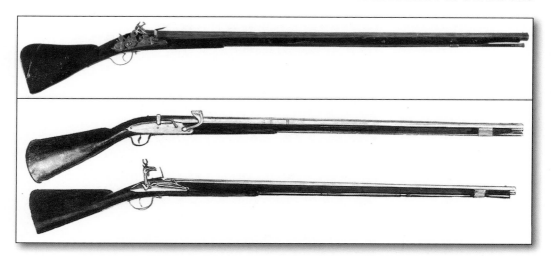

Regiment of Dragoons was also reduced to a strength of eight troops at this time and the missing troop undoubtedly became Somerset's sixth.[13]

The regiments of dragoons were now settled at six troops (eight in the Royal Regiment) with each troop's establishment as above. As mentioned above, the regiment's major was without a troop and the five regimental staff were on the strength of the colonel's troop.

In Ireland Colonel Richard Hamilton's Regiment of Dragoons appears to have absorbed the dragoon troops, which had previously been attached to the regiments of horse, and by January 1686 had a strength of 10 troops. The regiment and the troops were organised and officered exactly the same as their compatriots on the English establishment except that they retained the earlier 50 dragoons strength and appear never to have reduced to the 40 men of the English establishment.[14]

This establishment remained unchanged until in September 1688, as the relationship with the Netherlands deteriorated and William's intentions became plain, James ordered the augmentation of each troop of dragoons by 10 troopers to bring the strength back to 50 men,[15] plus officers, NCOs, etc. as above.

In 1688 no additional dragoons were ordered for either the English or the Scots Armies but on October 12 1688 a warrant was sent to the Earl of Tyrconnel in Ireland to raise three additional regiments of foot and one additional regiment of dragoons for the Irish Army.[16] Whether these regiments were ever raised is not known but it is possible that they became a part of James II's Irish Army.

Top: Snaphaunce musket *c*.1686. Typical of the 'munition quality' weapons in use by the army. Bottom: Dutch matchlock and snaphaunce muskets, *c*.1685.

The appearance of these would have been identical to those produced by English gunmakers. (Public domain)

---

13   Cannon also suggests this, in *Historical Records of the Third Light Dragoons* (London: Parker, Furnivall, & Parker, 1847), pp. 12.

14   National Archives, Kew, S P8/1, part 2, ff. 97–104.

15   Warrant 24 Sept 1688 to arm an augmentation of 10 men in each company of 'Horse, Grenadeers, Dragoons, and Foot', National Archives, Kew, SP 44/165 f. 66.

16   *Calendar of State Papers, Domestic Series*, James II, Volume III, June 1687–February 1689 (London: HMSO, 1972), p. 312. National Archives, Kew, SP 63/640, f. 304.

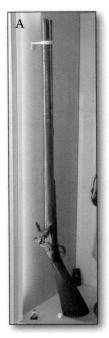

A. Late 17th century flintlock musket fitted with an English 'dog lock'. Somewhat outdated by James' reign, muskets such as this still remained on the Tower inventories and thus would still have been in use by the army.

B. Detail of the dog lock of the same musket.

(Collection of Shrewsbury Museum. Author's photographs)

Uniform

The uniform was generally the same as that worn by the regiments of horse. The table below gives the coat colours, facings, etc. where these are known. Headwear was the ubiquitous black felt hat but in the field a 'furred cap', similar to that worn by the grenadiers of some regiments of foot, was often worn. Some modern fantasies show the Royal Regiment of Scots Dragoons wearing a 'blue bonnet' but there is no contemporary evidence for such an item either in writing or in any illustration, and it seems likely that had it existed it would have attracted some comments, if only because of its uniqueness.

Dragoons wore the same black over-knee boots for both mounted and foot service. In appearance these were essentially the same as those worn by the Horse but they were actually made of more supple leather for ease of manoeuvre when dismounted. It is worth emphasising that the dragoons wore no armour, apparently not even a 'secrete'.

Armament

In 1685 the new companies of dragoons were issued with:

Snaphaunce musquets strapt for Dragoons	63
Cartouch Boxes with girdles	63

Boots or Sockets for ye muskets	63
Drummes for Dragoons	2
Bayonetts with Froggs and Belts	63
Halberts	2
Partizans	2
Saddles	63[17]

And a formal regulation dated 21 February 1687 laid out that the armament of the dragoons was to be a snaphaunce muskets 'strapt, with bright barrels of three foote eight inches long, cartouch-boxes, bayonetts, granado pouches, buckets, and hammer hatchetts.'

From other evidence however it would appear that flintlock muskets were not universal amongst the dragoons on the English establishment until the 1687 regulation; the regiments until then, like their counterparts in the regiments of foot, having to put up with a mixture of matchlock and flintlock. The Royal Regiment of Scots Dragoons was ahead of their English comrades in this respect in that they had been issued solely with flintlocks from their raising in 1681.

When the troop was mounted, muskets were carried butt-down in the 'buckets', mentioned above, attached to the front of the saddle. When dismounted the muskets could be slung across the back by means of their buff leather straps (in 1688 these straps are specified as being '4 inches broad … with large iron buckles and tin chapes'). Swords, bayonets and/or hatchets were suspended from a buff leather waist belt (in contrast to the shoulder baldric of the regiments of horse) but the grenade pouch (when worn) and cartouche box were worn on a strap over the left shoulder. All leatherwork was of buff or tan-coloured leather.

In 1672, when a dragoon regiment had been raised for the Dutch War, twelve men in each troop were given halberds and a pair of pistols in place of a musket and told off to act as horse holders when the regiment was dismounted (a dragoon troop had then mustered 80 men plus officers etc.). Whether a similar arrangement existed in the army of 1685 is not known but some similar arrangement must have existed even if all troops were now identically armed, certainly there are no issue warrant for halberds beyond those needed for the regiment's sergeants.

It is worth noting that Barthorp states that 'The wood work of all firearms at this time was painted black.'[18] Sadly I have not found this in any contemporary documents although Barthorp is usually an impeccable source.

---

17 The National Archives, Kew, WO47/15, quoted in Tincey, Sedgemoor 1685, p. 22. If correct, this warrant suggests that companies of dragoons were initially intended to have 60 rank and file and three corporals.

18 Michael Barthorp, *British Cavalry Uniforms Since 1660* (Blandford: Poole, 1984), p. 18.

Guidons of the eight senior troops of the Royal Regiment of Dragoons, 1685. (After C. C. P. Lawson)

The full guidon at centre is that of the colonel's troop with the badges of the lieutenant colonel's troop (left) and the 1st captain's troop (right). The row of badges below are those of the, left to right, 2nd to 6th troops. See text for more information. The guidons were carried on standard poles identical to that shown in the illustration of the standard of the 2nd Troop of the Royal Regiment of Horse Guards. Note the unique shape of these guidons, which was not used by any other regiment nor in any subsequent issues.

Sergeants

Sergeants were armed with a halberd and pistols in place of a musket and both they and the corporals were differenced from the common soldiery by the addition of white or yellow tape to pockets and buttonholes.

Officers

Crimson or red coats with linings and facings of the same, black hats with white feathers; coats and hats laced and edged with gold and/or silver lace. Like the officers of horse they wore crimson or red net sashes around their waist. Dragoon officers' armament was a sword and a pair of pistols, although it is probable that when serving on foot they carried half-pikes or partisans like the officers of foot and which were certainly issued to the troops, as evidenced by the above warrant. Company officers in the dragoon regiments wore 'gorgets of rank' in the same way as their colleagues in a regiment of foot (see below).

Drummers

Coats were usually the same as those of the regiment's rank and file with the addition of gold or silver lace in varying amounts of excess. It is possible that coats of the regiment's facing colour lined red may already have been coming into use – they were certainly the norm some decades later. The drums themselves were issued to the regiments from the Tower inventories. They were of wood, and distinctively different from those of the regiments of foot as they inventoried separately,[19] although exactly how they were different is unknown and it may simply have been a difference in size. They were probably painted with the colonel's cypher or badge on the front, but, of course, this would have been at the colonel's responsibility (and cost) and no records survive or at least have yet come to light.[20]

The Royal Regiment of Dragoons and the Royal Regiment of Scots Dragoons had the privilege of having their drummers dressed in royal livery although given the cost of these coats it is possible that the drummers may already have been issued with a heavily laced blue coat for 'service and everyday' wear as was the case a few years later. The drums in these regiments almost certainly had the royal arms painted on the front in the same way as drums used by the regiments of foot guards (and as the drums of the Lifeguard of Foot had during the English Civil Wars[21]).

Hautboys

Assuming the dragoons followed the system of the regiments of foot (see Table 2) it would have been at the regimental colonel's discretion whether the hautboys were dressed like the men or like the drummers.

Guidons

Each troop carried its own guidon of a swallow-tailed form somewhat different to what would be expected, and to the guidons of the Horse Guards. The guidons were 'two lengths in the hoist by five lengths flying' or approximately 2 feet 3 inches in the hoist by 5 feet 8 inches flying. The illustrations show the somewhat unusual shape of the guidons, which was uniform throughout the Regiment of Dragoons. Whether this had been the shape of the guidons of dragoon regiments under Charles II cannot be confirmed, although it does seem probable.

The Royal Regiment of Dragoons

The regiment, perhaps somewhat predictably, used various royal badges to differentiate the different troops' guidons. Colonel's troop: Charles II's cypher of two gold Cs interlaced; lieutenant colonel's troop: a gold escarbuncle. Captains' troops (in order of precedence): two silver ostrich feathers in saltire; a rose and pomegranate impaled proper, leaves and stalk green; the sun rising from a cloud, proper; a gold beacon fired; a gold heraldic lion passant spotted with roundels alternately black, yellow and red standing on a green mound; a phoenix in flames proper. All of these badges were surmounted by a gold Royal Crown (see illustration).

---

19 National Archives, Kew, WO55/1730, 'Survey of Arms, Stores, Cannon, etc.' is an inventory of the Ordnance Office dated 17 September 1686 and includes 'Drumms Ordinary 107, 91 repble, 40 uns[erviceable]. For Draggoons 99'.

20 See notes on this subject under 'Regiments of Foot'.

21 cf. the painting of Charles I and Sir Edward Walker by William Dobson in the National Portrait Gallery.

The field of all guidons was of crimson damask and was fringed in crimson and silver. These guidons were supplied 'against H.M.'s … Coronation by Thos Holford, Portcullis Pursuivant of Arms':

For 8 Colours for the Royal Regt. of Dragoons formerly commanded by the Ld. Churchill now by the Lord Cornbury at £7 5s each   58 0 0[22]

It is interesting to note that at the time that *The James II Colour Book* was compiled, probably in the summer of 1686, the regiment's colonel's guidon is shown as still carrying the cypher of Charles II, not, as might be expected, that of James II. These guidons were probably commissioned and made when the regiment was raised in 1684 but whether a replacement colonel's guidon was ever issued is not known but it seems unlikely. The badges carried on the other troops of the regiment are not recorded in *The James II Colour Book* and have thus far gone unrecorded.

Princess Anne of Denmark's Regiment of Dragoons
All guidons were of perfectly plain yellow silk damask, fringed and tasselled in mixed silver and yellow. The regiment's guidons were, like those of the other regiments of dragoons except for those of the Royal Regiment of Dragoons, of a similar size and shape to those of the Royal Regiment of Horse Guards (see line illustration).

Queen Consort's Regiment of Dragoons
The colonel's guidon was pinkish crimson, fringed and tasselled gold and bearing the Queen's cypher and crown in gold. The lieutenant colonel's guidon was identical to the colonel's, as were the captains' guidons.

The Royal Regiment of (Scots) Dragoons
This regiment does not appear in *The James II Colour Book*, and as yet no information has come to light regarding its guidons. Inferred evidence would however suggest that the regiment carried crimson guidons differenced by various royal badges, similar to the Royal Regiment of Dragoons, however there is no firm evidence of this.

John Berkeley's Regiment of Dragoons
This regiment does not appear in *The James II Colour Book* and again, as yet, no information has been found concerning its guidons.

Pay

All rates are per day and as with the other arms field officers were also paid separately as captains of companies.

Colonel (as Colonel)   15s 0d*

---

22 War Office State Papers, quoted in Walton, pp. 460–461.

Lieutenant Colonel (as Lieutenant Colonel)	9s 0d**
Major (as Major)	6s 0d***
Captain	1s 0d*
Lieutenant	6s 0d**
Cornet	5s 0d**
Adjutant	5s 0d
Quartermaster	4s 0d****
Chaplain	6s 8d
Gunsmith	5s 0d
Sergeant	2s 6d***
Corporal	2s 0d***
Drummer	2s 0d***
Private Centinel	1s 4d****

* Includes an allowance for 3 horses at 1s each.
** Includes an allowance for 2 horses at 1s each.
*** Includes an allowance for 1 horse at 1s.
**** Includes an allowance for 1 horse at 8d.

Dragoons paid 'off reckonings' of 4½ d per day.[23] Note that dragoon horses were valued at half of the value of those from a regiment of horse.

As in the regiments of horse the officers received an additional daily allowance for servants, the numbers were the same but were only allowed for at 1s 6d each.

---

23 For further details on 'subsistence' see John Childs, *The Army of Charles II* (London: Routledge, 1976).

5

The Royal Regiments of Foot Guards

Organisation

The First Regiment of Foot Guards was made up of 26 companies divided into two 13-company 'battalions'. The Second,[1] Scots and Irish Regiments comprised only one battalion each, 13 companies for the Second and Irish and eventually 15 for the Scots. One company in each battalion was a grenadier company, but the others were of mixed pike and musket in the proportion of one-third pike / two-thirds musket.

In 1685 on the accession of James II a company in all four regiments of foot guards had an establishment of:

1 Captain	1 Lieutenant
1 Ensign	
3 Sergeants	3 Corporals
2 Drummers	100 Guards

On James' accession in February 1685 the Scots Regiment of Foot Guards had comprised 10 companies plus one of grenadiers. An additional newly raised company, initially to be under Charles Carny although William Charters was commissioned in his place on 1 August 1685, was added on 12 June 1685. Another, under William Oliphant and also newly raised, was added on 7 November 1685 and then on 20 November the regiment added a previously independent company with Major Robert Middleton as captain. Middleton held the rank of major from his previous commission in Sir Edward Hales' Regiment of Foot. Prior to its incorporation into the Guards the company had been commanded by George Barclay.[2]

---

1 Although officially 'The Second Regiment of Foot Guards', even official documents called the regiment either 'The Coldstream Regiment of Foot Guards' or often, more simply, 'The Coldstream Regiment'. Cf. National Archives, Kew WO5/2, f. 157, warrant dated 30 April 1686.
2 Dalton, *The Scots Army, 1661–1688*, pp. 147–148.

A plug bayonet dated 1686. (Collection of the Royal Armouries. Author's photograph.)

The high quality of this piece suggests that it may have been for use by an officer, and thus probably from a grenadier company.

On July 16 1685,[3] in the general reduction of the army, the King ordered that the companies in the Regiments of Foot Guards were to be reduced to 80 men 'besides officers' or 90 'besides officers' in the Irish Regiment of Foot Guards. This order was followed up nine days later on 25 July 1685 when the companies in the English Regiments of Foot Guards were further reduced to an establishment of:[4]

1 Captain	1 Lieutenant
1 Ensign	
2 Sergeants	3 Corporals
2 Drummers	60 Guards

The King's own company in the First Regiment of Foot Guards was to have a third sergeant but was otherwise the same as above. The Scots Regiment kept to an strength of 80 guards in each company.

No official warrant has yet come to light that authorises a return to 80 guards per company but by March 1688 this seems to have been the strength of all regiments of foot guards (see below). It is seems likely therefore that, in fact, the four regiments of foot guards did not reduce their strength from that of the 16 July order. Some confirmation of this may be taken from the fact that in June 1686 at the camp on Hounslow Heath the companies of the regiments of foot guards are all given strength of 80 men.[5]

In all regiments the colonel, lieutenant colonel and the major were 'captains' of companies as was, in the First Regiment of Foot Guards and the Irish Regiment of Foot Guards, the King himself.

In addition to these companies there was a small regimental staff assigned to the colonel's own company. This staff comprised, for each regiment, an adjutant (two, in the case of the First Regiment of Foot Guards), quartermaster and provost marshal,[6] chaplain, chirurgeon and drum-major.

---

3   National Archives, Kew WO5/1, f. 167.
4   National Archives, Kew WO5/1, ff. 184–185.
5   *A LIST of KING JAMES's Army on Hounslow Heath … June 30th 1686*. Printed in *The Antiquarian Repertory*, Volume 1: Francis Grose and Thomas Astle (compilers), London 1807, pp. 229–232. All other company and troop strengths given in this list conform to the establishment warrants in force at the time.
6   It was normal for one officer to hold both positions.

Officer, sergeant and musketeers of the the Scots Regiment of Foot Guards 1685. Possibly celebrating the coronation of James II in Edinburgh. (Contemporary engraving)

The English and Irish Regiments of Foot Guards also had a chirurgeon's mate on their staff (two in the case of the First Regiment of Foot Guards).[7] Additionally, in the Scots and Irish Regiments of Foot Guards at least, there was also a piper on the regimental staffs, and on the staff of the Scots Regiment alone an additional four hautboys.[8]

Uniform

As with the horse Guards, Sandford gives a very full description of the two English Regiments at James' coronation (see Appendix I), but briefly the uniform was as follows.

Red coats lined and faced in blue (a few years earlier this had been described as 'light blue'[9]), blue breeches and stockings for the First regiment and red breeches and stockings for the Second. By 30 June 1686, when the army encamped at Hounslow Heath, the Second Foot Guards had also adopted blue breeches and stockings. The exact shade of blue used by both the foot and horse guards at this period was probably close to that still in use on the sash of the Order of the Garter. Black hats 'laced about in silver' with a blue hatband and bunch of ribbons for the First Regiment, and gold lace with red hatband and ribbons for the Second. The Scots Regiment had white facings and linings, white breeches and stockings and white hatband with silver lacing. The Irish Regiment had yellow facings and linings but breeches and stockings are, so far, unrecorded, although modern reconstruction either show them as yellow or red, and these two colours are indeed the most probable. Buttons were silver for the First Regiment and the Scots Regiment and gold for the Second Regiment and the Irish Regiment. Shoes were black. All belts, leatherwork, etc. was buff-brown. Sword scabbards were black.

Since 1683 the musketeers of the four regiments had been armed with snaphaunce muskets,[10] specified by a regulation of 21 February 1687 to have a barrel length of 44 inches.[11] Swords carried from waist belts, and 'collars of bandoliers' covered in natural-coloured leather. By a warrant dated 22 February 1686 James ordered the issuing of bayonets to all musketeers in the two English Regiments of Foot Guards, 'It being necessary, that all

---

7   National Archives, Kew, SP 8/1, Part 2, ff. 97–104; Nathan Brooks, pp. 11, 12.
8   *Calendar of State Papers*, 1684–1685, p. 208; National Archives, Kew, SP 8/1 Part 2, f. 257.
9   'All drest in red coats turned up with light blue (which is the colour of the Royal livery)'. *Travels of Cosmo the Third, Grand Duke of Tuscany*, p. 306.
10 Daniel MacKinnon, *Origin and Services of the Coldstream Guards* (London: Richard Bentley, 1833), p. 167.
11 *Ibid.*, p. 189.

the Musqueteers in Our two Regiments of Guards should for their more compleat arming be furnished with Bionetts.'[12]

This was the first general issue to any foot regiment in the British Army although Monck had tried to arrange the general issue of flintlocks to his own regiment in 1660.[13] A similar issue was not made to the Irish Regiment of Foot Guards until October 1688.[14] No evidence on this subject survives concerning the Scots Regiment of Foot Guards.

The bayonets in use in James' Army were of the so-called 'plug' variety; that is, they were fixed into the barrel and thus prevented the weapon being fired whilst it was in position, hence in the warrant for the arming of the grenadiers of the Second Regiment of Foot Guards reproduced below they are termed 'daggers'.

A print of late 1685 shows musketeers of the Scots Regiment of Foot Guards carrying cartouche boxes instead of bandoleers. If this changeover of equipment was reflected throughout the regiment then it is possible that a similar reform was carried out in the English regiments, and also perhaps the Irish Regiment. However a warrant dated 4 October 1688 authorised the issue of 'bandoleers' to the First Regiment of Foot Guards,[15] so it would appear that the change had not taken place in England.

Pikemen were armed with 16-foot pikes and carried their swords from buff shoulder baldrics. They still wore sashes around their waist: white fringed and edged blue in the First Regiment, white fringed and edged red in the Second. Of the Scots and Irish no information survives.

According to Sandford's description no armour was worn by the pikemen of the Regiments of Foot Guards at James' coronation. However this was a 'full dress parade' and it is possible that armour in the form of breast- and backplates was still available for active service if the colonels chose. Certainly in March 1687 the Tower still contained large amounts of 'Footmens Armor', comprising breasts, without tassetts, backs, 'HeadPeices', and Gorgetts.[16] However between 1685 and 1688 there are no issues of foot armour surviving in the records, although admittedly these records are not complete. Buff gauntlets were worn on active service.

Grenadiers were dressed identically to the musketeers except that they used a cartouche box in place of the latter's bandoliers and wore a cap instead of the hat. These caps were red turned up blue, laced and embroidered in silver for the First Regiment, and in gold for the Second. The Scots Regiment appears to have also had theirs red but turned up white and laced in silver. No information is recorded in respect of the Irish Regiment, but a guess would have them in red turned-up yellow and embroidered in gold.

The grenadier's musket was slightly shorter than that of the musketeers (the latter's musket barrels were 3 feet 8 inches compared to the grenadiers' 3 feet 2 inches) and also had a shoulder strap '4 inches broad', contemporary warrants

12 National Archives, Kew, WO44/164, f. 302.
13 Lawson, p. 53.
14 *Calendar of State Papers*, 1687–1689, p. 331; National Archives, Kew, SP 44/165, p. 122.
15 National Archives, Kew, SP 44/165, f. 97.
16 National Archives, Kew, WO55/1656, f. 28.

Officer, grenadier company of the First Regiment of Foot Guards, *c*.1685. (After C. C. P. Lawson)

Sketch after the painting of Captain Francis Hawley (see text). Note the patterned and laced belts, the pattern of the grenadier lacing and the fusil slung as well as the scabbarded plug bayonet.

often refer to it as a 'fusee'. Grenadiers were universally issued with bayonets, well in advance of their general issue in the army, and a 'hammer hatchet', both of which were carried attached to the waist sword belt. The grenades, from which they took their name, were carried in a pouch slung at the right hip; the pouch's capacity was four grenades. It is interesting to note however that grenades do not appear to have been general issue even to grenadiers, issue appeared to have required a specific application from the colonel.

A warrant for the total rearming of the grenadier company of the Second Regiment of Foot Guards, dated 11 March 1688, survives: 'to deliver to the Grenadiers of Our Coldstream Regimt of Foot Guards, Eighty three firelocks slung, Eighty three Cartouch Boxes, 83 Daggers.'[17]

NCOs

Uniformed identically to their men but with the addition of narrow silver or gold (depending on the button colour) lace to pockets and buttonholes. Sergeants wore crimson sashes and carried halberds, which was effectively their badge of rank.

Officers

Red, crimson or scarlet coats lined and faced in the same, embroidered and laced on edges, seams and buttonholes with silver lace for the First and Scots Foot Guards and with gold lace for the Second and Irish Foot Guards. All officers suspended their swords from shoulder baldrics, which were often of red or crimson leather and richly and elaborately decorated and fringed. crimson taffeta or net sashes, fringed and edged in gold and/or silver, were worn around the waist. Black hats, with tours of white feathers, laced in gold or silver and with hatbands of the same colour. Only field officers wore 'jackboots', company officers wore black shoes.

Although formal 'rank badges' of any sort were still a half-century in the future, an embryonic system of rank differentiation did exist for company officers. On 1 September 1684 Charles II issued an order laying down the design of the gorgets to be worn by the officers of the foot guards and the regiments of foot. From the meagre evidence that we have of James' reign this system was certainly still in use in the summer of 1686 and thus probably continued throughout the reign.

For the better distinction of Our Severall Officers serving Us in Our Companies of Foot, Our will and pleasure is, That all Captains of Foot wear no other Corselett

---

17   National Archives, Kew, SP 44/165, f. 27.

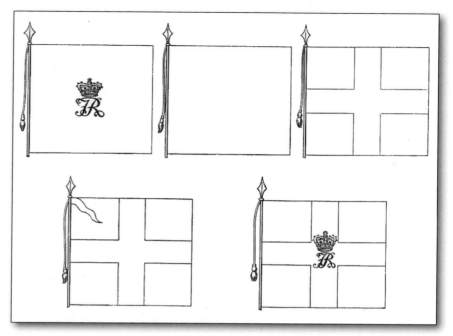

Colours of the First Regiment of Foot Guards, 1685 (after S. M. Milne)

From left to right: Royal Standard, colonel's company, lieutenant colonel's company, major's company, first captain's company. See text for colours and details.

than of the Colour of Gold, all Lieutenants black Corseletts studded with Gold. And the Ensigns Corseletts of silver. And Wee do likewise think fitt, that all Lieutenant of Foot, Carry Pikes and not Partizans, which We do hereby Order to be Redelivered into the Office of Our Ordnance. And Wee do further direct that authentique Copies hereof be sent to Our severall Colonells of Foot and transmitted to the Governors of Our Forts and Garrisons, To the end that the Respective Officers of Our Forces may Govern themselves accordingly. Given at Our Court at Winchester the First day of September 1684.[18]

'Corselets' in this warrant mean gorgets, not, as earlier, a back and breast. Company officers were armed with polearms. Captains usually carried half-pikes, whilst lieutenants carried partisans. Ensigns, of course, carried their company's colours, but no doubt a partisan at times when the colours were inappropriate. In the grenadier companies, however, it was becoming increasingly more common for the officers to carry muskets, similar to those of their men but shorter and lighter and always of the snaphaunce variety. In such cases a cartouche box would be worn on service and these were often highly decorated as was appropriate given their rank.

A contemporary portrait survives of Captain Francis Hawley of the grenadier company of the First Regiment of Foot Guards. This is privately owned and must have been painted shortly after his participation in the crushing of the Duke of Monmouth's rebellion.

Portraits of later 17th century junior officers in uniform are extremely rare, which makes this one all the more worth discussing,[19] it is one of only

---

18   National Archives, Kew, WO5/1, ff. 88–89.
19   The portrait was first brought to the notice of students of military uniform by C. Field: 'Uniform of a Grenadier Officer in the Army of James II', in *The Journal of the Society for Army Historical*

Musicians of the regiments of foot guards, *c*.1688. (After C. C. P. Lawson)

The sketch shows the full dress coat but whether such coats would have been worn in the field seems unlikely although a red (the Foot Guards never used facing colour coats for their musicians) coat would probably have been laced fairly similarly. Note the banner of the Royal Arms on the hautboys instrument – again it is unlikely that this would have appeared off the formal parade ground. See text for notes on the colour of the uniforms.

two known to date to James' reign. There may, of course originally have been more which have been quietly hidden away as James increasingly fell from favour after 'The Glorious Revolution', maybe others will surface in the future.

Hawley was captain of grenadiers in the First Regiment of Foot Guards from April 1684 until July 1685 when he was promoted major of the newly raised Princess Anne of Denmark's Regiment of Dragoons. As captain of the First Foot Guards' grenadiers he was present at the Battle of Sedgemoor on 6 July 1685. The evidence points to this portrait, by an unknown artist, having been executed shortly after the battle.

Captain Hawley is shown wearing a crimson velvet coat, faced in light blue velvet, with gilt domed buttons and gold lace on the buttonholes only. The cuffs are festooned with gold embroidery in a floral design. He wears a baldric over the left shoulder (presumably supporting a grenade pouch as he is portrayed in the act of lighting a grenade) and a waist belt supporting a cartridge box at the centre front (in the way of the 'belly box' in vogue amongst firelocks a half-century earlier) and a plug bayonet in a scabbard at the left front. Both belts, the cartridge box and the bayonet scabbard are covered in light blue velvet, edged with gold lace and decorated in gold lace in a zigzag pattern on the belts and pouch and a floral pattern on the box. The bayonet 'handle' is plain brown wood with a gilt ferrule and cross piece.

The cap is the usual 1680s low mitre but with an almost square front turn-up. It is blue, turned up blue velvet, with the front piece edged in broad gold lace and bearing the crowned royal cypher in gold embroidery; the entire front

---

piece field is covered with embroidered gold fleur-de-lys. Hawley's cravat is of fine white linen ended in gold and embroidered with a gold floral pattern.

Obviously Hawley was armed with a musket, hence the bayonet and cartridge box, and although the lack of a sash is unusual it is understandable considering the use of belly-box, which would have made it impracticable.

Drummers

The drummers of all the Regiments of Foot Guards were uniformed in royal livery of red coats, lined and faced with blue, blue breeches and stockings and a mass of gold and silver galoon and lace on all seams, edges, buttonholes etc. The royal cypher was embroidered in gold on the breast and back of the coat. Hats were edged in gold and silver lace. Buttons were gold.

The drums themselves were of painted wood and bore the royal arms on the front.

Colours

Each company (except the grenadier companies) had its own colour, which was 6 feet 6 inches square, and carried by the ensign. They were made of silk and the devices were, usually, painted on. Colour poles were approximately 10 feet in length and a pair of short bullion tassels was fastened just below the gilt pike head. The colours for the First and Second Regiments of Foot Guards were 'made and provided against H.M.'s ... Coronation by Thos Holford, Portcullis Pursuivant of Arms', and cost £8 each.[20]

The First Regiment of Foot Guards

The King's company's colours were crimson with the royal cypher and crown embroidered in the centre in gold. The colonel's colours were plain crimson. The remaining colours were based on the Cross of St George, viz.: lieutenant colonel's, a crown in the centre in gold; the major's the same as the lieutenant colonel's but with the addition of a crimson pile wavy; the 20 captains were each distinguished by the appropriate number of crowned royal cyphers, in gold, displayed on the arms of the cross, thus the 1st Captain had one, the 2nd Captain had two, etc. All colours had mixed crimson and gold cords.

The Second Regiment of Foot Guards

The colonel's company colours were plain white. The remaining colours were again based on the Cross of St George, viz.: the lieutenant colonel's carried no device; the major's added a crimson pile wavy in the canton; and the nine captains' colours each bore the appropriate Roman numeral, in white, below a gold crown in the centre of the cross. The colonel's and lieutenant colonel's colours had crimson cords with gold tassels; the remaining colours all had cords and tassels of crimson alone.

20 War Office State Papers, quoted in Walton, pp. 460–461.

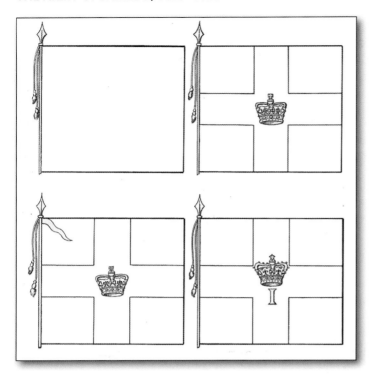

Colours of the Second Regiment of Foot Guards, 1685. (after S. M. Milne)

From top left: colonel's company, lieuenant colonel's company, major's company, first captain's company. See text for colours and details.

Colours of the Scots Regiment of Foot Guards, 1686 (after S. M. Milne)

From left to right: colonel's company, lieutenant colonel's company, major's company, first captain's company. See text for colours and details.

The Scots Regiment of Foot Guards

The colonel's colour was plain white. The remaining companies' colours were all based upon the Cross of St Andrew of a blue field with a white saltire. Thus the lieutenant colonel's colour was the plain cross of St Andrew. The major's was the same as the lieutenant colonel's but with the addition of a crimson pile wavy along the upper arm of the cross. The captains' colours were the cross of St Andrew with the appropriate roman numeral, in white, above the centre of the cross. The cords were gold and silver for the colonel's colour and blue and silver for the remainder of the stand.

The Irish Regiment of Foot Guards

There is no record of the colours of this regiment either during the latter years of the reign of Charles II or during the Reign of James II. However when the regiment had been formed in England in April 1662 colours had been ordered and the warrants specify:

> The Earl of Sandwich, Master of the King's Wardrobe, to deliver to the Duke of Ormond yellow taffety and transon for twelve colours for a regiment of foot; and that he cause badges to be painted and gilded thereon, and deliver the same parcels of taffety at the same rates as they were furnished for the King's Regiment of foot [Guards]. Likewise that he deliver twelve ensigns' staves with gilt heads, and twelve pair of tassels, crimson and gold, and that he cause the King's badges to be painted and gilded on 25 drums as they are painted on the King's regiment [of foot guards].[21]

In the period 1662–1685 the two English and the Scots regiments of foot guards made little changes to the general appearance of their colours and it is possible, indeed maybe even probable, that the colours of the Irish Regiment of Foot Guards in 1685 were little different from those of 1662.

Pay

As with the horse and dragoons, field officers also drew pay as captains of a company.

Colonel (as Colonel)	12s 0d
Lt Colonel (as Lt Colonel)	7s 0d
Major (as Major)	5s 0d
Captain	8s 0d
Lieutenant	4s 0d
Ensign	3s 0d
Chaplain	6s 8d
Adjutant	4s 0d
Chirugeon	4s 0d*

---

21 *Calendar of State Papers, Ireland*, 1660–1662 (London: HMSO, 1905); Dalton, *Irish Army Lists*, p. 28.

Chirugeon's Mate	2s 6d
Quartermaster	4s 0d
Provost	4s 0d
Drum Major	1s 6d
Sergeant	1s 6d
Corporal	1s 0d
Drummer or Hautboy	1s 0d
Private Centinell	10d (in London)
Private Centinell	8d (outside London)

* Plus an allowance of 2s 6d for a horse to carry his chest

'Off reckonings' for the foot at a rate of 2d per day were deducted from the pay of all except officers.[22] As a comparison an unskilled farm labourer would expect pay of 1s (12d) per day so whilst a soldier might seem underpaid, in a week he would be paid for seven days whereas a labourer would, at most, be paid for six.

As in the mounted regiments, all officers received an additional daily allowance for servants, although only at 8d per head. Colonels were allowed for 10 servants, the lieutenant colonel, major, and the captains for five servants and the lieutenants and ensigns one servant.

---

22   For details of 'off reckonings' and the mechanism of pay see Childs, *The Army of Charles II.*

6

The Regiments of Foot

Organisation

On James' accession the regiments of foot of the three standing armies were all organised basically along the same lines but with slight variations. Thus the line companies[1] in all regiments had an establishment of:

1 Captain	1 Lieutenant
1 Ensign	
2 Sergeants	3 Corporals
1 Drummer	
60 'private centinells'	

Except in the Royal Regiment of Foot where a company had two lieutenants, termed 'First' and 'Second', and three sergeants. In the three senior companies of a regiment, the colonel, lieutenant colonel and the major were the company captains.

Grenadier companies carried no colours and therefore their officers were a captain and two lieutenants, again termed as 'First' and 'Second'. Grenadier companies also had an establishment of three sergeants but the rest of the company make-up otherwise remained unchanged.

Grenadier companies' rank and file were obviously all grenadiers but in all other companies of foot (there were exceptions as noted below) the rank and file were mixed pikemen and musketeers at a ratio of 1:2. This had been the ideal composition of an infantry company as far back as 1642 and would not change for the bulk of the army until the last years of the century or, in some cases, the early years of the next.

The exact mixture of the armament of a company of foot is well exemplified by a warrant for the re-equipping of five companies late of The Duchess of York's Regiment of Foot (as it then was, being The Queen Consort's Regiment

---

1   To term the standard company as a 'line company' is an anachronism but is an ideal way to differentiate the normal company from a grenadier company.

of Foot after February 1685) before they were sent to Ireland in September 1684. The arms to be issued to each of the companies were:

> For 2 sergeants 2 halberts, for 3 corporalls 3 snaphaunce muskets and 3 collars of bandoliers and one drum and for the soldiers 20 long pikes, 12 snaphaunce muskets, 28 matchlock muskets and 40 collars of bandoliers.[2]

A similar issue to the new regiments of 1685 gave each company (after the 25 July reduction) 28 matchlock muskets, 6 snaphaunce muskets, 16 long pikes, 34 bandoliers. Both examples confirming the pike to shot ratio of 1:2, which had been the preferred in the army since at least the early 1640s.

The independent companies would appear to have been entirely musket armed, which would be entirely a logical organisation since the small number of ten or twenty men armed with pikes within a garrison would serve little tactical purpose. The independent companies raised in 1688 also appear to have been musket armed only, again logical if they were intended for garrison duty. This organisation may be why these companies were thought suitable for conversion to grenadier companies when they wee absorbed by the 'marching regiments'.

Even if the company establishment was, by 1685, uniform throughout the armies the actual regimental composition varied quite widely and in February 1685 looked like this:

The Royal Regiment of Foot[3]
Twenty line companies, plus one of grenadiers.

The Queen Dowager's Regiment of Foot
Ten companies of the regulation establishment, plus one of grenadiers.

The Holland Regiment
Twelve companies all of the above establishment. A company of grenadiers, commanded by Captain Thomas Cornwallis, was added to the regimental strength on 1 July 1685.

Prince George of Denmark's Regiment of Foot
Twelve companies with the standard establishment but all rank of file were musketeers. Prince George of Denmark's Regiment had been raised in 1664 as The Duke of York and Albany's Maritime Regiment of foot, 'to be in readiness to be distributed with H.M.'s Fleet, prepared for sea service',[4] and owes its lack of pikemen to this original purpose. By 1685 it was considered as an ordinary

---

2   *Calendar of State Papers*, 1684–1685, pp. 141–142. Warrant dated 13 September 1684 at Winchester. State Papers Domestic, Entry Book 164, p. 124.

3   A note from 1684 is interesting in respect of the titles of the senior regiments: 'New Commissions are issuing for re-establishing and continuing in the King's Service the three regiments that came from Tangier. Col. Kirke's is to be called the Queen's, lord Dumbarton's the King's and Col. Trelawney's the Duchess', *Calendar of State Papers*, 1684–1685, p. 7. In all events, whilst Kirke's and Trelawney's used their new titles, the Royal Regiment of Foot stayed as exactly that.

4   Lawson, p. 54.

regiment of foot although still often referred to as 'The Maritime Regiment' and officially rejoicing in the full title of 'Prince George, Hereditary Prince of Denmark's Maritime Regiment of Foot'. The establishment of a company of grenadiers in this regiment on 28 April 1685 is perhaps final evidence of its transformation into a standard regiment of foot. Because of its initial raison d'être the musketeers of this regiment were armed entirely with flintlocks long before this became the custom throughout the armies.

The Queen Consort's Regiment of Foot

Ten 'line' companies, all of the standard establishment, plus one company of grenadiers.

The Scots Fuzileers Regiment of Foot

Ten line companies with the regulation establishment, except with two drummers per company, but composed entirely of flintlock-armed musketeers, plus a company of grenadiers. This regiment had originally been raised as a 'standard' regiment of foot and issued with the usual mixture of pikes and muskets. The exact date of its change to a fuzileer regiment is unknown but Clifford Walton puts it at around 1680; it is termed as 'fuzileers' in a warrant of 3 August 1687.[5]

The foot regiments of the Irish Army were uniformly of a strength of 13 line companies, including one of grenadiers, a benefit of their recent creation from the numerous independent companies of that kingdom which had existed throughout most of Charles II's reign. The regiments had been created in 1684 from the formerly independent companies strengthened by a number of the veteran companies returned from Tangier that were in excess to those needed to create the new regiments on the English establishment.[6] These new 'Irish' regiments had grenadier companies added late the same year with the arms being shipped from England.[7]

In each case the small regimental staff of adjutant, quartermaster and provost marshal,[8] chaplain,[9] chirurgeon and chirurgeon's mate were carried on the strength of the colonel's company. On Nathan Brooks' 1684 list some of these positions are omitted but I take this as their being vacant rather than not existing.

As well as the above regiments on James' accession there were some 20 independent companies in various garrisons (see Table 3). Changes in internal organisation, strength, etc. in the regiments of foot were echoed and repeated in the independent companies.

On 20 May 1685 the Scots Fuzileers Regiment of Foot was augmented with an additional company under the command of Captain Walter Maxwell.

---

5   National Archives, Kew, WO5/3, f. 12.
6   These new regiments of foot were the Queen Consort's and the Duchess of York's, which in February 1685 had become the Queen Dowager's and Queen Consort's respectively.
7   *Calendar of State Papers*, 1684–1685, pp. 129–130.
8   In the English and Irish armies it was normal for one officer to hold both positions.
9   In Ireland some regiments had both a Protestant chaplain and a Catholic priest. *Calendar of State Papers*, 1686–1687, p. 254.

Playing card, 1704 (detail). (Public domain)

This card shows Marshal Tallard being escorted in captivity after the Battle of Blenheim. Although two decades later than James' reign, this card (the Four of Hearts), shows grenadiers of foot who are little different to how they would have appeared in 1685, except that the front of the cap is higher than it would have been in the earlier era.

Through the course of James' reign only one new regiment was added to the Scots establishment. Perhaps for cost reasons James chose to increase the Scots establishment by adding additional companies to the existing Regiments.

On 11 June 1685 the Earl of Dartmouth was commissioned to raise a new regiment, styled as 'Our Own Regiment of Fuzileers', for the English establishment. The regiment was to be composed of 12 companies of flintlock-armed musketeers plus, in place of a company of grenadiers, a company of miners. These wore grenadier caps, carried 'hammer-hatchets' and had their muskets 'strapt', and therefore may not have been too much different in practice from a grenadier company. The Regiment of Fuzileers was conceived as being a guard to the Train of Artillery and seems to have been used for this purpose throughout James' reign, escorting movements of artillery and at the Hounslow Heath musters drawing up with the train rather than the foot. That Dartmouth should have a regiment of foot had been suggested as far back as May 1684 when, at a review of the army in Hyde Park, it was noted that 'The several independent companies will be formed into regiments of which Lord Dartmouth will command one.'[10]

The Royal Regiment of Fuzileers had one additional 'officer' on its staff: a gunsmith who received pay at the rate of 5s per day, an extraordinary sum which is more than the ordinary pay of either a lieutenant or an ensign of Foot.[11]

On 13 June James issued a series of orders increasing the strength of all companies of foot on the English establishment to 100 private centinells and adding a third sergeant and a second drummer to each line company,[12] although still retaining the proportion of one third pikes and two thirds shot. Grenadier companies and all companies of the Royal Regiment of Foot already had three sergeants, and were thus specifically excluded from this part of the order. Initially the two companies of the Holland Regiment garrisoned on Jersey were ordered not to increase their establishment,[13] but they were quickly brought into line with the rest of the army.

Throughout June the expansion of the English army continued apace and between 19 June and 22 June James commissioned eight more colonels to raise further regiments of foot (see Appendix I). In all cases, company strength was to be at the increased establishment as above but initially at least no regimental establishment was laid down. Thus Henry Cornwall's was

---

10   *Calendar of State Papers*, 1684–1685, p. 22.
11   Walton, p. 646.
12   National Archives, Kew, WO5/1 f. 40.
13   *Ibid.*, f. 41.

raised with strength of 12 line companies plus one of grenadiers, the Earl of Bath's with 12 line companies only, and the other six regiments had a simple establishment of 10 line companies.

Unlike the horse, the new regiments of foot were commissioned as regiments and mainly raised in one geographical area:

The Royal Regiment of Fuzileers
Princess Anne of Denmark's Regiment of Foot
Henry Cornwall's Regiment of Foot
The Earl of Bath's Regiment of Foot (Nottinghamshire and Derbyshire)[14]
The Duke of Beaufort's Regiment of Foot (Devon, Somerset, Dorset)[15]
The Duke of Norfolk's Regiment of Foot (Norfolk and Suffolk)[16]
The Earl of Huntingdon's Regiment of Foot (Buckinghamshire)[17]
Sir Edward Hales' Regiment of Foot (Kent)[18]
Sir William Clifton's Regiment of Foot (Nottinghamshire)[19]

This county and regional association of the regiments of foot was obviously of some concern to the King, and when the Duke of Beaufort requested that his regiment of foot be quartered in the west, where it was raised and his lieutenancy was, his request was denied. Secretary at War William Blaythwayt set out the reasons in his reply of 28 August 1685:[20] 'To acquaint your Grace that in the removalls of all the Regiments His Majesty has made a rule that every one of them be removed some distance from the Country where they were raised.' Therefore Beaufort's Regiment 'cannot be quartered this year in the West or within your Graces Lieutenancy' and that it is to go to Yarmouth for winter quarters.[21]

The Battle of Sedgemoor was fought on 6 July 1685 and with the complete royal victory at that battle the whole of Monmouth's rebellion collapsed. As with the horse and dragoons James determined to keep the new regiments

---

14 Richard Cannon, *Historical Record of the Tenth, or the North Lincolnshire, Regiment of Foot* (London: Parker, Furnivall and Parker, 1847), p. 2.

15 Richard Cannon, *Historical Record of the Eleventh, or the North Devon, Regiment of Foot* (London: Parker, Furnivall and Parker, 1845), p. 9. A number of modern works, and some fairly shoddy regimental histories, refer to this regiment being raised as 'The Duke of Beaufort's Musketeers'; there is no evidence that it was ever anything other than a regiment of mixed pike and shot in the same way as most other contemporary English regiments of foot. There are no contemporary references to it as 'The Duke of Beaufort's Musketeers', or any similar title suggesting the same.

16 Richard Cannon, *Historical Record of the Twelfth, or the East Suffolk, Regiment of Foot* (London: Parker, Furnivall and Parker, 1848), p. 1. Cannon also adds that some companies were from the independent companies which had been garrisoned at Windsor and whose origins went back to the New Model Army.

17 National Archives, Kew, WO5/1, f. 101, orders that the Earl of Huntingdon's Regiment is to muster and rendezvous at Buckingham and Aylesbury.

18 National Archives, Kew, WO5/1, f. 95, dated 26 June, ordered that Edward Hales' Regiment was to rendezvous at Chatham, Sittingbourne, Feversham and Canterbury.

19 Richard Cannon, *Historical Record of the Fifteenth, or the Yorkshire East Riding, Regiment of Foot* (London: Parker, Furnivall and Parker, 1848), p. 1.

20 Blaythwayt held office as Secretary at War from 1683–1704: that is, under Charles II 1683–5, James II 1685–1689, William III 1689–1702, and Anne 1702–1704.

21 National Archives, Kew, WO4/1, ff. 14–15.

in being and turned his mind to restructuring his new army (all the new regiments were on the English establishment) in a logical fashion. The changes in establishments decreed over the following weeks, however, covered all three armies.

On 9 July 1685 the Royal Regiment of Foot, ahead of the general order to the Army cited below, was ordered to disband its new recruits and reduce all companies to a strength of 50 private soldiers.[22]

On 16 July 1685 the King ordered a general reduction in all companies of foot back to the 60 private soldiers of February,[23] and also that their establishment was to be reduced by one sergeant and one drummer. At the same time he gave orders that as the second lieutenancy in the companies of the Royal Regiment of Foot fell vacant it was to be considered abolished,[24] this regiment, however, retained its privileged three sergeants per company, as did the grenadier companies in all regiments.

On 18 July 1685 in line with his general intentions of a unified army organisation all of the regiments of foot were ordered to be of 10 companies only. Whilst the order does not specifically exclude the 'old' regiments all evidence is that they continued at their strength and establishment of February 1685,[25] with the exception that the Holland Regiment kept the company of grenadiers which it had been augmented by on 1 July.

As part of this rationalisation of structures of the armies, in late July the new regiments were ordered to absorb some of the independent companies that existed throughout the Kingdoms.[26] The following are specifically mentioned: the Duke of Norfolk's independent company to be absorbed into his regiment of foot;[27] three independent companies to be absorbed into the Earl of Bath's Regiment of Foot; Captain Roger Kirkby's independent company to be absorbed into Sir William Clifton's Regiment of Foot; Captain George Weld's independent company to be absorbed into Sir Edward Hale's Regiment of Foot;[28] Captain Charles Hatton's independent company to be absorbed into the Earl of Huntingdon's Regiment of Foot.

In all cases the colonels were to disband the appropriate number of their newly raised companies and absorb the erstwhile independent companies complete. The warrants also specify that all 'Partizans, halbirds and Drumms' from the disbanded companies be returned to the stores.

Also on 18 July Lord Dartmouth's and Major St Clare's companies were ordered to be discharged from Royal Regiment of Fuzileers but were to be retained as independent companies. This had the effect of reducing the Royal Regiment of Fuzileers to 10 line companies plus its company of miners. By

---

22 National Archives, Kew, WO5/1, f. 41.

23 *Ibid.*, f. 67.

24 National Archives, Kew, WO4/1, ff. 11–12.

25 See the lists of officers' commissions in Dalton, *English*, volume 2.

26 National Archives, Kew, WO5/1 ff. 170–3, orders dated 18 July unless otherwise specified.

27 This is probably a mistake for Captain Thomas Cheek's, which was in Norfolk's governorship of Windsor. There is no record that Norfolk himself commanded an independent company, and Cheek's disappears at around this time.

28 National Archives, Kew, WO5/1 ff. 187, orders concerning Weld's and Hatton's companies dated 27 July.

the middle of 1686 however both companies were back in the regiment, although St Clare was by now the lieutenant colonel, a rank that he had been promoted to on 1 May 1686.

On 25 July the establishment of a company of foot throughout the English Army was reduced further still,[29] and laid down as:

1 Captain	1 Lieutenant
1 Ensign	
2 Sergeants	3 Corporals
1 Drummer	
50 private centinells	

In the companies of grenadiers and in all companies of the Royal Regiment of Fuzileers the ensign was replaced by a second lieutenant. This lieutenant presumably carried the colours in the field officers' companies of the Royal Regiment of Fuzileers, the captain's companies did not carry colours, neither did grenadier companies, hence they need not require an ensign.

Grenadier companies in all regiments of foot and all companies of the Royal Regiment of Foot still kept the third sergeant of their establishment.

The Scots Fuzileer Regiment of Foot kept at strength of two drummers in each company.

In all cases it was the new recruits that were disbanded, the more experienced veterans being the men retained.

Despite, or perhaps because of, all of these changes the new regiments were still a long way from complete, and on 6 September 1685 Colonel Percy Kirke was ordered to delay the departure of the Queen Dowager's Regiment from Plymouth until the Earl of Bath's Regiment, which was also in garrison there, had received its arms![30] This is despite a circular letter that had gone out to all of the newly commissioned colonels on 23 July 1685 asking them for a return on the readiness and condition of their regiment.[31]

In January 1686 a complaint from the colonels of the regiments in Ireland that stated that they 'desire an additional drum and trumpet to each company and troop, there being but one established'.[32] There is, however, no record that any notice was taken of their complaint, either in the Irish Army or the English, the solitary Scots Regiment of Foot already had, and had retained, a second drummer to each company.

This company establishment remained unchanged throughout the rest of James' reign until, on the 2 September of 1688 as relations with the United Provinces continued to deteriorate, 10 additional men, one additional sergeant and one additional drummer were again added to the strength of each company of foot in the Three Kingdoms.[33] However, the new recruits

29 *Ibid.*, ff. 184–5.
30 National Archives, Kew, WO4/1 f. 13.
31 *Ibid.*, ff. 184–5.
32 *Calendar of State Papers*, 1686–May 1687, p. 10; National Archives, Kew, SP 63/351, ff.129–130.
33 National Archives, Kew, WO4/1, ff. 88–91. As was intended by the warrant, the Scots Fuzileers Regiment of Foot did not add the additional drummer of this order since they already had two.

were not authorised to be issued with arms until over three weeks later, which may say something about recruitment problems or it may simply suggest that bureaucracy was a little slow.[34]

The regimental establishments, however, went through two further significant changes.

The first change began in late 1686 and was calculated to have two effects, the first of which was to eliminate the most of the now obsolete independent companies. The second was to correct the anomaly that none of the new regiments of foot officially carried a grenadier company on their strength; this included Henry Cornwall's Regiment, which, as mentioned, had raised grenadiers as part of its original establishment. However in February 1686, as Secretary William Blaythwayt began to implement this strategy, he became aware that the Earl of Bath's Regiment of Foot already boasted a company of grenadiers on its strength, a situation with which he appears to have been none too happy,[35] although permission was granted for the company to be continued. Lord Arundell's Company from Pendennis which was to have become the grenadier company of the Earl of Bath's Regiment of Foot was therefore to be incorporated 'without being made Granadiers', and '[their] clothing to be stopt'[36] (presumably their new grenadiers' uniforms). Despite this latter order Arundell claimed the sum of 20 pounds to make good the damage to his men's coats that this change caused, a sum that Blaythwayt agreed should be reimbursed to him.[37]

The King's first action in this policy was to create all of the independent companies as grenadiers and then from February/March 1686 add these companies to the regiments of foot. These attached companies were not at this point part of the regiments but independent companies of grenadiers attached to them. There were some moves and variation in which companies were attached to which regiment until the system settled down over the next 12 months. However, what evidence there is suggests that even whilst they were technically independent these companies adopted the uniform and facings of the regiment that they were attached to.

In August 1686 there were five companies of grenadiers at Hounslow Heath muster and when the muster was dismissed these marched to the Tower as the garrison. Their captains were:[38] the Earl of Plymouth; Captain Henry Collier; Captain Thomas Cornwallis (of The Holland Regiment of Foot); Captain George Fitzjames (of Prince George of Denmark's Regiment of Foot); Captain John Grenville (of the Earl of Bath's Regiment of Foot).

Also mentioned in the records at the same time are the other independent companies of grenadiers, these were mostly descended from the companies shown in Table 3. Their origins and subsequent regiments are shown in Table 4.

---

34 Warrant dated 24 Sept 1688 to arm an augmentation of 10 men in each company of 'Horse, Grenadeers, Dragoons, and Foot', National Archives, Kew, SP 44/165 f. 66.

35 National Archives, Kew, WO4/1, f. 102.

36 National Archives, Kew, WO4/1, ff. 28–29.

37 *Ibid.*, f. 91. Letter from secretary at War William Blaythwayt to Baron Arundell of Trerice, dated 4 May 1686.

38 National Archives, Kew, WO5/2, f. 254.

These companies had been the garrison companies of February 1685 but by August 1686 were no longer in their 1685 garrison and are mentioned in the various marching orders either directing them to accompany a specific regiment of foot or directing them to take station as a garrison company. In this latter case they were still frequently moved around, as were all other garrisons.

The effect of all of the changes listed above was to add a grenadier company to the establishment of all regiments of foot by March/April 1687. These new grenadier companies, however, did not have the third sergeant that those of the old regiments had,[39] although they did have the second lieutenant in place of an ensign.

Around the same time the Queen Dowager's and the Queen Consort's Regiments of Foot both increased their establishments to 12 'line' companies and one of grenadiers. For these two regiments to affect this increase in strength they had, as can be seen from Table 4, each absorbed three independent companies although how the new companies were constructed from the three previous is yet to come to light.

By late 1685 the primary raison d'être of the independent companies had ceased to exist. Their origins lay in the fact that with a small army they were an effective cost saving exercise since the government could provide the necessary garrisons but without the overheads of a regimental staff and the higher pay of field officers. With the massive expansion of the army in England in 1685 the regiments existed and could do the job of the independent companies without the excess administration of a large number of small units. For purely financial reasons, however, many governors retained the captaincy of their old companies even when these had been absorbed into the regular regiments. A bonus to any governor's income was his pay as captain of one of his garrison's companies and initially many governors were loath to give this up, even though these companies were, strictly, no longer part of their garrison. However this situation did not continue, as new governors were appointed or new captains were required for these companies.

The second regimental establishment change took place in the summer and autumn of 1688 as England prepared for the imminent expected invasion by the King's son-in-law, William of Orange. To increase the army's strength the King commissioned additional companies to increase all regiments of foot to a new establishment of 12 'line' companies and one company of grenadiers.[40]

In the Royal Regiment of Foot this new 13-company battalion was echoed by the raising of five new companies to give it an establishment of two 13-company battalions, each the size of the other regiments of foot. Adam Cunningham was commissioned captain on 21 September, James McKraken on the 22nd, Alexander Pearson on the 23rd, David McAdam on the 24th and George, Lord Etrick on 24 October; all for companies 'to be

---

39   National Archives, Kew, WO4/1, f. 90.
40   For the dates of these companies' commissioning see Dalton, *English*, vol. 2.

raised'.[41] On 17 November all five companies received marching orders and must therefore have already been fairly complete: 'The 21 Old Companys to march tomorrow to Andover', and 'The 5 additional Companys to march from Maidenhead ... to Andover'.[42]

The National Archives contain similar marching orders around this time for many of these new companies, usually bringing them, as with the Royal Regiment of Foot, to join with their parent regiment, although National Archives WO5/4, which contains these orders, ends abruptly on 10 December.

With all of the above strength establishments it must be stressed that they are just that, establishments, and it is very doubtful if these theoretical company establishments were ever achieved. Contemporaries estimated that it took two full months to equip, train, arm and clothe a raw recruit,[43] so at best many of these additional men would not have been ready until December. From later practice it was possible to improve this time by building the company around an experienced cadre but we have no knowledge if this was done during the 1680s.

On 17 January 1688 James ordered the recall of the six regiments in the service of the Netherlands, the famous veteran 'Anglo–Scots Brigade', an order that William of Orange was loath to allow to be carried out. William was, however, incapable of totally preventing all officers and men of the brigade from returning and James gave order that three new regiments of foot were to be established to take in the returning officers and men. The regiments were split as one to each of the three armies: John Hales' Regiment in the English Army was commissioned on 10 March, John Wachop's of the Scots Army on 11 March, and Roger McElligott's on the Irish Army on 12 March. All three regiments were to be at establishment strength of thirteen companies including one of grenadiers, and arms were ordered to be issued to the colonels for a regiment of this strength on 23 March 1688.[44] James' order concerning the English officers and men returning from Dutch service was issued from Whitehall on 18 May 1688 and was sent by Secretary Blaythwayt to David Crawford, Chief Deputy Commissary Generall of Musters:

> Any English Soldier or Non Commission Officer of what fitness Soever he be to Serve ... upon giving them Pay as aforesaid to list them of the Regiment of Colonel Hales and to send them down to the Quarters of that Regiment.[45]

A similar order must have been issued regarding the returning Scots and Irish officers and men but McElligott's was also to receive recruits in another way.

---

41 *Ibid.*, pp. 163–195. Etrick was Dumbarton's son and heir and only 18 months old at the time of this commission.
42 National Archives, Kew, WO5/4, ff. 1–2.
43 Childs, *The Army, James II and The Glorious Revolution*, p. 3.
44 *Calendar of State Papers*, 1687–1688, p. 170; National Archives, Kew, SP 44/165, f. 29.
45 'Letters on the Administration of James II's Army', edited with notes by Godfrey Davies, *Journal of the Society of Army Historical Research*, volume XXIX, London, 1951, pp. 69–84.

Perhaps using this same source of recruits two additional companies, under Captains John Bell and John Ramsay, were added to the Scots Fuzileers Regiment of Foot on 23 April 1688. John Ramsay had previously held the same rank in the Anglo-Scots Brigade, Bell had been the regiment's captain lieutenant.

In the autumn of 1688 a yet further increase in the regiments of foot was also ordered and between 27 September and 8 November a further seven regiments of foot were commissioned for the English establishment. All seven regiments were to be of the now usual 13-company establishment, and armed identically to the 'old' regiments; the regiments themselves are listed in Appendix II. A warrant, dated 3 October 1688, for the arming of Colonel Henry Gage's Regiment survives:

> To arm Colonel Gage's Regiment of 13 companies of 60 private soldiers apiece, including one of grenadiers with … such numbers of Musquets & Piques as shall be necessary for Arming twelve of the said Companies, and sixty fusees, granados pouches & Bayonetts for Arming the said Company of Grenadeers.[46]

Gage had only been commissioned as colonel six days earlier!

On the 19th of the same month Henry Gage's Regiment of Foot was directed to muster at Chester,[47] a further indication that it may already have been fairly complete.

A similar warrant for the arming of Colonel Solomon Richards' and the Duke of Newcastle's Regiments of Foot was issued on the following day, 4 October 1688:

> Thirteen Companies in each Regiment
> Colonell Richards Regiment whereof one Company Granadoes
> Duke of Newcastles Regiment as the same number as the old Regiments[48]

However there is some evidence that the new regiments were not immediately armed exactly as they were intended to be, or as their colonels thought they should be. Thus the letter from Secretary Blaythwayt to the Duke of Newcastle, one of the new colonels, sent from Whitehall on 1 November 1688 and obviously a reply to a now missing letter of complaint from the Duke:

> The Officers of the Ord'nance do assure me, there are Orders sent to Hull, for the delivering out to the Regiment under your Grace's Command, a full number of Matchlocks and all other necessarys. And that in a short time your Graces Regiment will be furnisht with the usuall number of Firelocks in exchange for so many Matchlocks.[49]

---

46 National Archives, Kew, SP44/165, f. 94.
47 National Archives, Kew, WO5/3, f. 280.
48 National Archives, Kew, SP 44/165, ff. 104, 108.
49 Davies, 'Letters on the Administration of James II's Army', pp. 69–84.

Other notes within this letter make it clear that the Duke of Newcastle's Regiment of Foot is either complete or at least near so.

An eighth additional regiment was authorised on 11 October 1688 when Sir Thomas Haggerston, lieutenant governor of Berwick, was given a colonelcy to raise a regiment of eight companies. A full set of commissions was sent to Haggerston, but no trace remains of the activation of these commissions or of the regiment's ephemeral existence, presupposing that it ever had one.[50]

The following day, on 12 October, a warrant was signed and sent to the Earl of Tyrconnel in Ireland authorising him to raise a further three regiments of foot for the Irish Army.[51] Whether these were ever put on foot is not known since a number of regiments were created over the next few months to aid in James' restoration and when each was authorised is not accurately known.

According to Cannon, Colonel Francis Luttrell's Regiment of Foot (later the 19th Foot) was raised in 1689 from the independent companies commissioned by James in the autumn of 1688,[52] see Appendix VII.

Two further regiments of foot were ordered during James II's reign. The most interesting and unusual commission issued by James was that signed at Whitehall on 18 June 1685 and given to Colonel Thomas Strangways to be

> Colonell of a Regiment of foot to bee forthwith raised for Our Service, and to bee drawn out of the Militia of Our County of Dorsett, & likewise to bee Captain of a Company in the said Regiment.[53]

There is, however, no evidence that anything further was done towards the raising of this regiment and there is no record of any further commissions in it being issued. Dalton comments that 'The Regt … was never raised.'[54]

During the general expansion independent companies again made an appearance, presumably to take over garrison duties again and release the regulars for field service, and on 4 October 1688 31 new independent companies were ordered to be raised 'at the same strength as the old Companies'.[55] Perhaps most interesting, though, is the warrant dated 2 October 1688:

> To George, Lord Dartmouth, Master general of the ordnance, to cause to be delivered sixty snaphaunce muskets, and sixty collars of bandoleers to each of the two companies (of sixty in each company) which have been formed out of the Royal Hospital, with drums, halberts and ammunition proportionable, the captains indenting for the same.[56]

It is interesting to note that these were formed as musket-only companies.

50   Dalton, *English*, vol. 2, p. 192.
51   *Calendar of State Papers*, 1687–1688, p. 312; National Archives, Kew, SP 63/340, f. 304.
52   Richard Cannon, *Historical Record of the Nineteenth, or the First Yorkshire North Riding, Regiment of Foot* (London: Parker, Furnivall and Parker, 1848).
53   National Archives, Kew, SP 44/164, f. 203.
54   Dalton, *English*, vol. 2, p. 45.
55   National Archives, Kew, SP 44/165 f. 104.
56   National Archives, Kew, SP 44/165 f. 95.

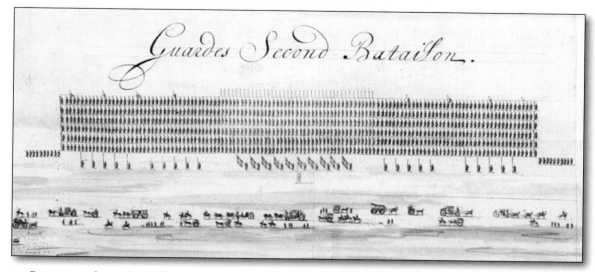

Guardes Second Bataillon.

Raising independent companies from the Pensioners of the Royal Hospital was a common wartime expedient over the next two centuries giving the government ready access to trained and experiences veterans; ideal troops for garrisons, which in turn released the regulars for service in the field. This warrant of 1688 was, however, the first instance of this expedient and came even before the hospital was fully finished (in 1690)[57] or fully occupied. Walton believed that the Royal Hospital had not begun to be occupied until after a general muster of men 'disabled by wounds' was held in 1689. The evidence of the creation of these two companies, however, suggests that the hospital was in use and substantially functioning by the autumn of 1688, although even the official history of the hospital says that it did not '[admit] the first Chelsea Pensioners until February 1692.'[58]

Detail from a contemporary coloured illustration of a battalion of the Foot Guards on Hounslow Heath in 1687. (Public domain)

The full series of illustrations shows many of the regiments although without the legend it would be almost impossible to differentiate. Of note here, however, is the positioning of officers and the six ranks of both muskets and pikes.

Tactical

Whatever the regimental and company establishment, it seems that tactically a body of around 500–600 men was considered a 'battalion' which would have fought tactically together in battle if needed. This body size is the same as that in use during the English Civil Wars and was originally advocated by Maurice of Nassau in the first years of the century.[59] It is likely that, once the grenadier company was detached, most regiments would have formed a single battalion of this approximate strength; it is noticeable that the units sent west to confront Monmouth in 1685 were all initially of around this strength and usually termed

---

57 Inscription in the colonnade of the hospital: *In subsidium et levamen emeritorum senio belloque fractorum condidit Carolus II, auzit Jacobus II, perfecere Giulielmus et Maria, rex et regina, MDCVC.*

58 <http://www.Chelsea-Pensioners.co.uk>. Accessed January 2016.

59 Conforming as it does to the Roman cohort of 480 men and the Spartan unit of 600 men, as well as numerous other ancient and later military 'units', as well as the English Civil War's 'full regiment of 500'.

Frontispiece of *Military Discipline and the Art of War*, London 1688. (Author's collection)

The illustration shows, left to right, an ensign, a lieutenant, and a captain of a company of foot. Whilst some aspects of the illustration, such as the overall style of the clothing, is correct for *c*.1688, others were already out of date when the book was published. In this latter respect it is unlikely that, by 1688, the captain would have been wearing a back and breast although, it is not impossible. However the pikemen shown in the background are also wearing armour (and may even be supposed to be wearing helmets) and there were no issues of armour to the foot during James' reign. It may simply be that the engraver for Stearne's book reused an old plate, a not uncommon practice.

Stearne's book never had the official endorsement of Bill's 1685/6 book and was published privately for commercial reasons. *An Abridgement...*, by comparison, was printed by the Charles Hill, Henry Hills and Thomas Newcomb, 'Printers to the Kings most Excellent Majesty', and was 'Printed by Especiall Command, for the Use of his Majesties Forces'.

as 'battalions' (although the King later refers to them as 'weak battalions' at Sedgemoor). On 27 March 1686 'a *battalion* of our Scotch Guards' (author's emphasis) arrived in London by sea en route to that year's Hounslow Camp; the 'battalion' is listed as being of 560 men, as always 'besides officers'.

An Abridgement of English Military Discipline sets out six ranks for both pike and musket, and *Fortification and Military Discipline*[60] confirms this as being the normal depth for the foot. However musketeers more usually reduced to 'half files' of three ranks in action and *An Abridgement* gives instructions for firing by various combinations of the three ranks as well as how to fire when still in a full six ranks.[61] It also gives instructions for firing by two ranks at a time and also for a single rank at a time. With the varied methods in the army's drill the regiments could presumably choose whichever resulted in the most advantageous to serve the prevailing tactical situation. Platoon firing would not be introduced into the army until after 1688.

James employed the Dutchman Willem van de Velde to make a series of drawings of the Hounslow camps and these are now in the collections of the National Army Museum and Boynam's Museum in Rotterdam.[62] These drawings show the battalions of foot formed in six ranks with pike

---

60 Captain J. S., *Fortification and Military Discipline In Two Parts* (London, 1688).
61 For a more in-depth discussion of the development of firing methods see David Blackmore's superb study, *Destructive and Formidable: British Infantry Firepower 1642-1765* (London: Frontline Books, 2014). Even into the 18th century the full depth was considered to be six ranks and the usual three ranks were 'half files'.
62 There is a full set of photographs of the Rotterdam drawings in Hounslow Public Library.

in the centre and two 'wings' of musketeers, an identical formation to that of the English Civil Wars a half-century before. As might be expected, what information we have suggests that this formation was the way that the battalions formed and fought at Sedgemoor in 1685.

Regimental Artillery

On 8 August 1686 the King issued a warrant ordering that 14 brass 3 pdr guns 'with requisite equipage' were to be sent to the camp at Hounslow:

> To be in readiness to march with the regiments of foot hereafter mentioned … at the breaking up of the camp, viz., the battalion of Scotch Guards, Dumbarton's battalion, The Queen Dowager's Regiment, Prince George's Regiment, the Holland regiment, The Earl of Bath's Regiment and the Marquess of Worcester's Regiment.[63]

These, no doubt, were to act in much the manner as the 'Battalion Guns' that were attached to the infantry regiments of many European armies throughout the course of the 18th century. No 'gunners' or 'mattrosses' were added to the regimental establishments so presumably the new guns were to be crewed by musketeers. Four days later, on 12 August, as the Royal Regiment of Foot marched through the city on their way to their winter quarters, it was noted that they were accompanied by two small field pieces and a wagon of ammunition.[64]

The experiment, if that is what it was, must have been considered a success, for at the Hounslow Heath camp in June 1687 two 3 pdr guns were issued each to:

The Queen Consort's Regiment of Foot
Princess Anne of Denmark's Regiment of Foot
Colonel Henry Cornwall's Regiment of Foot
Colonel Edward Hale's Regiment of Foot
Colonel William Tufton's Regiment of Foot
The Royal Regiment of Scots Fuzileers

It is worth noting however, that there is no record of the issue of similar guns to the new regiments raised in 1688, but that may be because few of them were complete before the King fled in December (see also Chapter 7 on this subject).

Uniform

The table below sets out the facing colours and coat hues etc. for the regular regiments of James's army, although some regiments are known to have had a grey 'fatigue coat' as well. Whether this was ever worn in the field is a matter

---

63 *Calendar of State Papers*, 1686–1687, p. 231; National Archives, Kew, SP 44/164, p. 351.
64 *Ibid.*, p. 234; Adm. 77/3, no. 24.

of some conjecture but Hollar certainly shows it as being worn on service in Tangier during the previous decades. The coat itself had buttons all the way to its lower edge and a 1686 bill for coats for the Scots Fuzileers Regiment of Foot says that each coat had 'five dozen of buttones'.

Waistcoats are a troublesome point. No documents record their issue but there are, nonetheless, several references to them; however it should also be noted that, to date, no issue document for the coats themselves has come to light either, although at least one bill does survive. One clue comes from a notice for a deserter from Prince George of Denmark's Regiment in January 1667 which describes his attire as 'a red coat lined with yellow and an old yellow coat worn under it'. As this regiment is known to have worn yellow coats in 1685–86 it is not unlikely that, as in the 18th century, this 'old yellow coat' represents his issue coat for the previous year which had been cut down, and waistcoats were provided throughout the foot regiments by the expedient of cutting down last year's coat.

Hats for both musketeers and pikemen were black with either white or yellow binding around the edge, probably according to the button colour, and facing-colour hatbands – although it must be stressed that to be pedantic on these points might be unwise, given the paucity of surviving information on such details. The buttons themselves, on the evidence of the large numbers recovered from the site of Feversham's camp at Westonzoyland, were simple flat-faced examples, undecorated, and with the shank on the reverse cast integral.[65]

Leatherwork for all arms was of buff-brown colour and shoes were black, without decoration. Sword scabbards were black.

Musketeers

The musket carried by James' regiments of foot fired a ball of 12 to the pound and had a barrel of 'about foor foote long',[66] or according to a regulation of 21 February 1687, 42 inches[67] (why it should be two inches shorter that the muskets specified for use by the regiments of foot guards in the same regulation is a mystery). It was kept 'bright', that is, not browned or blued. Barthorp's assertion that 'the wood work of all firearms at this time was painted black'[68] would also, of course, be applicable to the muskets of the foot. Until late 1688, in the majority of regiments muskets were issued in proportions of approximately two matchlocks to one flintlock, although there is some evidence that the pre-1685 raised regiments had a higher proportion of flintlocks. A 1683 order gave two companies in each regiment to be armed completely with flintlocks,[69] and

---

65   This archaeology was carried out by Tony Pollard and Neil Oliver for series two of the TV programme 'Two Men in a Trench', first broadcast on 3 April 2004. An outline of the results appeared in the accompanying book, *Two Men in a Trench II: Uncovering the Secrets of British Battlefields*, Tony Pollard and Neil Oliver (London: Michael Joseph, 2003). The book, of course, misses out on Andy Robertshaw's excellent insights from the original TV episode.

66   Regulations of King Charles II, National Archives, Kew.

67   MacKinnon, p. 189.

68   Barthorp, *British Cavalry Uniforms Since 1660*, p. 18. See, however, the comment on this in chapter 4.

69   MacKinnon, p. 167.

Musketeers of foot, *c*.1688. (After C. C. P. Lawson)

Sketch by C. C. P. Lawson after an original illustration in the Royal Library in Windsor Castle. The individuals are, obviously, from four different units and are two musketeers (upper) and two grenadiers (lower). Unfortunately the 'badges' on the various cartouch boxes are so unclear as to give no indication as to what they actually represent. The illustration of these soldiers is, however, an excellent idea of the appearance of the English, Scots and Irish armies of James' reign, noticeably though there is no indication of, even the obvious grenadiers, carrying a grenade pouch.

This illustration is often dated '1689' and described as being of Dutch foot but the sword carried from a waistbelt, rather than the baldric used by the Dutch foot suggests that these are actually English soldiers.

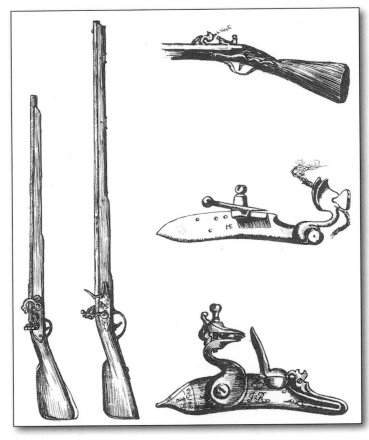

Muskets, *c*.1685. (After C. C. P. Lawson)

Matchlock and flintlock bearing the monogram of James II. Detail, from top to bottom: matchlock from the back, detail of the lock on the matchlock, detail of the lock on the flintlock.

it may be that by 1685 this number had been expanded (although I have not found any warrant on this). Memorably, James II comments in his account of the Battle of Sedgemoor that the Royal Regiment of Foot was the only unit using matchlock muskets,[70] perhaps suggesting that the companies sent west were, in most regiments, specifically chosen to be those that were flintlock armed – or, of course, the King could have been exaggerating the equipment of his army.

Musketeers carried their powder and ball in the collar of bandoleers mentioned above, with the actual wooden bottles painted green, blue or black. Swords were in general issued to all foot and carried from buff-leather waist belts by the musketeers. Bayonets were not, however, universally issued to the musketeers of regiments of foot until 1689, which is after the period under consideration in this study. The musket carried by musketeers did not have a shoulder strap, which was still the preserve of grenadiers and dragoons.

Prince George of Denmark's Regiment and the Royal Regiment of Fuzileers are exceptions to this, in that they were both armed entirely with snaphaunce muskets with plug bayonets, and carried their ammunition in cartouche boxes, presumably in the form of paper cartridges.

In late November 1688 there was a movement to replace the matchlocks in the regiments of foot, and amongst the State Papers in the National Archives at Kew is the following warrant, dated 7 November 1688, directed to Lord Dartmouth, Master of the Ordnance:

> Wheras Our Generall Officers have represented to us yt ye change of ye Match-lock Musquets belonging to Our Regiments of Foot for Snaphaunce will be of great advantage to Our Service. Our Will and pleasure is & Wee do hereby authorize and require you to cause Snaphaunce Musquets to be delivered to Our severall Regiments of Foot in exchange for so many Matchlocks as shall be by them returned into Our stores.[71]

---

70 Quoted in Tincey, *Sedgemoor 1685*, p. 23.
71 National Archives, Kew, SP 44/165, f. 134.

How far this change was put into effect before James' first flight of 11 November is open to debate. The likelihood is that little had been done but this warrant does serve to demonstrate an intention.

Pikemen

Pikemen carried their swords from brown leather shoulder baldrics and were armed with 16-foot pikes, usually made of ash. Whilst armour was still in use in many of the county trained bands,[72] it had generally dropped out of use amongst the foot and there are no issues from the Tower Armouries during James' reign. Pikemen still wore thick, buff leather gauntlets. Additionally, in most regiments, pikemen wore red or white waist sashes, usually fringed and edged in the regimental facing colour.

Grenadiers

Grenadiers were armed and equipped similarly to the musketeers except that they replaced the hat with the grenadier cap, the bandoleer with the cartouche box, and were always armed with flintlock muskets 'strapt'. The 1687 regulation cited above which gave the musketeers' muskets barrels of 42 inches stated that grenadiers should be armed with muskets with a 38 inch barrel. And of course they carried a pouch of four grenades, from which they took their name. How often grenadiers actually carried grenades, however, is cast into some doubt by a letter from Secretary at War William Blaythwayt to Percy Kirke on 21 July 1685: Kirke had requested an issue of grenades for his regiment, then campaigning in the West against Monmouth. The request itself suggests that these were not normally part of the regiment's armament but Blaythwayt denied the request and said that he 'hopes that you will have no use of [them]'.[73]

The appearance of the various regiments' grenadier caps has largely gone unrecorded but what evidence we have suggests that these varied widely from regiment to regiment since they were supplied by the order of the colonel. Whereas the caps seem sometimes to have been almost simple woollen caps with a fur edging around the bottom, within a few years even the 'line' regiments had low caps with heavily embroidered front pieces, similar to that worn by Captain Hawley of the Guards in the well known painting and to the rare surviving example (dated to *c.*1690) in the Collection of the National Museums of Scotland, and as evidenced in the Deserters' Notices in Appendix X, this style was already coming into use under James II in some regiments at least.

Grenadier of a foot regiment, *c.*1685. (After C. C. P. Lawson)

This individual could, aside from the furred cap, also be from one of the regiments of foot guards. The grenadiers of the foot guards wore an early form of grenadier cap, but at this period some regiments of foot, including the Queen Dowager's Regiment, still used this style of 'furred cap'. also in use in some dragoon regiments. Note the slung fusil, plug bayonet and hatchet as well as the slightly curved sword.

---

72 See Christopher Scott, *Military Effectiveness of the West Country Militia at the Time of the Monmouth Rebellion*, unpublished PhD thesis, Cranfield University, 2011.

73 Davis, 'Letters on the Administration of James II's Army', pp. 69–84.

In most cases the coats of grenadiers were fringed about the buttons and buttonholes with a distinctive regimental lace (see table below). In Nathan Brooks' 1684 *A General and Compleat List Military*, the grenadiers are stated to be 'without swords',[74] presumably the hatchet taking its place, as its use is suggested by Bill's instructions for the grenadiers in combat.

Officers and NCOs

For general information see the appropriate section above in Chapter 5. Officers of the regiments of foot followed the same fashions and styles as those of the foot guards and there may have been little to differentiate the two. Company officers wore the same gorgets of rank and carried the same polearms as their brother officers in the foot guards. Officers of the regiments of foot appear not to have used regimental or coloured linings to their coats but preferred instead red or crimson, although as in the horse, regimental distinctions were beginning to be used. As in the foot guards, sergeants carried halberds, effectively as their badge of rank.

Although dating to slightly before James' reign, a tailor's bill for clothing for Francis Luttrell when he was appointed as a colonel in the Somerset Militia in 1681 is highly indicative of how richly dressed senior officers might be:

Making a rich laced cloath suite	1 / 18 / 0
Silk and galloone	5 / 0
Buckles to the britches	3 / 6
Silk to line the britches	10 / 0
Pockets and staying tape	3 / 6
A sett of rich gold buttons	4 / 6
Rich gold brest buttons	4 / 6
Fine drawing the suite	3 / 6
2½ yards of superfine gray cloath	2 / 12 / 6
Buckram and canvas	1 / 3
5½ yards of rich Florence satin to line the coate	4 / 14 / 0
Scarlett plain ribbon	1 / 5 / 0
4 yards rich gold and scarlet ribbon	6 / 5 / 0
18 yards rich gold orar lace for coate and britches	18 / 00 / 0
Gold chaine to the suite	14 / 9
Rich gold needle for the gloves	10 / 5 / 0
A pair of gloves, making and facing	9 / 0
A scarlet fether	1 / 8 / 0
Rich gold needle gold fring for a scarffe	35 / 5 / 0
Silk for a scarffe and making it	18 / 0[75]

---

74 Nathan Brooks, *A General and Complete List Military of Every Commission Officer of Horse and Foot now commanding in His Majesty's Land Forces of England*, London, 1684, p. 11.

75 Sir H. C. Maxwell-Lyte, *A History of Dunster and of the Families of Mohun and Luttrell* (London: St Catherine Press, 1909), pp. 204–210. Quoted in Scott, *Military Effectiveness of the West Country Militia at the Time of the Monmouth Rebellion*, p. 220.

Colour Plates
See colour plate commentaries for full captions

Plate P1. King James II in the uniform of a general officer c.1686.
Godfrey Kneller, oil on canvas. National Army Museum London Collection
© NAM, Reproduced with permission

Plate P2. Captain Francis Hawley of the First Royal Regiment of Foot Guards, 1685.
Oil on canvas. © Private collection, reproduced with permission.

Plate P3. An unknown captain of the Earl of Bath's Regiment of Foot, *c.*1685/6.
Oil on canvas, private collection. © Author's photo

Plate W1: The Regiments of Guards

Watercolours by Mark Allen. © Helion & Company

Plate W2: The Regiments of Horse and Dragoons

Watercolours by Mark Allen. © Helion & Company

PLATE 3

Regiments of Foot. (1)

Plate W3: The Regiments of Foot
Watercolours by Mark Allen. © Helion & Company

Plate W4: Colours of the Regiments of Foot

Watercolours by Mark Allen. © Helion & Company

Plate R1: A musician of the Royal Regiment of Dragoons
(Reconstruction: Alan Larsen)

Plate R2: A trooper of the Royal Regiment of Dragoons (Reconstruction: Alan Larsen)

Notably this does not include any weaponry or equipment and Colonel Lutterell would still have to add his sword, baldric, gorget, etc. as well as his hat, boots, horse, and saddlery to what was, for the time, the immense sum of £74 / 3 / 0, and he was serving only in the county militia!

A painting of what is almost certainly an officer of the Earl of Bath's Regiment c.1686,[76] shows a blue coat with red cuffs and, just visible, red waistcoat. Although his gilt gorget, still of the older 'full gorget' pattern,[77] demonstrates his rank of captain, his coat is surprisingly not heavily laced. It has, however, an overly large number of ornate silver buttons at the front, five or six (it is unclear) on each of the large cuffs, and eight or nine along each of the horizontal pockets; each corresponding buttonhole has a small amount of silver lace around it. The officer wears a pinkish red scarf fairly low on the waist, knotted on the right side and very heavily fringed with fine gold wire. His most ornate item is this baldric which suspends the sword low on the left hip, the belt is so heavily laced with gold and silver designs that the actual colour cannot be made out.

Although this painting is, at the time of writing, the only one known of an officer of a 'line regiment' during James' reign there is no reason to suppose that it is atypical of the appearance of other officers of the army.

Drummers and Musicians

Perhaps unsurprisingly drummers were not recruited in the same way as the rest of a regiment's recruits, indeed they were apparently not even recruited by the regiment but on its behalf by the 'Drum Major Generall'; this was John Maugridge during the period in question. Thus on 21 June 1685 a Warrant was issued to:

> Our Drumm Major General ... [to] Raise or Impress 24 Drummers for Twelve Companies in Our Right Trusty and right Welbeloved Cousin and Councillor John Earl of Bath's Regimt of Foot.[78]

Presumably similar warrants were issued for Maugridge to provide drummers for other regiments, although the warrants only survive for the newly raised regiments of foot of the Duke of Norfolk and Sir William Clifton (24 June),[79] Sir Edward Hales (26 June),[80] and the Earl of Huntingdon (27 June).[81] These warrants were all for him to provide 20 drummers and the reduction to one drummer per company ordered on 25 July would therefore have given Maugridge more than enough drummers than he would have needed to provide for the other three new regiments.

---

76 Stephen Ede-Borrett, 'A Captain of the Earl of Bath's Regiment', in *Journal of the Society for Army Historical Research*, volume 88, London, 2010, pp. 1–4.
77 That is ,it has a back piece and is not just the front plate suspended from ribbons.
78 National Archives, Kew, WO5/1, f. 83.
79 *Ibid.*, WO5/1, f. 88.
80 *Ibid.*, f. 95.
81 *Ibid.*, f. 102.

Top right: detail from plate XVIII / 14 from *Grosse Uniformenkunde* by Richard Knötel, published in Germany *c*.1895. (Author's collection). The original plate is titled as 'Netherlands : Infantry 1680-90' but as with the plate of French cavalry the overall appearance of the two soldiers is little different from that of the foot of James II's army. The only noticeable difference is that the Dutch were still carrying the sword in the old-fashioned method of a baldric whereas the English used the more 'modern' waistbelt. The use of the baldric can be seen on the pictures of the regiments of the Anglo-Dutch Brigade that William sent to aid James in the suppression of the Monmouth Rebellion in 1685.

Top left, bottom left: details from Knötel, plate XIII / 09 (author's collection). The original plate shows foot of the Electorate of Brandenburg, but the general cut of the uniform, shape of the hats, etc. is the same as that of the rank and file of James' army.

Top: a musketeer armed with a flintlock and a equipped with a cartouch box in place of the more common collar of bandoliers.

Bottom: drummers. The lace and braiding on the coats is typical of that in use by all European armies of the period but, of course, very much was at the whim of the regimental colonel. The flame design on the drums is typically German and unlikely on the drums of other nations although the use of the colonel's arms or badge on the front of the drum was common if not near universal.

A similar warrant was issued on 28 September 1688 when the army was further augmented with new regiments of foot and Maugridge was ordered to 'Impress Drums and Fifes … as shall be necessary for Our Service'.[82] Interestingly in both this and the 1685 warrant Maugridge is empowered to 'impress' recruits, not just recruit them. The mention of 'fifes' in the 1688 warrant is the first mention in this context of the formal recruitment of fifers although where they fitted into the establishments is a mystery.

Maugridge had originally been appointed to the post of Drum Major Generall by Charles II and his commission is dated 20 June 1660. He was succeed by (presumably) his son, also John Maugridge, on 1 May 1688. This latter was, in turn, succeeded by R. (almost certainly Robert) Maugridge Jnr on 24 April 1705, probably the son of Robert Maugridge who was kettledrummer to the 1st Troop of Horse Guards in 1684. Robert Maugridge Jnr held post until 18 February 1720 when he was succeeded by John Clothier, and the family's more than half-century tenure of the post ended.[83]

The advantage, of course, of a drum major generall 'recruiting' and training all of the army's drummers is that there would have been a single march in use throughout the army. This was probably the English March, which was certainly in use by the army in Ireland as noted in a letter from the Earl of Sutherland to the Lord Deputy of Ireland, in which he directs that the King 'would not have the march in Ireland changed from the English march nor any alteration in the colours.'[84]

Presumably 'the English March' referred to was still the same as that ordered to be used by Charles I in 1642.[85]

Drummers in the regiments of foot probably wore coats of the regimental facing colour lined and faced red, except for the Royal Regiment of Foot, 'Our Regiment of Fuzileers', and possibly the Queen Consort's Regiment, where royal livery, as worn in the regiments of foot guards, was in use. Drummers also added metallic or coloured lace to seams, edges, buttonholes, etc. on their coats and, normally, the crest or device of the regimental colonel to the breast and back of their coat. There is little firm evidence for the use of 'reversed colours' (that is a coat in the regiment's facing colour lined red) during James' reign, or during the earlier reign of Charles II, although it was common two decades later and it is probable that some colonels already provided their drummers with these coats.

Some regiments had hautboys and/or fifers on strength during the 1680s but these seem to have worn a regimental uniform with lace added, rather than a drummer's-style coat.[86] However there is no formal acknowledgement of their existence on the establishments.

---

82 National Archives, Kew, SP 44/165, f. 78.

83 Stephen Ede-Borrett, 'The Post of Drum-Major-General', in *Journal of the Society for Army Historical Research.*, vol. 92, 2014.

84 *Calendar of State Papers*, 1686–1687, p. 368; National Archives, Kew, SP 63/340, p. 217.

85 Lewis Winstock, *Songs and Marches of the Roundheads and Cavaliers* (London: Leo Cooper, 1971), and *Songs and Music of the Redcoats* (Harrisburg, Pa, 1970).

86 A notice for a deserter from the Earl of Bath's Regiment, in the *London Gazette* of August 11 1690, gives the following information: 'Frenchman, a hautboy, wears a blue coat lined with red, with a

The Queen's Cypher Crowned.
(Author's drawing)

From as early as 1662 the Royal Regiment of Foot had a piper on its regimental establishment as part of the colonel's company, but the dress of this individual remains obscure beyond the fact that in 1680 he had worn a red coat faced white, without lacing.[87] Musicians' headwear was as the rest of their company but with the addition of gold and/or silver lace and galoon.

Little information has survived concerning the drums themselves. They were issued to the regiments and companies from the stores in the Tower,[88] and were to be returned there if no longer required (see above). It is obvious, therefore, that they must have been made to a standard pattern. Whether they were decorated in any way is uncertain, principally because, as with so much of James' army, after issue from the Tower any adornment would have had to have been done at a regimental level, ordered and paid for by the Colonels. In the British Library, however, is a herald painter's record book in which is recorded '2 drums for his grace ye Duke of Norfolk', accompanied by a sketch of the Howard Crest, exactly as it appears on the regiment's colonel's colour, encircled by the Garter which is in turn surmounted by a ducal coronet.[89] The entry is approximately of the right date, although itself undated, but as only two drums were ordered it might be that these were for the colonel's own company.

One contemporary military drum does survive, however. In All Souls College, Oxford, is a drum from the colonel's company of the 'Oxford Volunteers', raised in 1685 as part of the Monmouth emergency.[90] This has red upper and lower hoops and a plain wooden barrel adorned with the arms and mantling of the college (not 'the College Crest' as is often stated), and the usual double row of gilt dome-headed nails fastening the barrel where the ends join. The cords and ties are white rope (although this could have been whitened at a later date). The drum is 56 cm (22 inches) high and 51 cm (21¼ inches) in diameter. This drum is probably typical of the size and appearance of the Army's drums although there is no record that it was issued through the Ordnance Office (and the fact that at the unit's disbandment the drum was given to the college rather than being returned to the Ordnance Office suggests that it was a private purchase).

It is perhaps worth noting that the decoration of the drum with the colonel's arms is in line with what is believed to be the earliest English

narrow silver edging down the seams red breeches and stockings, a red waist-belt and black hat, both with silver lace.'

87   P. D. Clendenin, 'Two Early Pipers', in *Bulletin of the British Model Soldier Society*, December 1950.

88   National Archives, Kew, WO55/1730, 'A Survey of Arms, Stores, Cannon, etc.' stored in the Tower of London, dated 17 September 1686, lists 107 drums serviceable, 91 in need of repair, and 40 unserviceable (excluding drums designated as 'for draggoons').

89   British Library Add. MSS 26683, f. 57v; cf. also Stephen Ede-Borrett, 'Drums for the Duke of Norfolk's Regiment', in *Journal of the Society for Army Historical Research*, volume LXIX, London, 1991, p. 137.

90   The unit saw no action but was employed in patrolling the roads of Oxfordshire against any rebel activity – they are not recorded as having encountered any.

military drum to survive, the so-called 'Drake's Drum' in the collection of the National Trust. Although this drum is probably from the Devon Trained Bands c.1630 (as, most probably, are six of the eight 'Drake Colours' in the same collection) it is once again plain wood with the colonel's arms (i.e. those of the Drake family) painted on the front.

The uniforms and equipment of the independent companies have gone totally unrecorded, although in general they would, of course, have followed the style as the regiments of foot. It may, however, be safely assumed that most, if not all, of these companies wore the almost ubiquitous red coat.

The Grey 'Undress Coat'

As well as the red coat there is are numerous accounts of soldiers in a grey coat, usually stated as being faced with black, even when we know that the regiment wore red. Given the amount of evidence it is undeniable that this coat existed but its use or purpose has yet to come to light, and there are no surviving warrants or order for its making or issue.

It has been suggested that this coat was issued to all rank and file to be worn on an everyday basis to prevent wear, and thus extend the life, of the red coat which in turn would have been worn only on duty or on parades. However, if this were the case it might be expected that a great many more of the deserters would have left wearing their grey coat rather than the red, which latter would have suggested that they were on duty (thus making desertions somewhat harder) whereas the former would have been far less conspicuous.

It seems far more likely that the grey coat was issued in small numbers to each company for guard duty or for wear on colder duties, in the form of a 'watch coat' to be shared and used as needed, as was certainly the situation with such coats later.

However, from evidence of the Tangier Garrison and of those officers shown on the painting of the Second Regiment of Foot Guards on parade on Horse Guards c.1680,[91] officers certainly did have an undress grey coat, often faced in black. Since they were expected to pay for their own, not inexpensive coats (cf. the bill reprinted above), having such an item would make good economic sense.

Colours

As with the regiments of foot guards each company of a regiment of foot, except the grenadiers, carried its own colours. Sizes etc. were the same as for the regiments of foot guards (see above). Yet again, the Royal Regiment of Fuzileers was an exception (but not the Scots Fuzileers Regiment of Foot), in that they had colours only for the field officers' companies.[92]

---

91 In the collection of the Duke of Roxburghe, and discussed in detail in Major P. R. Adair, 'The Coldstream Guards c.1680', in *Journal of the Society for Army Historical Research*, volume XL, No. 163, September 1962, London, 1962, pp. 111–113.

92 Although arguing against this is the fact that the Windsor *Colour Book* actually records a single captain's colour for the regiment.

The Royal Regiment of Foot

The colonel's company colour: plain white with, all in gold in the centre, a thistle below a crown all surrounded by the motto NEMO ME IMPUNE LACESSIT. The lieutenant colonel's colour blue with a St Andrew's Cross and the main device as the colonel's in the centre. The major's the same as the lieutenant colonel's but with the addition of a crimson pile wavy. The various captains' company colours were the same as the lieutenant colonel's but with the addition of a silver Roman numeral above the cross. All colours had mixed blue and silver cords.

The Queen Dowager's Regiment of Foot

Colonel's colour: plain sea green with the Queen Dowager's crowned cypher, in gold, in the centre. The lieutenant colonel's: sea green with an overall cross of St George, fimbriated white, the cypher in the centre and five gold rays issuing from the centre of the cross. Major's: the same as the lieutenant colonel's with the addition of a gold pile wavy. Captains': the same as the lieutenant colonel's with the appropriate Roman numeral, in silver, above the cypher. All cords gold. An illustration in the Officers' Mess of the present-day descendant Regiment of the Queen Dowager's shows the Roman numeral to have been carried in the upper canton instead of on the cross, but to date no contemporary source for this has to come to light.

Prince George of Denmark's Regiment of Foot

When James ascended the throne this regiment's colours were as follows. Colonel's: plain yellow. Lieutenant colonel's: yellow with a red cross edged white overall. Major's and captains: all identical, being white with the cross of St George overall and five gold rays issuing from the corners of the cross. Whether these colours were changed when the regiment's coats were altered from yellow to red is not known.

The Holland Regiment

In 1684 this regiment's colours were as follows. Colonel's: plain green. Lieutenant colonel's: green with the cross of St George overall, fimbriated white. Major's: as lieutenant colonel's with the addition of a gold pile wavy in the upper canton. Captains': as lieutenant colonel's but differenced by a gold Roman numeral in the upper canton.

By June 1686, when the Windsor *Colour Book* was produced, new colours had been issued, viz., colonel's: black with a gold sun in splendour in the centre. Lieutenant colonel's: black with the cross of St George overall, fimbriated white, and the same sun in splendour as on the colonel's. Major's: same as the lieutenant colonel's with the addition of a silver pile wavy. Captains': differenced by a silver Roman numeral in the upper canton.

Colours of the first captain's company of the Holland Regiment. (*The James II Colour Book*, Windsor Castle)

The Queen Consort's Regiment of Foot

In 1684 this Regiment's colours are described by Nathan Brooks as 'of yellow silk, with a red cross bordered white, and the rays of the sun issuing from the angles of the cross', and with the royal cypher in the centre.

In August 1686 James presented new colours to the Queen Consort's Regiment of Foot at Portsmouth. The bill for these 10, from Thomas Holford and amounting to £206 5s 6d, is preserved in the official records in the War Office and the authority to pay it is dated 21 August 1686.[93]

> Or will and pleasure is, That out of such moneys as shall come into your hands for the pay and contingent uses of Our guards and garrisons, you pay to Thomas Holford the sum of Two Hundred and Six Pounds Five Shillings and Six Pence, for Ten Colours made and provided by him for Our dearest Consort, the Queen's Regiment of Foot, and for so doing this, together with the acquittance of the said Thomas Holford, shall be your warrant and discharge.
>
> Given at Our Court at Windsor this 21st day of August 1686
> By His Majesty's command

After the regiment's expansion to 12 'line' companies in 1686, the Queen presented two further colours to the regiment, although the bill for these two additional colours has yet to come to light.

The quality of these colours is evidenced by the fact that the 36 colours for the Regiment of Foot Guards supplied by Holford in 1685 'against H.M.'s … Coronation' cost only £8 each,[94] and in a 1689 bill from Thomas Holford for the making and painting of the 24 colours for the 1st Royal Regiment of Foot Guards the total cost was only £157 6s – and that price included the cloth, staves, tassels (these alone cost £18), etc.[95] That the colours for the Queen Consort's were painted (i.e. not embroidered) is confirmed by the 1689 bill for the Foot Guards where Holford is referred to as 'Tho. Holford Herald Painter'.

The regiment evidently celebrated their new colours:

> Letter from Plymouth of the 27th [August, 1686] say that the officers of Colonel Trelawney's Regiment, having received their new colours, carried them to the royal citadel where they were saluted with 21 great guns and three volleys of small shot, after which the regiment was exercised by the colonel who was extremely well satisfied with them.[96]

These colours are illustrated in *The James II Colour Book* at Windsor, viz., colonel's colour: plain white with the Queen's cypher in the centre in gold and surmounted by a gold crown. Lieutenant colonel's: white, with the cross of St George overall and five black eagles beaked and legged gold in each canton. Major's: the same with the addition of a red pile wavy. Captains': all identical with no differencing between the companies, being as the lieutenant colonels

---

93 Richard Cannon, *Historical Record of the Fourth, or the King's Own, Regiment of Foot* (London: Longman, Orme, and Co., 1839), p. 10.

94 War Office State Papers, quoted in Walton, pp. 460–461.

95 'Great Wardrobe Accounts, Bills', Royal Archives, Windsor Castle, f.79997v.

96 *Calendar of State Papers*, 1686–1687, p. 253; Adm. 77/3, no. 28.

Princess Anne of Denmark's Regiment of Foot, 1685 (after S. M. Milne). Major's company.. See text for colours & details.

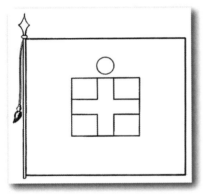

Colonel Henry Cornwall's Regiment of Foot, 1685 (after S. M. Milne). First captain's company. See text for colours and details.

The Earl of Bath's Regiment of Foot, 1685 (after S. M. Milne). First captain's company. See text for colours and details.

but with the addition of the royal cypher and crown in gold at the centre of the cross.

The Royal Regiment of Fuzileers

The colonel's company colour was white with a 'trophy of arms' in gold and a gold shield and stag's head. The lieutenant colonel's was white with the overall cross of St George and a gold 'trophy of arms'. The major's exactly the same but with the addition of a crimson pile wavy. The Windsor Colour Book states that 'the Regiment has but three colours of such kind of trophee' but then goes on to show an illustration of a captain's colours of the regiment; this is the same as the lieutenant colonel's but with the addition of a gold cannon at the centre of the cross. Nonetheless all evidence is that these colours were never issued and this may be presumed to be a projected colour or, and it has to be accepted as a possibility, the captains' companies did indeed receive colours and somehow the statement, and with it the ongoing tradition, is in error and the evidence of their existence has simply not survived.

Princess Anne of Denmark's Regiment of Foot

The colonel's colour was a dark pinkish crimson with the Princess' crowned cypher, in gold, in the centre. The lieutenant colonel's was the same with the addition of an overall cross of St George, fimbriated white. The major's: as for the lieutenant colonel's, with the addition of a white pile wavy. The captains': as for the lieutenant colonel's but differenced by white Roman numerals in the centre of the first canton (I, II, etc.), all cords gold.

There is, however, an alternate source for the colours of this Regiment. British Library Add MS 6832 shows the twelve colours of a regiment of foot under 'Lord Ferrers Colonel'. Ferrers was colonel of Princess Anne of Denmark's Foot from its raising in 1685 until the end of 1686. The colours shown are orange but with a manuscript note that they were changed to rose, cherry or pink. Colonel's: orange with a gold coronet and cypher in the centre. Lieutenant colonel's: orange with an overall red cross edged white. Major's: the same with a white pile wavy. The 1st captain's: as the lieutenant colonel's but with a gold coronet and cypher in the centre of the cross. The 2nd captain's: the same with two cyphers side by side. The 3rd captain's: three cyphers. The 4th captain's: four cyphers in a diamond arrangement. The 5th captain's: five cyphers forming a similar pattern. The 6th, 7th, 8th and 9th captains': the appropriate number of cyphers extending along the arms of the cross. The likelihood of two different stands of colours being issued in less than 18 months is slim, and from later and Civil War evidence a stand of colours should have lasted between three and seven years. Bearing in mind the note that the hue of the field has been changed it is probable that this manuscript is the design for a stand of colours, but when actually made the decision was taken to simplify them into the form shown in the Windsor Colour Book.

Henry Cornwall's Regiment of Foot

Colonel's: plain orange. Lieutenant colonel's: orange with a cross of St George on a white square in the centre. Major's: the same with a white pile wavy. Captains': the same as the lieuenant colonel's with differencing of white roundels above the cross, one for the 1st captain, two for the 2nd captain, and so on. Orange and silver cords.

The Earl of Bath's Regiment of Foot

Colonel's colour: plain yellow. Lieutenant colonel's: yellow with red cross bordered white. Major's: the same with a red pile wavy. Captains': as for the lieutenant colonel's but with the addition of an 'organ rest' and without any form of differencing between companies. Silver and gold cords.

The Duke of Beaufort's Regiment of Foot

Colonel's colours: plain crimson. Lieutenant colonel's: crimson with an overall cross of St George, bordered white. Major's: the same with the addition of a white pile wavy. All captains bore identical colours, being the same as the lieutenant colonel's but with the addition of a gold portcullis and chains in the centre of the cross. Crimson and silver cords.

The Duke of Norfolk's Regiment of Foot

Colonel's colours: crimson with a central device of a gold crowned lion standing on an ermine cap of maintenance. Lieutenant colonel's: crimson with the usual Cross of St George, fimbriated white. The captains' colours were all the same as the lieutenant colonel's, but with the addition of a single cross crosslet fitchée in the centre of the cross. Crimson cords.

The Duke of Norfolk resigned command of this regiment in June 1686 (see Appendix I) and the field of the colours was then changed to white. Unfortunately, aside from the fact that they had an overall red cross in the usual form no other details are recorded.[97]

The Earl of Huntingdon's Regiment of Foot

Colonel's colour: plain yellow. Lieutenant colonel's: yellow with the Cross of St George overall, bordered white. Major's: the same but with a crimson pile wavy. Captains': as for the lieutenant colonel's with no distinguishing or differencing. Mixed gold and silver cords.

Sir Edward Hales' Regiment of Foot

Colonel's colour: plain crimson. Lieutenant colonel's: crimson with the Cross of St George bordered white overall and three gold flames issuing from the corners of the cross. Major's: the same with the

The Duke of Beaufort's Regiment of Foot, 1685 (after S. M. Milne). Captains' companies colours. See text for colours and details.

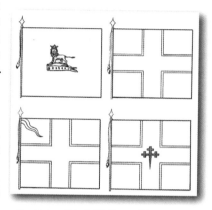

The Duke of Norfolk's Regt. of Foot, 1685 (after S. M. Milne). L-R: colonel's, lt colonel"s, major's, and captains' companies. See text.

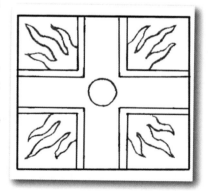

Sir Edward Hales' Regiment of Foot, 1685 (after S. M. Milne). First captain's company. See text for colours and details.

97 Cannon, *Historical Records of the Twelfth, or the East Suffolk, Regiment of Foot*, pp. 2–3.

addition of a white pile wavy. Captains': as for the lieutenant colonel's but with differencing of varying numbers of white roundels along the arms of the cross.

Sir William Clifton's Regiment of Foot

Colonel's colour: plain turquoise with, in the centre, the Clifton crest 'out of a ducal coronet gules, a demi-peacock argent'. Lieutenant colonel's: turquoise with the Cross of St George overall, fimbriated white, and five white cinquefoils in each quarter. Major's: the same with the addition of a white pile wavy. Captains' colours: all identical, being the same as the lieutenant colonel's with the Clifton crest at the centre of the cross. Turquoise and silver cords.

Archibald Douglas' Regiment of Foot

One modern source gives the colours of this regiment as having a white field with all, except the colonel's, having the Cross of St George overall; no other details are given. I have been unable to trace the original source for this.

John Hales' Regiment of Foot; Henry Gage's Regiment of Foot; Solomon Richards' Regiment of Foot; Duke of Newcastle's Regiment of Foot; Bevil Skelton's Regiment of Foot; John Carne's Regiment of Foot; the Earl of Stafford's Regiment of Foot.

No information has come to light concerning the colours of these seven regiments and it is not improbable that, in some cases, colours were never issued.

Regiments on the Scottish Establishment:

The Scots Fuzileers Regiment of Foot

Colonel's colours: white with, in the centre, a crowned thistle within the motto NEMO ME IMPUNE LACESSIT in gold, all on a circular patch of blue. Lieutenant colonel's: blue with the Cross of St Andrew and a single flame of white issuing from each angle of the cross, in the centre the same device as on the colonel's colour. Major's: the same as the lieutenant colonel's but with a crimson pile wavy. Captains' colours: as for the lieutenant colonel's but with the addition of silver Roman numerals on the upper inner arm of the cross as differencing. Cords of mixed blue and gold.

John Wachop's Regiment of Foot

Although no definite identification of any colours for this regiment has come to light, there is some evidence to suggest that its colours were blue with the Cross of St Andrew and the same motto as borne on the colours of the Scots Regiment of Foot Guards and the Scots Fuzileers Regiment of Foot

The Scots Fuzileers Regiment of Foot, 1685 (after S. M. Milne). First captain's company. See text for colours and details.

Regiments on the Irish Establishment:

No firm evidence has yet come to light on any of the colours of the regiments of foot on the Irish Establishment during James' reign. However the engraving of the army on Hounslow Heath in September 1688, by William Van de Velde, shows what is most probably the Earl of Granard's Regiment of Foot. The regiment is shown carrying white colours with what is almost certainly a red St Patrick's Cross. Although no other details are shown it might not be too fanciful to suggest that the company distinctions were simple numerals similar to those on the colours of the Scots Fuzileers Regiment of Foot.[98]

There is also an interesting note in a letter from the Earl of Sutherland to the Lord Deputy of Ireland in which he directs that the King 'would not have the march in Ireland changed from the English march nor any alteration in the colours',[99] This suggests either that the colours of the regiments in Ireland may have been the St George Cross like the English regiments of foot, carrying on the fantasy that this was not an 'Irish Army', or that someone had made the suggestion that a change to that form should be made.

Pay

The regiments of foot and the independent companies of foot were paid at the same rate as the regiments of foot guards (see above), although they received no additional allowance for being quartered in London.

However there were two ranks which did not exist in the Foot Guards, but only in specific regiments of foot:

In The Royal Regiment of Foot	
Piper	1s 0d per day
In The Royal Regiment of Fuzileers	
Gunsmith	5s 0d per day

---

98 Stephen Ede-Borrett, 'The de Velde Drawing at the National Army Museum', *Arquebusier*, volume XXVIII No. 1, Farnham, 2004, pp. 2–10. The Museum catalogue puts the drawing at 1687 but the presence of an Irish regiment firmly places it as being from 1688 since no Irish regiments served in England until that year.

99 *Calendar of State Papers*, 1686–1687, p. 368; National Archives, Kew, SP 63/340, p. 217.

7

The Artillery

Although there had been a small number of gunners and gunners' mates on the 'Guards and Garrisons' establishment as early as the reign of Henry VIII, there were to be no formal, regular companies of artillery ('batteries' by modern usage) until the Royal Artillery was raised in 1716. Prior to this date a 'train' was organised by the Ordnance Department for each new campaign or war and was disbanded at the end of it.

Even after the formation of the Royal Artillery the Ordnance Department itself came under the direction of the Master General of the Ordnance; both it and its personnel were answerable only to the Master General, and, theoretically at least, not even to the general commanding the army.[1]

The core of any train of artillery was the one hundred professional gunners of the department's permanent staff, although these were not the professionals they are often claimed to be – see the pay scale below; however, as can be seen in Table 6, the majority of these were allocated to the various permanent garrisons in England. In addition to these gunners could be added such gunners' mates and others as had some experience or as could be quickly trained. The third component of a train was the mattrosses, who seem to have been largely semi-skilled labourers responsible for the manhandling of the guns in action, and suchlike duties. Lastly it was usual to add a number of pioneers to any train to emplace guns, dig defensive works, etc.

On James' accession the distribution of gunners in the kingdoms' garrisons was as per Table 6.

Additionally, of course, in 1685 many of these garrisons had independent companies permanently based within them. For details of these companies see chapter 6.

In action men from the regiments of foot seem to have been attached to the guns to aid the working and manoeuvring of them. The conductors and their carts (together with carpenters, coopers etc.) were hired civilians and not subject to military discipline: thus, it was not unknown or unusual for then to disappear in a homeward direction when the shooting started.

---

1   Hence the reason why shrewd generals, like Marlborough and Wellington, ensured their appointment as Master General as well as their army rank, although the pay of £1,500 per annum may also have provided some attraction.

Details of a number of trains of James' reign survive but the most detailed is that for Feversham's Army during the Sedgemoor Campaign of summer 1685. The armament of the personnel of this train is listed in the manuscript in the Blake Museum in Bridgwater:

For 2 Gun^es Mates & 32 Gun^es	Field Staves	34
	Hangers	34
	Belts to do	34
32 Matrosses	Half Pikes	32
	Hangers wth Belts	32
Capt of ye Pioneers	Partisan	1[2]
Serg^t	Hanger wth Belt	1
Corporall	Halbert	1
	Hanger wth Belt	1
20 Pioneers	Hangers wth Belts	20
Drumer	Drume	1
	Hanger wth Belt	1
For the Pioneers to march with	Pick-axes	8
	Shovels	6
	Spades[3]	6
Hangers with Belts for	Conductors	6
	Wheelwrights	3
	Carpenters	5
	Cooper	1
	Smiths	4
	Coller-maker	2
For ye Provost Marsh^ll	Hand-Cuffs	4
	Pistols	2 pr
	Holsters	1 pr
	Hangers with Belts	2

The train itself comprised 26 guns brought together as follows:

From The Tower
Two 12 pdrs (brass)
Eight 9 pdrs (brass)
Four 6 pdrs (brass)
Four 4 pdrs (brass)

From Portsmouth[4]
Four 3 pdrs (iron)
Four Falcons (2½ pdrs) (brass)

The warrants for this train are complete but I have only transcribed and reprinted the more important items from that warrant. A full list including

---

2   Although this is what the warrant calls for, I think that there is an error in the original. I believe that the partisan, etc., is for the captain and the halberd etc. for the sergeant, and that the corporal's arms – probably a field stave and a hanger – have been missed from the list. There is no other time that a corporal is given a halberd, nor a sergeant a partisan.
3   Suggesting that the sergeant and the corporall also marched with tools.
4   National Archives, Kew, SP 44/164, f. 242, warrant dated 16 June 1685.

the candles, grease oils and starch was transcribed by Bill Carman and reprinted in the *Journal of the Society for Army Historical Research*.[5]

From the Tower was ordered:

Office of Ordnance

A Proporcon of Ordnance Carriages & other St[res] and Habiliaments of Warr to be forthwith issued out of his Maj[es] Stores being for a Traine of Artillery of 16 peeces of Ordnance to attend on his Maj[es] Forces according to his Maj[es] Warr[t] dated 21st June 1685

Brass Ordnance	12 Pound[e]	2
	D Culvering	4
	6 Pound	4
	Saker	4
	Minion	2
Travell Carriage wth ffore Carriages comp[et]	12 Pound[e]	2
	D Culver	4
	6 Pound[e]	4
	Saker	4
	Minion	2
	Block Carriage wth Shodd wheels & ffore Carriage compleat	1
Spare field Carriages mount[d] on Shodd wheels wth ffore Carr[s] Compl[t]	12 Pound[e]	1
	D Culver	1
	6 Pound[e]	1
	Saker	1
	Minion	1
Spare Extrees barr'd	12 Pound[es]	1
	D Culver	2
	6 Pound[e]	2
	Saker	2
	Minion	1
Spare Extrees Unbarr'd	12 Pound[es]	1
	D Culver	2
	6 Pound[e]	2
	Saker	2
	Minion	1
	12 Pound[es]	1 p

5   W. Y. Carman, 'The Train of Artillery in the Monmouth Rebellion' in *Journal of the Society for Army Historical Research*, vol. LXVI (1988), pp. 212–223.

Spare wheels Shodd for	D Culver	1 p
	6 Pound^e	1 p
	Saker	1 p
	Minion	nl

Equipage for the Traine

		la	sp
	12 Pound^{es}	2	5
Ladles & Sponges with	D Culver	4	4
Staves Heads & Rames	6 Pound^e	4	4
	Saker	4	4
	Minion	2	2

Cases of Wood for	12 Pound^e	3
	D Culver	5
	6 Pound^e	5
	Saker	5
	Minion	4

To be putt into ye boxes	Hamer Hatchets	20
of ye Carriages	Pincers	18 p
	Nailes of Sorts	25,000

Brass Gages for Shott	1 sett
Baskets	12
Hand-spikes	16
Hand-crow-leavers	16
Field tampeons	16
Linstocks wth dble heads	16

There then follows a list of quantities of smaller items like Mortar & Pestill (1), Powder-hornes (16) etc., a list of the various pieces of harness required for both the guns and the wagons and items such as horseshoes (2,000) and horseshoe nails (12,000). Then:

Municon for ye Traine

Corn Powder	40 barr^{ls}
Match	40 lb w^t

Round Shott for	12 Pound^{er}	80	
40 Rounds	D Culvering	160	
	6 Pound^{er}	160	
	Saker	160	
Minion			80

Tin cases of d^{ble} plate	12 Pound^{es}	30
fill'd with Musq^t Shott	D Culvering	60
for ---- 15 Rounds	6 Pound^{es}	60

Saker	60	
Falcon	30	

Hand grandadoes with ffuzes	1,000 incl 500 fixt
Parchment Skins for Cartridges	40
Leather Bags to carry Powd^r	20
Spare ffuzes	200

Carriages

Waggons open	15 & 4 hired
Waggons cover'd	23
ffaire Carts	1 & 7 hired
Tumbrils close	8 & 1 Ice cart
Tumbrils open	1
Gin Cart	1
Sling Cart	1

Materialls

Spades	300
Shovels	610
Turfe Spades	50
Pick-axes Steeld	300
Wheel-barrows	60
Hand barrows	30
Hand-hatchets	100
Hedgeing bills	20
Felling-axes	20

This is then followed by a full listing of all of the minor necessaries of the train including 'Sheep Skins (3 doz), Oyls (2 gall), Needles (4 doz)', etc. but towards the end of the list are two very interesting items:

Defences before Trenches	
Turn Pikes furn^d	8
Stockadoes	200

The Tower train document also lists the individual personnel and their daily pay, but not covered elsewhere are:

Capt of ye Pioneers   4s
    1 Serjeant   2s
    1 Corporal   1s 6d
    1 Drummer   1s
    20 Pioneers at 12d each
    Drivers 118 at 12d each

The warrant for the Portsmouth train orders:

A Proporcon of Powder, Shott, Match and other Stores to attend a Train of Artillery consisting of Eight Guns hereafter menconed as likewise for foot services. By Express Order and Comand from his Maj^{ts} Signisfyed by ye Rt Honble ye Lord Dartmouth Mas Gen^{ll} of his Maj^{ts} Ordnance 16 June 1685

To be issued out of his Maj^{ts} Stores at Portsmouth

Iron Ordnance	
Neild & Turn'd 3 Pound^s of 5 foot	4
Brass Ordnance ffalcon of 6 foot	4
Travels Carriages 3 Pound^s	4
Compleat for ffalcon	4
Round Shot for 3 Pound^s	200
ffalcon	200
Tin cases ffill'd wth 3 Pound^s	40
Musq^{tt} Shott for	
Spare field carriages 3 Pound^s	1
wth fore Carriages comp^t ffalcon	1
Spare Wheels for 3 Pound^s	1 pr
ffalcon	1 pr
Spare Extras barr'd 3 Pounds	2
ffalcon	2
Spare Extras unbarr'd 3 Pounds	4
ffalcon	4
Field Budels for 3 Pounder	4
ffalcon	4
Coines	16
ffield tampeons	16
Muncon	barr^{ll}
Corne Powder	20 incl 6 in ½ Barr'ls

Match	10 lb wᵗ		
Musqtt shott	20 lb wᵗ		
Hand Granadoes fix't	1000		

Equipage			
Linstocks	8		
Browne Bills	16		
Hatchets	25		

Carriages			
Waggons cover'd	2		
Tumbrils	4		
Pack sadles	4		
Crooks	4 pr		

Materials			
Shovels	200	Hurdles	1 cart load
Spades	200	Malt ladles gr	1
Pickaxes	200	do small	1

Apparently the train was also expected to function as an 'Ordnance Office out station in the field', in other words for an Army of this size not to be able to equip this many men, since amongst the items listed for it to carry are:

Spare Armes for Three Thousand Foot & One Thousand Horse, Three Hundred Granadeers, Three Hundred Dragoons
As also Materialls, for One
Thousand Men to work at one time,
wᵗʰ Waggons & Tumbrills for the Same.

Vizt.

Match Lock Musqᵗˢ	300		
Pikes	250		
Pistols with Holsters	100 pr		
Snaph Musqᵗˢ Strapt for Granadeers	50		
Snaph Musqᵗˢ Strapt for Dragoons	50		
Municon for ye ffire Armes		Powder	23 barrels fine
		Musqtt Shot	20 lb wᵗ
		Pistol Shot	6 lb wᵗ
		Match	1½ Tn
		Flints	9000
Working Materialls		Spades	250
		Shovels	250
		Pick-axes 250	

Close Waggons for yᵉ Minicon & Armes	5

Close Tumbils for yᵉ Small Shott	2
Open Waggons for yᵉ Pikes & Materials	1

The list of weaponry and the 'spare armes', suggests that one in four of the foot's weapons would be expected to need replacing but that the horse would not lose any of their swords. The list also highlights the fact that dragoon and grenadier musket were different enough for the Ordnance Office clerk to record them so.

The Ordnance Office also supplied the tents for the Army:

Tents with their Furniture
for the Army vizt.

Trench Tents		50
Mallets		750
Tent-pins		12,600
Tent-Spikes		1,000
Tent-Line		1 lb of
Stand Poles		1,600
Ridge Poles		800
Materialls sent	Shovels	100
With ye Said Tents	Spades	50
	Pick-axes	50
	Hatchets	6
	Pikes, unserv[ble] 24[6]	

In preparation for a possible landing in the north, two months earlier another train had been sent to Berwick:[7]

Consisting of ten Peeces of Brasse Ordnance; viz 4 Demy Culvering, 2 Sakers, & 4 three Pounders with the severall Carriages belonging to the same, and all the necessaries whatsoever.

However this train was without personnel, who would presumably have been sent from London if and when the train had been activated.

A Scots train was organised to accompany the Scots Army into England in the Autumn of 1688, but it was ordered to return to Scotland on 31 October under escort of the garrison of Berwick.[8] The composition of this train is unknown.

Information of the train organised for the army on Salisbury Plain in 1688 is sketchy, but on 28 September 26 cannon and four mortars were ordered from the Tower to Finchley Common in readiness. The train eventually

---

6   These details are all taken from a manuscript in the collection of the Blake Museum in Bridgwater.
7   National Archives, Kew, WO44/164, f. 177. Warrant dated 24 May 1685.
8   National Archives, Kew, WO5/3, f. 308.

moved west with the Earl of Feversham and was with the Army at the camp on Salisbury Plain on 15 November.

The most common guns in use in the field (that is, distinct from siege pieces) were still sakers (6–7 pounders) and demi-culverins (9–10 pounders). Although 8–12 inch mortars were available, they were not common. To these field pieces a siege train could add cannon as large as 62 pounders, mortars, and howitzers as large as 18 inches.

The carriages of the guns themselves were painted a 'redd lead' colour. This has sometimes been interpreted as a dark brick-red colour but is more likely to have been the mid grey that the Artillery used from at least as early as the first years of the 18th century,[9] and which English guns are recorded as being painted during the reign of Henry VIII and during the Civil Wars.

At the camp on Hounslow Heath in the July and August of 1686 a contemporary newsletter recorded that:

> The cannon, consisting of 28 brass pieces, is placed just in the centre of the army, each gun having a gunner and two warders to attend it and a party of foot besides.[10]

The 'warders' here are the warders of the Tower.[11]

For the annual muster on Hounslow Heath in 1687 a train was ordered and organised by a warrant dated 5th June 1687.[12] It was to comprise:

2 Demi Culverin of 10 foot long
4 Minion of 10 foot long
6 Three-pounders of 6 foot long
6 Brass Mortars of 7¼ inch diameter

2 Three-pounders 'new' to be issued to
The Queen Consort's Regiment of Foot
The Princess Anne of Denmark's Regiment of Foot

2 Three-pounder Drakes to be issued to
Colonel Henry Cornwall's Regiment of Foot

2 Falconetts to be issued to
Colonel Sir Edward Hale's Regiment of Foot
Colonel Sir William Tufton's Regiment of Foot

2 Three-pounders to be issued to
The Scots Fuzileers Regiment of Foot, 'Col Buchans Batalia'.

(For these latter issued 'battalion guns' see 'The Regiments of Foot' above.)

---

9   The guns on the Blenheim Tapestries are shown as having their woodwork painted light to mid grey.
10 *Calendar of State Papers*, 1686–1687, p. 193; Adm. 77/3, no. 13.
11 *Ibid.*, p. 176; Adm. 77/3, no. 9a.
12 National Archives, Kew, SP 44/164, ff. 397–399.

17th century artillery piece
(modern trail)

The barrel actually dates to
the Civil War but is displayed
on a modern reproduction
carriage. The overall
appearance, however, is still
that of the 1680s when guns
still retained the distinctive
'long trail', typical of the 17th
century.

Photograph © Serena Jones,
reproduced with permission
of Tyger's Head Books

Uniform

The gunners and gunners' mates on both the English and Scots establishments wore red or crimson coats with blue linings and facings. Their headgear appears to have been the same form of cap as worn by dragoons and some grenadiers. 'Hanger' in the above list refers to the short infantry sword as worn in the regiments of foot and presumably of the same pattern. The gunners in the Tower garrison are, however, in 1688 recorded as having red coats faced with black velvet,[13] but given the cost of velvet it is doubtful if this was commonplace throughout the Army.

Officers

The officers probably wore red coats like the gunners but these may have been faced in red or even in black. Bill Carman noted a painting of Anthony Payne, 'Captain of the Guns in Plymouth', by Sir Godfrey Kneller, in which the sitter is portrayed in a red coat guarded black 'somewhat in the style of the yeomen of the Guard',[14] although I would be hesitant to suggest that this is other than the attire of a unique individual.

The normal 'arquebusier armour' of back and breast plates and pott helmet was obviously impractical for officers of the train but there are two interesting issue of armour amongst the 1688 warrants that cast some light on this subject:

To Jacob Richards for his owne use in the Traine of Artillery
By order of the Board and Proporton 30th of October 1688
      Silk Armour   1 suite[15]

To Sr Martin Beckham Lent him for his use, By order
and Proporton of ye 1st Decemb 1688
      Silke Armour   One suite[16]

13   National Archives, Kew, WO51 / 32.
14   Carman, 'The Train of Artillery in the Monmouth Rebellion, 1685', pp. 212–223.
15   National Archives, Kew, WO55/1656, f. 36.
16   *Ibid.*, f. 40.

Jacob Richards is so far unidentified, but 'Sir Martin Beckham' is almost certainly the Swedish captain of artillery who had come to England in 1667 and who had been appointed 'Engineer to the Ordnance' by royal warrant of 19 October 1670. On 14 June Beckham was additionally commissioned as a captain in the Royal Regiment of Fuzileers,[17] and on 30 November 1685 he had succeeded Sir Bernard de Gomme as Chief Engineer.

For notes on 'silk armour' see Chapter 3 on the regiments of horse. Silk armour is surprisingly effective especially against the low velocity weapons of the period, although even in the 21st century experiments are being carried out around its effectiveness for issue to some police forces in the Far East. It may have been more expensive than iron armour in 1685, but in 2015 it is considerably cheaper than Kevlar!

Sir Henry Shere's armour issue mentioned above may be significant in this respect only as he is termed 'Lt Gen^{ll} of y^e *late* Traine of Artillery'[18] (author's italics), in other words he is serving as a general officer rather than an officer of the train.

Pay

Unlike the other arms the personnel of the Ordnance Office were generally paid an annual salary (gunners being the exception to this – see below). Note: these pay rates are as at 1683 but few other rates of pay in the army changed from 1680–1690 and there is no reason to suppose that those of the Ordnance Office did so during the same period.

Master General	£1,500
Lieutenant General	£ 800
Surveyor General	£ 400
Clerk of the Ordnance	£ 400
Storekeeeper General	£ 400
Clerk of Deliveries	£ 300
Treasurer	£ 500
Secretary	£ 200
Office Clerks	£ 40 to 75
Armoury Keeper	£ 60
Armourer	£ 20 to 25
Keeper of Small Guns	£ 80
Furbisher of Small Guns	£ 30 to 40
Storekeeper	£ 20 to 120
Principal Engineer	£ 300
Second Engineer	£ 250
Third Engineer	£ 150
'Young Men to be bred up as Engineers'	£ 100

---

17   See Dalton, *English*, vol. 1, p. 157 and vol. 2, p. 28.
18   National Archives, Kew, WO55/1656, f. 41.

Master Gunner	£ 190
Master Gunner's Mate	£ 45 10s
Firemaster	£ 150
Firemaster's Mate	£ 80
Fireworker	£ 40
Petardier	£ 40
Proof Master	£ 20
Wagon Master	£ 100
Clerk of the Cheque	£ 60
Purveyor of Transport	£ 40
Gunner	1s 0d per day[19]

The train for the Sedgemoor campaign adds one further officer to this list, in addition to the carpenters (2s per day), wheelwrights (2s per day), master cooper (2s 6d per day), and sundry other workmen:

Gentleman of the Ordnance	5s per day

The train had three of these 'officers'.

The relatively low pay of the gunners themselves, no more than that of a drummer in a regiment of foot, is comparable to the level of pay of gunners during the English Civil Wars and suggests that they were not considered as valuable professionals. Comparably the pay of the master general is just above £4 per day, equivalent to the pay of a lieutenant general in the army.

Interestingly, despite their appearance on the list of troops in the Sedgemoor train and with the artillery on Hounslow Heath there is no pay specified for a 'matross' and we can only guess that his pay rate must have been perhaps equivalent to a private soldier, i.e. 8d per day.

19 Walton, p. 650.

8

The Royal Army at Sedgemoor, 6 July 1685

This is not intended as a narrative of either the campaign or the battle of Sedgemoor,[1] but as the only full action that James' army undertook during his brief reign. A look at the army during the campaign perhaps sheds light on the army as a whole.

The Duke of Monmouth landed at Lyme on the morning of 11 June 1685 and the news reached the King in London within 36 hours. He was not slow to react and on the 13 a force comprising four troops of the Royal Regiment of Horse, two troops of the Royal Regiment of Dragoons and five companies of the Queen Dowager's Regiment of Foot left London for the West Country as the advance guard of the royal army. This advance party was put under the command of Lord Churchill, later to become famous as the 1st Duke of Marlborough, but on 19 June the King appointed Lord Feversham to overall command of the expedition. Given the advance warning that James had received of Monmouth's intentions it seems likely that these two forces had already been 'readied' to move to the invasion point as soon as this was known.

Further troops were sent west, and by 6 July the order of battle of the royal army on the field of Sedgemoor was as follows:

One troop of the Royal Regiment of Horse Guards[2]
Seven troops of the Royal Regiment of Horse

---

1   There are a number of first class works on the campaign and battle but perhaps the best are David Chandler's *Sedgemoor 1685, An Account and Anthology* (London: A. Mott, 1985), which although fairly poor and often inaccurate on the army and military does benefit from its reprinting of almost all of the contemporary accounts; Tincey, *Sedgemoor 1685* is an excellent up-to-date analysis; and Peter Earle's *Monmouth's Rebels: The Road to Sedgemoor 1685* (London: Weidenfeld and Nicolson, 1977), is also invaluable. John Childs' account of the battle in *General Percy Kirke and the Later Stuart Army* is perhaps the most concise and readable of all, although, as he readily admits, he makes 'no claim to originality'.

2   James II says that this was 'one hundred and fifty commanded out of the three troops of Gards [and] sixty Gran. on Horseback commanded by Villars'. This had also been the method previously adopted for the provision of such a unit, as in the case of the troop that was sent to France with Monmouth in 1672. Note that the strength that James gives for this unit is almost certainly exclusive of officers.

Four troops of the Royal Regiment of Dragoons

Thirteen companies of the First Regiment of Foot Guards
Six companies of the Second Regiment of Foot Guards
Five companies of the Royal Regiment of Foot
Five companies of the Queen Consort's Regiment of Foot
Five companies of the Queen Dowager's Regiment of Foot

All regiments, except the Second Regiment of Foot Guards, had their grenadier companies with them, as the composite troop of horse guards had a company of horse grenadiers (whether this was a composite company or one of the three complete, which seems the more likely option, is unknown). The 13 companies of the First Regiment of Foot Guards were deployed as two battalions.

In a letter to the Prince of Orange, his son-in-law, James wrote that his army at the battle:

> Consisted of about two thousand foot in six battalions, and some seven hundred horse and dragoons and eighteene smal feild peeces.[3]

Allowing for the troops of horse not being quite up to strength, 700 does not seem far wrong, however for 34 foot companies to muster only 2,000 men, would give an average strength of around 58 each, which seems fairly unlikely under the circumstances. These figures do however become more credible if we take it that James has excluded all 'officers' from his calculations, as was often done by contemporaries (and as James had done in citing the Horse Guards at 150 men and 60 grenadiers – see note above); 'officers' in the late 17th century were considered to include any soldier who was not actually a private centinell or trooper, and thus included NCOs and drummers, as well as commissioned officers. At full strength each company of foot had an establishment of 10 'officers', so if we recalculate to include these then we can add up to 10 to each company to a total of up to a further 340 men, which would give an average company strength nearer 70.

In October 1684 the regiments reviewed at Putney Heath averaged between 71 and 74 men per company, or approximately full establishment strength at that time, not too far from the above suggested strength. James had been aware of his nephew's intentions since mid April at the latest and it seems inconceivable that he would not have taken the opportunity and time given him to recruit his army back to at least its establishment strength, if not to the increased establishment levels ordered on 13 June.[4] After the battle, it suited James' purposes to play down the number of troops Feversham had used to crush Monmouth's army, for both propaganda and prestige purposes.

With all this in mind it is possible that the foot companies at Sedgemoor may indeed have averaged nearer to their full February establishment

---

3   The National Archives, Kew, SP 8 / 3, f.144.
4   To 100 'private centinells' per company, see 'Regiments of Foot'. National Archives, Kew, WO5/1 f. 40.

THE ARMY OF JAMES II, 1685–1688

Playing cards from 1685 (author's collection)

From a pack printed to celebrate the defeat of Monmouth's Rebellion. The face of each card showed a different incident from the rebellion although most are of non-military subjects.

V: The narrative for this, the Five of Clubs, reads: 'The three Eng: Regiments that came out of Holland returning back'

As the threat of invasion increased James II had recalled the regiments of the Anglo-Scots brigade, which was in the service of the Netherlands. These regiments had not proceeded further than London when the victory at Sedgemoor made their presence no longer necessary and they were allowed to return to Netherlands service.
Interestingly the musketeers are shown with their swords carried from baldrics in the manner of the Dutch Army, giving them a distinctive 'cross belt' appearance, although they are still shown with collars of bandoliers for their powder and not yet cartouche boxes.

I: The narrative for this, the Ace of Diamonds – the 'I' by contemporary parlance – reads: 'Two troopes of ye Rebells horse cutt of att Cansham Bridge by Coll: Ogilthorpe'

Note the 'cross belts' indicative of a regiment of horse (Oglethorpe was colonel of the Royal Regiment of Horse). It is notable that the troopers are not wearing back and breast or helmet but this may be because the engraver would only have seen the regiment in London in a non-campaign situation.

VIII: The narrative for this, the Eight of Clubs, reads: 'Severall of ye Kings Forces in search after Ferguson'

The nearest figure is a sergeant, wearing a military scarf (a 'sash'). The musketeers clearly show the collar of bandoliers and the sword worn from a waist belt (or suspended in mid air below the waist belt!) The small size of the brim on the hats, which is common throughout the figures on the set, is an interesting aspect.

Rebells Marching out of Lime

The Rout of a 1000 of the Rebells horse Comãnded by ỹ Ld: Gray

VIII: The narrative for the Eight of Spades, is: 'Rebells Marching out of Lime'

Monmouth's Rebels are shown looking the same as the army except for having cross belts, that is the sword carried on a baldric, in the Dutch style, rather than on a waist belt. This may, or may not be accurate but Monmouth had bought much of his equipment in the Netherlands and more had come from the Trained Bands - in both cases the older style of carrying the sword was still in use. Perhaps the most interesting thing about this illustration is the officer carrying a half-pike (the figure at the rear of the forces) who is shown correctly in the second movement of shouldering his weapon, hence the apparently strange position of his right hand. That the engraver should be so precise about this detail is most remarkable but does suggest some knowledge of the military.

V: The narrative for this, the Five of Hearts, reads: 'The Rout of a 1000 of the Rebells horse Comãnded by yᵉ Ld: Grey'

As on the Ace of Diamonds, horse are clearly identified by their cross belts, a style apparently imitated by Monmouth's Horse from this illustration. The low crown and narrow brim on the hats is again evident.

IV: The narrative for this, the Four of Hearts, is: 'The Battaile att Bridgwater'

This extremely naive view of the Battle of Sedgemoor is interesting for a number of points although it is very strangely wrong in so many ways. The army's musketeers are shown with their collar over the wrong shoulder, no waist belt and the sword apparently being worn on a belt below the coat with the hilt emerging through the panels at the coat's side.
Worth noting however are the army's colours, which are illustrated with the St George's Cross in a canton, as it had been before 1660, and not in the post 1660 form of overall – suggesting that perhaps the engraver had seen only the colours of the Trained bands where the earlier style was still in use. By contrast the colours of Monmouth's army are shown totally without the St George Cross, an almost subliminal assertion that they were rebels and not a truly English force at all.

The Battaile att Bridgwater

The Late Duke of M: taken near the Ld Grey

Williams ye D: of M:s Sarvant taken with his Coat &c

The late D of M.s Standard

I: The narrative for this, the Ace of Hearts, reads: 'Williams ye D: of M:s Sarvant taken with his Coat &c'

An interesting, a fairly detailed view of two musketeers of the army clearly showing the collar of bandoliers, the sword from the waist belt, the position of the coat's pockets and the buttons running all the way to the lower edge. Yet again the hats have a fairly narrow brim and a low crown.

III: The narrative for this, the Three of Spades, reads: 'The Late Duke of M: taken near the Ld Grey'

This card shows a fairly detailed view of two troopers of horse, identifiable by the cross belts and the heavy boots. The close detail of this card suggests that the low crown of the hat was indeed the fashion.

Queen: The narrative for this, Queen of Spades, reads: 'The late D of M.s Standard'

The card clearly shows this as a standard with fringing, i.e. a cornet of horse. There is no indication, contrary to many 21st century reconstructions, that this motto was carried on the colours of Monmouth's Foot: something that would have been contrary to both contemporary practice and to what Monmouth himself would have considered as usual.

strength of 69 officers and men; which would have given Feversham a force of around 2,400 foot, which with addition of 800–900 horse, would have meant that the royal army was about 3,300– 3,400 at the start of the campaign. In support of this strength is the warrant for the train from the Ordnance Office which orders it to carry 'Spare Armes for [an Army of] Three Thousand Foot & One Thousand Horse, Three Hundred Granadeers, Three Hundred Dragoons,'[5] which at least suggests that the army was intended to be at, or near, that strength.

Casualties at Philip St Norton (27 June) and elsewhere had probably reduced Feversham's strength by some 200–300 although many of these were wounded and some may have been back with their regiments by Sedgemoor. All of this should have resulted in an actual battlefield strength on the day of Sedgemoor of perhaps around 3,000, fairly close to the Monmouth's own strength on the field. Monmouth, of course, also had some 1,200–1,500 men unarmed, or armed with improvised weapons at best, who were not on the field of Sedgemoor and had been left behind when his night march had begun. Edward Dummer, who was serving with the train at Sedgemoor, puts the strength of these 'left behind' men at 2,000.[6]

Feversham also had other troops additional to the main regular army units listed above; the 'regular' Queen Consort's Regiment of Horse, or at least some part of it, arrived with Feversham on 7 July, and must have been fairly close by the night before (as has been mentioned, this regiment had been commissioned somewhat ahead of the other new regiments), and there were approximately 1,500 men of the county trained bands in and around the village of Middlezoy, fairly close if not actually present in Feversham's camp. Elements of these county forces, including the militia horse units, had been campaigning with Feversham almost since their first mustering between 11 and 17 June.[7] At least one troop of militia horse under the command of Colonel Orpe was present on the field and fought alongside the regular horse on Feversham's right.[8]

Adam Wheeler's account of his service with the Wiltshire Militia makes it clear that the regiment both fully supported James II and was more than willing to actually fight if called upon to do so,[9] although of course brave words in a 'memoir' may not reflect the actual situation on the field at the time. The assertion, however, that these militia 'could not be trusted … And if Monmouth had made a success would probably have joined the rebels at once and killed their officers',[10] whilst often stated, is quite simply the rubbish of later Whig historians, which cannot be supported by any contemporary

5   An Account of the Traynes of Artillery Issued out of His Majts Stores …. For the late Expedition against the Rebells in ye West …, Admiral Blake Museum, Bridgwater, Somerset.
6   Dummer's account has been reprinted many times but the easiest to access is that in David Chandler's Sedgemoor 1685: An Account and Anthology, pp. 124–130.
7   See Scott, Military Effectiveness of the West Country Militia at the Time of the Monmouth Rebellion.
8   Childs, General Percy Kirke and the Later Stuart Army, p. 92.
9   See Adam Wheeler, 'Iter Bellicosum', printed in Camden Miscellany Volume XII (London: Royal Historical Society, 1910), pp. 153–166.
10   Sir Edward Parry, The Bloody Assize (London: Benn, 1929), p. 166. It is not difficult to find similar types of assertion in histories of Monmouth's Rebellion.

Monument to the Battle of Sedgemoor, 6 July 1685.
The only major engagement fought by James' Army during his short reign. (Author's photograph)
The monument reads:

'To the Glory of God
And the Memory of all Those who
Doing the Right as They Saw it
Fell in the Battle of Sedgemoor
6th July 1685
And Lie Buried in This Field
Or Who For Their Share in This Fight
Suffered Death Punishment or Transportation
Pro Patria'

accounts. The militia, as Chris Scott has persuasively argued, were not quite the ineffective rabble that they are sometimes portrayed as, and served the valuable purpose of guarding Feversham's rear and supply lines and thus freeing the Army's units for actual combat.

In addition to these units of horse and foot, Feversham's artillery train at Sedgemoor comprised 26 guns made up as follows:

From The Tower
Two 12 pounders (brass)
Eight 9 pounders (brass)
Four 6 pounders (brass)
Four 4 pounders (brass)

From Portsmouth
Four 3 pounders (iron)
Four 2½ pounders (brass)

All manned by around 200 personnel of the Ordnance Department.[11]

During the 18th century it was customary for men to be detailed from the infantry regiments to serve as mattrosses and labourers with the guns and there is some evidence that this happened at Sedgemoor. After the battle the King awarded a gratuity of £40, a very large sum representing almost 10 years pay for a sergeant,[12] to Sergeant Weems of the Royal Regiment of Foot for his services in working the guns during the battle.

What little information we actually have of the army during the battle suggests that they fought very much in line with the usual tactical doctrine of the period and of 'the drill book'. That Feversham/Churchill was able to redeploy battalions from the left of the line to the right during the course of the action, never an easy manoeuvre and complicated by the darkness, says much about the discipline and professionalism of both officers and men. The other aspect of the army's tactics on the field, which is rarely mentioned, is the probable use of the separated musketeers as 'commanded shot' by Feversham when it would have been as easy simply to dismiss them back to the line of foot. This may show some 'memory' of the effectiveness of this tactic during the English Civil Wars, only three decades before.

The royal army is estimated to have lost around 80 soldiers killed and 230 wounded during the course of the battle. A good proportion of the army's casualties were from the Royal Regiment of Foot, which lost 30 killed and 77 wounded, the regiment was to the right of Feversham foot. In contrast the Queen Dowager's, towards Feversham's left, suffered no fatalities at all, although Childs records four men (James Barnes, John Rosse, James Resin, John Pawling) who received 10 marks each from the Chelsea Hospital out-pension fund for wounds suffered at the battle.[13]

---

11 Feversham's train and its equipment are the subject of a study by W. Y. Carman in *The Journal of the Society for Army Historical Research*, vol. LIV, pp. 212–223.
12 A sergeant's daily rate of pay at the time was 1s 6d, before off reckonings and deductions. Childs, *Army of Charles II*, p. 258.
13 Childs, *General Percy Kirke and the Later Stuart Army*, p. 94.

Officers and men wounded at Sedgemoor:[14]

Regiment	Number Wounded	Admitted to Chelsea Hospital[15]
Royal Regiment of Horse Guards	37	1
Royal Regiment of Horse	15	0
First Royal Regiment of Foot Guards	70	12
Second Royal Regiment of Foot Guards	26	3
Royal Regiment of Foot	81	12
Queen Dowager's Regiment of Foot	4	4
Total	233	32

The comparative numbers are indicative of the point of attack of Monmouth's army and the subsequent intensity of the fighting. It is interesting that no casualties are recorded for either the Royal Regiment of Dragoons or the Queen Consort's Regiment of Foot, a confirmation of the collapse of Monmouth's right as the Royal Dragoons attacked.

Arni gives a more detailed analysis of the casualties from the First Royal Regiment of Foot Guards who were not admitted to Chelsea:

1 Captain
4 Lieutenants
1 Ensign
1 Sergeant
3 Corporals
2 Drummers
46 Private Soldiers[16]

A noticeably high proportion of 'officers'; over 20 percent of the casualties whereas they formed less than 10 percent of the strength.

In contrast Monmouth's rebel force lost approximately 1,000 dead,[17] and a further 500 prisoners; although no doubt many of these rebels were killed in the pursuit by Feversham's numerous and effective horse.

One interesting footnote is that in a cavalry skirmish at Ashill on 19 June the Royal Regiment of Horse, which had been on the establishment since 1661, suffered its first recorded wartime casualty when Lieutenant Phillip

---

14 Eric Gruber von Arni, *Hospital Care and the British Standing Army, 1660–1714* (Aldershot: Ashgate, 2006), p. 42. Original source MacKinnon, p. 182.
15 These men are included in and not additional to the number of wounded.
16 Arni, pp. 42–43.
17 John Oldmixon's claim that Monmouth lost 'only 300' dead against the army's loss of 400, although often quoted, is a complete fabrication (Oldmixon, *History of England during the Reigns of the House of Stuart* (London, 1730)).

Monoux was mortally wounded by a pistol shot. He is buried in St Mary's in Ashill.[18]

Notes on, and analysis of the artillery shot recovered from on and around the battlefield of Sedgemoor

Some years ago I was privileged to be given access to the collection of pieces of artillery shot in Bridgwater Museum,[19] that had been, over the years, recovered from the battlefield of Sedgemoor. By analysing the weight and diameter of these it is possible to tell which army fired the piece.[20] There are, of course, almost certainly many other pieces of shot both still in the ground and also in 'private collections' neither of which (obviously in the former case) I had access to, nonetheless the shot so far recovered suggests that the royal artillery managed to fire more than a few rounds.

Museum Acc. No.[21]	Diameter (inches)	Weight (pounds)	Material	Class of Gun	Probable Origin
BWRAB 1993/38	4½	12 lb	Iron	'twelve pounder' demi culverin	Royal
	4½	12 lb	Iron	'twelve pounder' demi culverin	Royal
	4	9 lb	Iron	Nine Pounder	Royal
A137	3½	6 lb	Iron	'six pounder' saker	Royal
	3½	6 lb	Iron	'six pounder' saker	Royal
	3½	6 lb	Iron	'six pounder' saker	Royal
	3½	6 lb	Iron	'six pounder' saker	Royal
A132	3	3 lb 14 oz	Iron	'four pounder'? minion	Royal
	3	3 lb 14 ox	Iron	'four pounder'? minion	Royal
A136	2¾	2 lb 8 oz	Iron	Falcon	Royal
	2¾	2 lb 8 oz	Iron	Falcon	Royal
	2½	2 lb	Iron	Falconet? (Note 1)	
	2¼	1 lb 8 oz	Iron	Falconet? (Note 1)	
85/65	2	1 lb 8 oz	Iron	Note 1	
	1½	12 oz	Iron	Note 1	
1991/31	1	8 oz	Iron	Robinet (Note 2)	Rebel

18   My thanks to Alan Larsen for calling my attention to this snippet.

19   My sincere thanks to the staff of the museum for their help and cooperation in this exercise, which I am sure they thought was more than a little eccentric.

20   Sincere thanks to Cliff Mitchell, whose knowledge of 17th century artillery is unmatched and who provided the reproductions of contemporary gunners' tools which allowed these measurements.

21   Not every piece of shot has been given a formal number by the museum, only those acquired in more recent years.

The royal train at the Battle of Sedgemoor consisted of two parts (see above):[22]

From the Tower
Two 12 pounders (brass)
Eight 9 pounders (brass)
Four 6 pounders (brass)

From Portsmouth
Four 3 pounders (iron)
Four falcons (brass)
Four 4 pounders (Brass)

The metal in parentheses is that from which the piece's barrel was cast.

Note 1: These pieces of shot do not fit any of the known royal guns from the battle and it would therefore seem likely that they were from Monmouth's guns.

Note 2: An intelligent guess for the origin of this small calibre gun would suggest that this might have been one of the 'parish militia guns' which had existed since the end of the 16th century. Whilst many disappeared during the English Civil Wars it is not unlikely that perhaps either Monmouth or the royal army, maybe even the royal trained bands, found the gun and brought it to the field.

---

22   National Archives, Kew, SP 44/164, f. 242. Warrant dated 16 June 1685.

Tables

Table 1. The Uniforms of the Regiments of Horse

Regiment	Coat	Linings	Officers' Lace	Buttons	Breeches	Raised	Notes
The Royal Regiment	Blue	Red	See text		Buff	1661	Blue velvet housings and holster caps with 'silver twist.' Carbine belts 'laced with gold upon buff with red edging.'
The Queen Consort's	Crimson	Yellow	Silver	Gold	Buff	1685	In 1687 a quartermaster is recorded as wearing a 'white waistcoat.'
Earl of Peterborough's	Crimson	Red	Silver?		Buff	1685	Hats edged with silver lace.
Earl of Plymouth's	Crimson	Green			Buff	1685	Waistcoats: grey in 1692 but blue in 1694.
Lord Dover's	Crimson	Blue			Buff	1685	
Earl of Thanet's	Crimson	Red	Red		Tawny	1685	
Earl of Arran's	Crimson	White		Pewter	Buff	1685	White waistcoats? Officers wore white scarves in place of crimson.
Earl of Shrewsbury's	Crimson	Buff		Pewter	Buff	1685	The regimental facings had changed to white before spring 1689. Buff coloured waistcoats in 1685/6.
Princess Anne of Denmark's	Crimson	Yellow			Tawny	1685	Holster caps embroidered with the Princess' cypher.
Queen Dowager's	Crimson	Sea Green	Silver	Silver	Buff	1685	At the Hounslow review on August 22 1685 officers are recorded with ostrich feathers in the hats and all ranks had sea green ribbons tied in the manes and tails of their horses.
Marquis de Miremont's	Crimson					1688	
Lord Brandon's	Crimson					1688	
Henry Slingsby's	Crimson					1688	
George Holman's	Crimson					1688	
Earl of Salisbury's	Crimson	Orange				1688	
On the Scots Establishment							
Royal Regiment of (Scots) Horse	Red	Yellow	Gold	Brass	Buff	1683	Coats 'laced and faced with yellow' (Dalton, *The Scots Army*, p. 81 n1). Armour recorded as 'all blackened.'
On the Irish Establishment							
Duke of Ormonde's	Red	Blue	Silver	Pewter	Red	1684	Blue housings and holster caps embroidered with the crowned royal cypher in silver.
Earl of Tyrconnell's	Red	Green?				1684	Blue housings and holster caps embroidered with the crowned royal cypher in silver.
Earl of Ossery's	Grey	Red	Gold	Brass	Grey	1684	Blue housings and holster caps embroidered with the crowned royal cypher in white.

Regiment	Coat	Linings	Buttons	Breeches	Raised	Notes
Table 2. The Uniforms of the Regiments of Dragoons						
The Royal Regiment of Dragoons	Red	Blue	Brass	Blue	1679	Housing and holsters: red embroidered in blue and yellow
Princess Anne of Denmark's Regiment of Dragoons	Red	Carnation (pink)		Blue	1685	
The Queen Consort's Regiment of Dragoons	Red	Yellow		Blue	1685	'white silver' lace about the hat in 1687
On the Scottish Establishment						
The Royal Regiment of (Scots) Dragoons	(Early 1685) Grey	Red	Tin	Red?	1681	Red cloth for the regiment's coats was imported from England in the summer of 1685.
	(Late 1685) Red	Blue	Tin	Blue		
On the Irish Establishment						
John Berkeley's Regiment of Dragoons	Red				1685	Raised on the English establishment in June 1685 but transferred to the Irish in September of that year.

Table 3. The Independent Companies in February 1685

Garrison	Governor	Lt. Governor	Captains
Berwick	Henry Cavendish, 2nd Duke of Newcastle	Ralph Witherington	Ralph Witherington
Carlisle	Sir Christopher Musgrave		Sir Christopher Musgrave
Chester	Peter Shackerly		Peter Shackerly
Chepstow	Henry Somerset, 1st Duke of Beaufort		Henry Somerset
Guernsey[I]	Chr. Hatton, 1st Viscount Hatton		Chr. Hatton; Chas. Hatton
Gravesend & Tilbury Fort	Sackville Tufton	Robert St Clare	Sackville Tufton
Hull	Thomas Windsor, 1st Earl of Plymouth	Lionel Copley	Thomas Windsor, 1st Earl of Plymouth
Jersey	Thomas Jermyn, Lord Jermyn		Thomas Jermyn, Lord Jermyn
Plymouth[II]	John Grenville, 1st Earl of Bath	Sir Hugh Pyper	John Grenville; Sir Hugh Pyper
Portsmouth	Edward Noel, Earl of Gainsborough	Henry Slingsby	Edward Noel, E. Gainsborough
Scilly Isles	Francis Godolphin		Francis Godolphin
Sheerness	Sir Charles Littleton	Robert Crauford	Sir Charles Littleton
Twr of London	George Legge, 1st Lord Dartmouth	Thomas Cheek	George Legge, 1st Lord Dartmouth
Tynemouth	Sir Edward Villiers	Henry Villiers	Sir Edward Villiers
Upnor Castle[III]	Robert Mynors		Robert Mynors
Isle of Wight[IV]	Sir Robert Holmes		Sir Robert Holmes
Windsor	Henry Howard, 7th Duke of Norfolk, Constable	Charles Potts	Thomas Cheek

Table 3. The Independent Companies in February 1685			
Garrison	Governor	Lt. Governor	Captains
York & Clifford's Tower	Sir John Reresby		Sir John Reresby
Blackness Castle[V]	No governor	Alexander Livingstoun	
Dumbarton Castle[VI]	Charles Fitzroy, Duke of Lennox	Major George Arnott[IX]	Charles Fitzroy, Duke of Lennox
Edinburgh Castle[VII]	William Douglas, Duke of Queensbury	Major Andrew White[X]	William Douglas, Duke of Queensbury
Island of Bass[VIII]	James Drummond, Earl of Perth	Charles Maitland	James Drummond
Stirling Castle	Charles Erskine, Earl of Mar	Captain Archibald Stuart[XI]	
James's Fort 'to be built near Stirling Bridge'	Captain George Barclay	Captain George Barclay	
Inverary Castle	Wm. Drummond, Viscount Strathallan	Wm. Drummond, Viscount Strathallan	Raised 1687. Independent.

Notes to Table 3

I   Incorporated into the Earl of Huntingdon's Regiment of Foot on 27th July 1685.

II   Both companies incorporated into the Earl of Bath's Regiment of Foot on 18 July.

III   Not a full company. Aside from the governor and captain, it comprised only 1 lieutenant, 1 corporal and 30 soldiers (National Archives, Kew, WO25/3206).

IV   In 1684 there was an additional separate garrison of 30 soldiers at Sandown Fort.

V   Company remained independent. The establishment of the garrison company of Blackness Castle was: deputy governor, 1 sergeant, 1 drummer, and 39 soldiers (National Archives, Kew, SP 8/1, f. 259).

VI   Company remained independent. The establishment of the garrison company of Dumbarton Castle was: 1 captain, 1 lieutenant, 1 ensign, 2 sergeants, 3 corporals, 2 drummers, 1 scrivener, and 43 soldiers (National Archives, Kew, SP 8/1, f. 258).

VII   Company remained independent. The establishment of the garrison company of Edinburgh Castle was: 1 captain, 1 lieutenant, 1 ensign, 3 sergeants, 3 corporals, 2 drummers, 1 scrivener, 1 chaplain, 1 surgeon, 1 gunsmith and 79 soldiers (National Archives, Kew, SP 8/1, f. 258).

VIII   Company remained independent. The establishment of the garrison company of the Island of Bass was: deputy governor, 1 sergeant, 1 corporal, 23 soldiers (National Archives, Kew, SP 8/1, f. 259).

IX   Arnott was commissioned as lieutenant of the garrison company on 30 March 1685, the same day as his commission as lieutenant governor.

X   White was commissioned as lieutenant of the garrison company on 26 February 1685, the same day as his commission as lieutenant governor.

XI   Stuart was commissioned as lieutenant of the garrison company on 30 March 1685, the same day as his commission as lieutenant governor.

The designation of the independent companies

By August 1685 a number of the companies were already being referred to as 'companies of grenadiers', although the King did not order the official change until later in the year. By late 1686 all references to the independent companies refer to them as 'grenadiers', although whether they were truly grenadiers is open to dispute since there is no real evidence either way and it may simply be a term of prestige in preparation to their absorption into the regiments of foot. It is also possible that this may be a way of indicating that the rank and file were all musket armed and the company had no pikemen – which does indeed seem to have been the case.

'James's Fort'

George Barclay was commissioned on 2 May 1685 to be 'Capt of the Independent Cy. of Foot to be raised for garrisoning James's Fort … to be built near Stirling Bridge'. It is unclear if this fort was ever actually built or the company raised, as on 28 November 1685 Barclay was commissioned as Major of Sir Edward Hales' Regiment of Foot in the English Army, and there is no record of any successor Governor or further mention of the Fort (Dalton, *The Scots Army 1661–1688*, p. 162).

'Inveraray Castle'

Strathallan's commission is dated 16 May 1687 'to be Capt. of the Cy. of Foot which is to be raised and put into the Castle of Inverary of which he is Governor.' Unlike James' Fort, this company does appear to have existed as Strathallan was succeeded in both posts by Sir John Drummond who was commissioned on 7 May (governor) and 19 May (Captain) 1688 when the latter commission refers to 'that Cy. of Foot lately put in garrison in Our Castle of Inverary' (Dalton, *The Scots Army 1661–1688*, p. 163).

Table 4. The Independent Companies of Grenadiers, August 1686 and their subsequent incorporation into the Regiments of Foot[I]			
1685 Garr'sn	**1685 Captains**	**1686 Captains**	**Regt. Associations**
Carlisle	Sir Chr. Musgrave	Sir Chr. Musgrave	Absorbed into Queen Consort's Regt as a 'line' company[II]
Chester	Peter Shackerly	Captain Peter Shackerly	Became gren. company of Sir Edward Hales' Regt[III]
Chepstow	Henry Somerset, 1st Duke of Beaufort		
Gravesend & Tilbury Fort	Sackville Tufton	Captain Sackvile Tufton	Became gren. company of Sir Wm Clifton's Regt[IV]
Guernsey	Christopher Hatton	Christopher Hatton	Became gren. company of Earl of Huntingdon's Regt; incorp. into that regt 27 July 1685[V]
Hull	Tho. Windsor, 1st E. Plymouth; Lionel Copley (comm. 25 June 1685)	Tho. Windsor	Became gren. company of Duke of Beaufort's Regt[VI]
Jersey	Thomas Jermyn, Lord Jermyn	Thomas Jermyn	Became gren. company of Duke of Norfolk's Regt[VII]
Pendennis Castle	Rich. Arundell, Baron Arundell of Trerice (comm. 22 June 1685)	Richard Arundell	Incorp. into Earl of Bath's Regt 17 March 1686 as a 'line' company
Plymouth	John Grenville, 1st Earl of Bath; Sir Hugh Pyper	Both companies incorp. into Earl of Bath's Regt 18 July.	Earl's own company presumably became company of grenadiers regt. not 'supposed' to have (see above)
Portsmouth	Edward Noel, Earl of Gainsborough	Edward Noel	Absorbed into Queen Dowager's Regt as a 'line' company[VIII]
Scilly Isles	Francis Godolphin		
Sheerness	Sir Charles Littleton		
Tower of London	George Legge, 1st Lord Dartmouth	Col's company of Royal Regt of Fuz., June 1685	Disch. from Royal Regt of Fuzileers in July; back in regt by autumn.
Tynemouth	Henry Villiers	Captain Henry Villiers	Became gren. company of Henry Cornwall's Regt[IX]
Isle of Wight	Sir Robert Holmes	Sir Robert Holmes	Absorbed into Queen Dowager's Regt as a 'line' company[X]
York & Clifford's Twr	Sir John Reresby	Sir John Reresby	Became gren. company Princess Anne of Denmark's Regt[XI]

Table 4. The Independent Companies of Grenadiers, August 1686 and their subsequent incorporation into the Regiments of Foot[I]			
1685 Garr'sn	**1685 Captains**	**1686 Captains**	**Regt. Associations**
Berwick	Sir Thomas Haggerston[XII] (comm. 26 June 1685)	Sir Thomas Haggerston	Probably absorbed into Queen Consort's Regt as a 'line' company
		Captain Henry Collier	Absorbed into Queen Dowager's Regt as a 'line' company
		Captain Richard Carter	Absorbed into Queen Consort's Regt as a 'line' company[XIII]

Notes to Table 4

I This only refers to the English companies, the Scottish garrison companies were never regimented and in Ireland the process had been carried out a year earlier.

II National Archives, Kew, WO5/3, f. 21. Order for the company to march to Carlisle, dated 4 August 1688.

III *Ibid.*, ff. 20–21. Order for the company to march to Chester dated 4 August 1687.

IV Dalton, *English*, vol. 2, p. 145.

V National Archives, Kew, WO5/3, f. 118. Order dated 7(?) May 1688.

VI Dalton, *English*, vol. 2, p. 141.

VII National Archives, Kew, WO5/3, f. 81. Order dated 16 February 1687.

VIII *Ibid.*, f. 21. Order for the company to march to Portsmouth, dated 4 August 1688.

IX *Ibid.*, f. 16. Order for the company to march to Tynemouth, dated 3 August 1687. Richard Carter's company had previously been associated with Cornwall's.

X *Ibid.*, f. 80. Order dated 15 February 1688.

XI *Ibid.*, f. 21. Order for the company to march to York, dated 4 August 1687. This association between Reresby's Company and Princess Anne's Regiment goes back to at least the spring of 1687, cf. WO5/2, ff. 172, 176.

XII Lieutenant governor of Berwick.

XIII National Archives, Kew, WO5/3, f. 79. Order dated 15 February 1688.

Table 5. The Uniforms of the Regiments of Foot								
Regiment	**Coat**	**Linings**	**Buttons**	**Breeches**	**Stockings**	**Grenadier Lace**	**Raised**	**Notes**
The Royal Regt	Red	White	Pewter	L. Grey	L. Grey	White edged blue	1633[I]	Ex-Scots in Swedish Service. Pikemen's sashes white, white fringe. Gren.caps of white cloth with a lion's face proper embroidered on the front.
The Queen Dowager's Regt	Red	Sea Green	Pewter	Green	White	Green & White	1661[II]	Ex-Old Tangier Regt. Grenadier caps red cloth edged in brown fur
The Holland Regt[III]	Red	Buff	Pewter	Buff	Buff	No Lace	1572[IV]	
Prince George of Denmark's Regt[V]	Yellow (early 1685)	Red	Brass	Red	Red		1664	Armed entirely with snaphaunce muskets & cartr.boxes. Hats edged with 'broad gold lace'. Yellow waistcoats 1687.
	Red (by June 1686)	Yellow	Brass	Grey	Grey			

Regiment	Coat	Linings	Buttons	Breeches	Stockings	Grenadier Lace	Raised	Notes
The Queen Consort's Regt	Red	Yellow	Brass	Yellow	White	Yellow	1680[VI]	Ex-New Tangier Regiment
The Royal Regt of Fuzileers	Red	Yellow	Brass	Grey	Grey	No grenadier company	1685	Armed entirely with snaphaunce muskets and cartridge boxes. Red grenadier type hats with a yellow turn up for all other ranks.
The Royal Regt	Red	White	Pewter	L. Grey	L. Grey	White edged blue	1633[I]	Ex-Scots in Swedish Service. Pikemen's sashes in white, with a white fringe. Grenadier caps of white cloth with a lion's face proper embroidered on the front.
The Queen Dowager's Regt	Red	Sea Green	Pewter	Green	White	Green & White	1661[II]	Ex-Old Tangier Regiment. Grenadier caps of red cloth edged in brown fur
The Holland Regt[III]	Red	Buff	Pewter	Buff	Buff	No Lace	1572[IV]	
Prince George of Denmark's Regt[V]	Yellow (early 1685)	Red	Brass	Red	Red		1664	Armed entirely with snaphaunce muskets and cartridge boxes. Hats edged with 'broad gold lace'. Yellow waistcoats in 1687.
	Red (by June 1686)	Yellow	Brass	Grey	Grey			
The Queen Consort's Regt	Red	Yellow	Brass	Yellow	White	Yellow	1680[VI]	Ex-New Tangier Regiment
The Royal Regt of Fuzileers	Red	Yellow	Brass	Grey	Grey	No grenadier company	1685	Armed entirely with snaphaunce muskets and cartridge boxes. Red grenadier type hats with a yellow turn up for all other ranks.
Princess Anne of Denmark's Regt	Red	Deep Yellow	Brass				1685	
Henry Cornwall's Regt	Red	Orange	Brass	Grey	White		1685	
Earl of Bath's Regt	Blue	Red	Pewter	Red	Red	Red & White	1685	Grenadier caps 'white'

Table 5. The Uniforms of the Regiments of Foot

Table 5. The Uniforms of the Regiments of Foot								
Regiment	Coat	Linings	Buttons	Breeches	Stockings	Grenadier Lace	Raised	Notes
Duke of Beaufort's Regt	Red	Tawny	Pewter	Tawny	Tawny		1685	Grenadier caps of red cloth edged with white and carrying 'the King's cypher'. Tawny hat bands.
Duke of Norfolk's Regt	Red	White	Brass	Blue	Blue		1685	Pikemen with white sashes. The regimental linings were changed to green between summer 1686 and summer 1687.
Earl of Huntingdon's Regt	Red	Yellow	Pewter	Yellow	Grey		1685	
Sir Edward Hale's Regt	Red	Red	Pewter	Grey	Grey		1685	
Sir William Clifton's Regt	Red	Red			White		1685	
John Hale's Regt							1688	Ex-English of the Anglo-Scots Brigade in Netherlands service.
Henry Gage's Regt							1688	
Solomon Richards' Regt	Red	Red	Pewter	White			1688	
Duke of Newcastle's Regt							1688	
Archibald Douglas' Regt	Red	Grey or White	Pewter	Buff or White	White		1688	White waistcoats
Bevil Skelton's Regt							1688	
John Carne's Regt	Blue?	White?		White?			1688	
Earl of Stafford's Regt							1688	
On the Scottish Establishment								
The Scots Fuzileers Regt	Red	Red	Brass	Grey	Grey		1678	
John Wachop's Regt	Red	Yellow					1688	Ex-Scots of the Anglo-Dutch Brigade in Netherlands service.
On the Irish Establishment								
The Duke of Ormond's Regt	Red						1684	
The Earl of Granard's Regt	Red						1684	

Regiment	Coat	Linings	Buttons	Breeches	Stockings	Grenadier Lace	Raised	Notes
Viscount Mountjoy's Regt	Red						1684	
Sir Tho. Newcomen's Regt	Red						1684	
Sir William King's Regt	Red						1684	
Thomas Fairfax's Regt	Red						1684	
Roger McElligott's Regt	Red						1688	Ex-Irish of the Anglo-Dutch Brigade in Netherlands service.

Table 5. The Uniforms of the Regiments of Foot

Notes on Table 5

I   Added to the English establishment in 1679. Ironically the regiment was never a part of the Scots Army.

II   Added to the English establishment in 1684.

III   A deserter's notice in *The London Gazette* of 25 January 1686 records the following additional information: 'A new red coat lined with a buff coloured lining, surtout sleeves, cross pockets with 3 scallops, large plain round pewter buttons, breeches of the same colour as the coat lining.'

IV   Added to the English establishment in 1665.

V   In his account of the Monmouth Rebellion, Adam Wheeler records the execution after the battle of 'A Yellow-coate souldier that ran out of his Maties Army to Monmouth'. This has always been taken as being a militiaman, but it is more likely to have been a soldier from this regiment who had been 'drafted' into one of the regiments which had marched west to bring the companies up to strength. In this it is significant that Wheeler's words are 'out of his Maties Army', whereas, had he indeed been a militiaman one would have expected Wheeler to record that and perhaps even which county he was from.

VI   Added to the English establishment in 1684.

Garrison	Governor	Master Gunners on Strength	Gunners on Strength
Berwick	Henry Cavendish, 7th Duke of Newcastle	1	6
Calshot	James Halsall	1	3
Carlisle	Sir Christopher Musgrave	2	3
Chester	Peter Shackerly	1	2
Chepstow	Henry Somerset, 1st Duke of Beaufort	1	1
Dartmouth Castle	Sir Joseph Tredenham	1	1
Gravesend & Tilbury Fort	Sackville Tufton	2	15
Guernsey	Christopher Hatton, 1st Viscount Hatton	1	4
Holy Island	Sir John Fenwick, Bt	1	1
Hull & the Block Houses	Thomas Windsor, 1st Earl of Plymouth	1	7
Hurst Castle	Sir Robert Holmes	1	3

Table 6. The Distribution of Gunners in Garrison, February 1685[I]

Table 6. The Distribution of Gunners in Garrison, February 1685[I]			
Garrison	Governor	Master Gunners on Strength	Gunners on Strength
Jersey	Thomas Jermyn, Lord Jermyn	1	8
Landguard Fort	Sir Roger Manley	1	6
Pendennis Castle	Richard Arundell, 1st Baron Arundell of Trerice	1	2
Plymouth	John Grenville, 1st Earl of Bath	2	22
Portland Castle	Major Bonham Stangways		1
Portsmouth & St Nicholas Island	Edward Noel, Earl of Gainsborough	1	29
St Mawes[II]		1	1
Scarborough Castle	Sir Thomas Slingsby	1	3
Scilly Isles	Francis Godolphin	1	10
Sheerness	Sir Charles Littleton	1	13
Tynemouth	Sir Edward Villiers	1	4
Clifford's Fort nr. Tynemouth		1	4
Tower of London	George Legge, 1st Lord Dartmouth	1	4
Upnor Castle & its dependencies	Robert Mynors	4	14
Isle of Wight Carisbrooke Cowes Sandown Fort Yarmouth	Sir Robert Holmes Captain Captain Captain Captain	 1 1 1 1	 4 2 2 4
Windsor Castle	Henry Howard, 7th Duke of Norfolk	1	6
North Yarmouth Fort		1	2
York & Clifford's Tower	Sir John Reresby		1
Blackness Castle	No governor		
Dumbarton Castle	Charles Fitzroy, Duke of Lennox		1
Edinburgh Castle	William Douglas, Duke of Queensberry		3
Island of Bass	James Drummond, Earl of Perth		1
Stirling Castle	Charles Erskine, Earl of Mar		1

Notes on Table 6

I   Taken mainly from National Archives, Kew, WO25/3206, and SP 8/1, part 2. Governors principally from Dalton, English, volume 2, pp. 37–38, 66.

II   Sir Joshua Tredenham was appointed 'Captain and Keeper of St Mawes' on 30 April 1686 but whether in place of his governorship of Dartmouth, or as well as, is not known.

Appendices

Appendix I

Extracts From Sandford's Description of the Coronation of James II

Francis Sandford, Lancaster Herald of Arms, wrote an extremely detailed description of many of the military aspects of the James' Coronation.[1] His coverage of the dress of the regiments of horse guards and foot guards present on that occasion is particularly useful and is well worth reproducing here:[2]

The First Troop of His Majesties Horse Guards
Commanded by His Grace
Christopher Duke of Albemarle, Colonel and Captain

The Officers of this Troop were richly Habited, either in Coats of Crimson Velvet Imbroidered with Gold and Silver, or of Fine Scarlet Cloth Imbroidered or Laced with Gold or Silver. or both intermixed. They wore Scarfs about their Wastes, either of Gold or Silver Network, or Crimson Taffeta, richly Fringed with Gold or Silver on the Edges, and with a deep Fringe of the same at the Ends.

Their Cloaks were also of Fine Scarlet Cloth, Imbroidered on the Capes end down before with Gold or Silver, or both intermixed.

In their Hats they wore Tours of White Feathers; Their Housses end Holster-Caps being of Crimson Velvet, were richly Imbroidered end Embossed with Gold and Silver: And the Manes, Cruppers and Tayls of their Horses were garnished with large knots of Blew Taffeta Ribband.

The Gentlemen of this Troop (Two Hundred in Number) were all new Clothed in Coats and Cloaks of Scarlet Cloth, lined with Blew Chalon: The Facings of their Sleeves, of the same Stuff, were laced about with a Figured Galoon of Silver (edged with Gold) two Inches broad: Their Buttons were of Silver Plate: They had each of them a good Buff Coat, and a large Pair of Gantlet Gloves of the same: And in their Hats (which were Black, and turned upon one side, end edged about with a broad Silver Lace) they wore large Blew Knots of broad Taffeta Ribband; which Blew being the Distinguishing Colour of their Troop from the others, the Heads of their Horses were adorned with knots of the like Ribband.

They were extraordinary well Mounted, and excellently well equipped. having their Housses and Holster-caps of Scarlet Cloth, Imbroidered with the Kings Cypher end Crown within a Border of Foliage.

Each of these Gentlemen was Armed and Accoutred with a good broad sword, and large Buff Shoulder-Belt, a Case of Pistols, a Carabine, with a Carabine Belt of Blew Velvet five Inches broad,

---

1 *A List of the Several Commanders … on the Day of Their Majesties Coronation* (London, 1685).
2 Because the Coronation took place in London the Scots units of Guards were not, sadly for us, present.

bordered with figur'd Silver Galoon, (edged with a narrow Gold Lace) in bredth two Inches, so that not above an Inch in bredth of the Velvet appeared.

The Cornet of Crimson Damask doubled, being Two Foot Six Inches flying, and two Foot Three Inches on the Staff, was Fringed about, with Silver end Gold intermixed, Three Inches deep. with Strings and Tassels suitable; end in the middle was Imbroidered the Kings Cypher. Ensign'd with a large Imperial crown of Gold, within a Scroll of Silver. whereon the Kings Motto, viz. DIEU ET MON DROIT, was wrought in Black Silk: and under the Scroll three lesser Imperial Crowns of Gold were Imbroidered.

The Guydon was also of Crimson Damask, made up and Imbroidered in all respects as the Cornet, from which it differed only in Form, having a forked Tail, to the Points whereof from the Staff it was about a yard and three inches flying...

The First Troop of His Majesties Horse Grenadiers

The Officers of this First Troop of Horse-Grenadiers were richly Habited and equipped, agreeable in Colour to the First Troop of Horse-Guards, being very well Mounted and Accoutred. The Lieutenants lead the Troop, when it marched on Foot, with Half Pikes. The Sergeants were Armed with Partisans, and the Corporals with Halberts.

The Granadiers (Sixty in Number) were Cloathed in Coats of Fine Red Cloth, Lined and Faced with Blew Chalon, and Buttoned with White Mettle hatched with Silver. On the Brest, Arms, and Facings of the Sleeves, they wore large Loops of Fine Blew Worsted, Edged and Tufted with Black and White.

The Crowns of their Caps were raised high to a point falling back at the top in Form of a Capouch. which were turned up before and behind, Triangular, and Faced with Blew Plush; and on the back of the Crowns was a Roundel or Granada-Ball also of the same.

Their Cloaks were of Fine Red Cloth, Lined with Blew, and their Hats being Black, and Laced about with Silver, were buttoned up, end adorned with Knots of Blew Taffeta Ribband as were the Heads of their Horses. Their Holster-caps and Housses (scallopt on the Edges) of Red Cloth, were Imbroidered with the Royal Cypher and Crown, and bordered with Foliage; so that being annexed or depending upon His Majesties First Troop of Horse-Guards, this Troop was agreeable unto them in all their Colours.

Each of these Granadiers was armed and Accoutred with a long Carabine strap'd, a good Sword. with a Waste Buff Belt, a case of Pistols. cartouch-Box, Bucket, Bionet, and Granada-Pouch.

They usually Paraded with the First Troop of Horse-Guards in the Piazza of Covent-Garden; but being commanded to do Duty (the Coronation day) on Foot, as were also the two other troops of Granadiers, they were all Three drawn up in St. James's Park near the Horse-Guard; from whence being lead by Captain John Parker the Eldest Lieutenant, with a Spanish Half-Pike, (who that Day appeared in a Fine Scarlet coat exceeding richly Laced and Paned with Point de Venice, and Scarff of the same) they marched through Kings-Street to their several Stations...

The Second Troop of His Majesties Horse-Guards
Commanded by His Grace
George Duke of Northumberland. Colonel and Captain

The Officers of this Second Troop were very richly Habited and equipped, in like manner as were those of the First Troop, from whom they differ'd only in the Colour of their Housses and Holster caps, which were of Green Velvet; and in the garnishing of the Manes, Cruppers and Tails of their Horses, which was with Green Taffeta Ribbands, whereas the Distinguishing Colour of the First Troop was Blew.

The Gentlemen of this Troop, were also 200 in Number, all new Cloathed, Armed end Equipped in like manner as were the First Troop, differing only from them in the Lace of their Hats, of their Sleeve-Facings, and their Carabine Belts, all of which was Gold edged with Silver, rind in the Colour of their

Ribbands in their Hats and Horses Heads, which were Green, as were also their Housses and Holster-Caps, end Carabine Belts; only the Kings Cypher on the said Housses end Holster-Caps was within a border of the Royal Badges.

Their Cornet of White Damask doubled, being Two Foot Six Inches Flying and as much in depth upon the Staff, was Fringed about with Gold Three Inches deep, with Strings and Tassels suitable; rind in the middle was Imbroidered the Kings Cypher, Ensigned with an Imperial Crown sustained by Two Angels of Silver, That on the Right Side having a Sword in his Hand, and That on the Left a Palm Branch: Under the Cypher was the Year of our Lord 1685 wrought in Figures of Gold; rind below maid figures a Scroll of Gold with the Words DIEU ET MON DROIT, in Black Silk, and under the Scroll were Imbroidered three lesser Imperial crowns, also of Gold.

The Guydon was of the same Silk, made up and Imbroidered as the Cornet, differing from it only in Form, having a Forked Tail, which, from the Staff to the Points thereon, was about Three Foot and Three Inches...

The 2nd Troop of His Majesties Horse-Granadiers

The Officers of this Second Troop of Horse-Granadiers were richly Habited, and suitable, in the Colour of their Housses and Holster-caps (which were of Green Velvet, and in their Ribbands of Green Taffaty) to the Officers of the Second Troop of Horse-Guards; being also excellently well Mounted and Equipped.

The Granadiers also (Sixty in Number) were Cloathed, Armed and Accoutred in all respects answerable to the First Troop of Horse-Granadiers, but were differing from them in the Colour of their Housses, Holster-Caps, Linings, Facings,[3] and Worsted Loops, (Edged and Tufted with Black and White) which were all Green, (the Distinguishing Colour of their Second Troop of Horse-Guards) and their Caps Faced with Green Plush. They wore Gilt Buttons, and their Hats, Edged about with Gold Lace were adorned with large Knots of Green Taffeta Ribband, their Horse-Heads being garnished with the same...

The Third Troop of His Majesties Horse-Guards
Commanded by the Right Honourable
Lewis Earl of Feversham. Colonel and Captain

The Officers of this Third Troop of Guards were richly Habited and excellently well Mounted and Equipped, in like manner as were those of the First Troop, from whom they differed only in the Colour of their Horses and Holster caps, which were of yellow Velvet; and in the garnishing of the Manes, cruppers and Tails of their Horses, being yellow Taffeta Ribband: Whereas the Distinguishing Colour of the First Troop was Blew, and that of the Second Troop Green.

This Third Troop consisted also of 200 Gentlemen, who were all new Cloathed and Armed, and extraordinarily well Mounted and Accoutred, after the same manner as were the First and Second Troops of Horse-Guards; but differing from both in the Lace of their Hats, of their Sleeve-Facings, and their Carabine Belts, which was of Silver; rind in the Colour of the Ribbands in their Hats and Horse-Heads, which were Yellow, as was also the Cloth of their Housses and Holster-Caps. and the Velvet Facings of their Carabine Belts.

---

3   Sandford is not here referring to the linings and what we would call facings, these remained blue throughout the Regiment. Facings here and as referred to in the other troops is simply the 'troop colour'.

Their Cornet of Yellow Damask doubled. being Two Foot Six Inches square, was Fringed about with Gold and Silver Paned, Three Inches deep, with Strings end Tassels suitable; and in the middle was Imbroidered the Kings Cypher of Silver, Ensigned with a large Imperial Crown of Gold, within a Scroll also of Silver, whereon the Kings Motto, DIEU ET MON DROIT, was wrought in Gold; rind under the Scroll Three lesser Imperial Crowns of Gold were Imbroidered. The Guydon was' also of Yellow Damask, made up and Imbroidered in all respects as the Cornet, differing from it only in Form, by having a Forked Tail, to the Points whereof from the Staff it was about a Yard and Three Inches flying.

The 3rd Troop of His Majesties Horse-Granadiers

The Officers of this Third Troop of Horse-Granadiers were richly Habited and suitable, in the Colour of their Housses and Holster-caps, to the Officers of the Third Troop of Horse-Guards, being Yellow Velvet, and their Ribbands of the same Colour, and were excellently well Mounted and Equipped.

These Granadiers also, Sixty in Number, were clothed, Armed end Accoutred in all respects as were the First and Second Troops of Granadiers, but differing from both in the Colour of their Housses, Holster-caps. Linings, Facings and loops, all of which were Yellow, only the Loops were Edged and Tufted with Black and White, as those of the First and Second Troops were.

Their Buttons were White Mettle hatched with Silver, rind their Hats edged with Silver Lace, like those of the First Troop, but their Ribbands were Yellow...

The First Regiment of Him Majesties Foot-Guards
Commanded by His Grace
Henry Duke of Grafton, Colonel and Captain

The Officers of this First Regiment of Foot-Guards (consisting of 24 Companies and two Companies of Granadiers) were exceedingly richly Habited: some in Coats of Cloth of Gold, others in Crimson Velvet Imbroidered or Laced with Gold or Silver; but most of them in Fine Scarlet Cloth, Buttoned down the Brest and on the Facings of the Sleeves with Silver Plate.

Their Scarffs (which they wore about their wastes) were either Network of Gold or Silver, or Crimson Taffeta richly Fringed with Gold or Silver, find their Hats were adorned with Tours of White Feathers.

The Captains were distinguished by Corselets or Gorgets of Silver Plate double gilt; The Lieutenants by Corselets of Steel Polished and Sanguin'd, and studded with Nails of Gold; and the Ensigns had their Corselets of Silver Plate.

The Private Soldiers Lined were all new Clothed in Coats of Red broad Cloth, Lined and Faced with Blew; Their Hats were Black, Laced about with Silver, turned up and garnished with Blew Ribbands. Their Breeches were Blew Broad Cloth, and their Stockings of Blew Worsted.

The Musquetiers were Armed with Snaphance Musquets, with Sanguin'd Barrels, Three Foot eight Inches in length; good Swords in Waste Belts, and Collars of Bandiliers; And the Pike-Men with Pikes Sixteen Foot long, each headed with a Three-Square Point of Steel, and good Swords in broad Shoulder-belts, wearing also about their wastes, Sashes, or Scarffs of White Worsted, Fringed with Blew.

The Granadiers (viz. Two Companies) were Cloathed as the Musquetiers, but distinguished by Caps of Red Cloth Lined with Blew Shallon, and Laced with Silver Galoon about the Edges: And on the Frontlets of said Caps (which were very large and high) was Imbroidered the Kings Cypher and crown. Each of these Granadiers was Armed with a long Carabine Strapt, the Barrel thereof Three Foot Two Inches in length: a Cartouch-Box, Bionet, Granada-Pouch, and a Hammer-Hatchet.

The Colours or Ensigns of this First Regiment (Twenty-Four in Number), were of a large size, viz. Two yards and Three Quarters, Flying and Two Yards and a half on the Ensign Staff ...

The Second Regiment of His Majesties' Foot-Guards, called the Coldstreamers
Commanded by the Right Honourable William Earl of Craven, Colonel and Captain

The Officers of this Second Regiment of Foot-Guards (consisting of Twelve Companies, and One of Granadiers) were exceeding richly Habited, but differing, in their Imbroideries, Laces and fringes, which were of Gold, and their Buttons of Gold Thread, from the Officers of the First Regiment of Foot-Guards, which had them of Silver.

The Captains, Lieutenants and Ensigns were distinguished by Corselets or Gorgets as those Officers of the First Regiment, and their Hats were also adorned with Tours of White Feathers.

The Private Soldiers, viz. Musquetiers, Pikemen and Granadiers, were in all Points Armed and Accoutred as the First Regiment, and agreeable to them in their Clothing, except their breeches, which were of red broad Cloth, and their Stockings of Red Worsted.

Their Hats were Black, turned up and laced about with Gold Galoon, in which they wore Red Ribbands, and their Shashes or Waste-Scarffs of the Pikemen being of White Worsted, were fringed on the Sides, and at the Ends with Red Worsted.

The Granadiers had their caps Lined and Faced with Blew Chaloon, and laced with Gold Galoon, and Imbroidered on the Frontlets with the Kings Cypher…

Appendix II

The Succession of Colonels in the Armies of James II

Except for those few regiments that rejoiced in an official title (e.g. 'The Royal Regiment of Horse' or 'The Queen Dowager's Regiment of Foot') it was usual for a regiment to be known by the name of its colonel. Even this methodology, though, is far from foolproof since the 'Queen Consort's' is often encountered as 'The Queen Majesty's'. To further complicate matters many officially titled regiments were also often called by the name of their commanding officer (hence the Queen Consort's Regiment of Foot is more normally known encountered 'Trelawney's' and the Queen Dowager's as 'Kirke's'). Throughout the main body of the text as well as here, for purposes of clarity, regiments are always referred to by their title, if they had one, or by the name of their colonel on James' accession or the regiment's raising. The lists below however should allow those interested to follow the actual succession of colonels up to the end of 1688.

	Date of Commission
1st Troop of the Royal Regiment of Horse Guards	
Christopher Monk, 2nd Duke of Albemarle	29 November 1679
Louis de Duras, 2nd Earl of Feversham	1 August 1685
2nd Troop of the Royal Regiment of Horse Guards	
Sir Philip Howard	23 November 1659
George Fitzroy, Duke of Northumberland	11 February 1685
3rd Troop of the Royal Regiment of Horse Guards	
Louis de Duras, 2nd Earl of Feversham	7 June 1685
John Churchill	1 August 1685
4th Troop of the Royal Regiment of Horse Guards (disbanded November 1688)	
Henry Jermyn, 1st Baron Dover	22 May 1686
The Royal Regiment of Horse	
Aubrey de Vere, 20th Earl of Oxford	26 January 1661
James Fitzjames, Duke of Berwick	4 February 1688
James Hamilton, Earl of Arran	29 November 1688
Aubrey de Vere, 20th Earl of Oxford (reappointed)	31 December 1688

	Date of Commission
The Queen Consort's Regiment of Horse	
Sir John Lanier	6 June 1685
The Earl of Peterborough's Regiment of Horse	
Henry Mordaunt, 2nd Earl of Peterborough	20 June 1685
Hon. Edward Villiers	31 December 1688
The Earl of Plymouth's Regiment of Horse	
Thomas Windsor, 1st Earl of Plymouth	15 July 1685
Sir John Fenwick Bt.	6 November 1687
Richard Savage, 4th Earl Rivers	31 December 1688
The Lord Dover's Regiment of Horse (Disbanded Spring 1686)	
Henry Jermyn, 1st Baron Dover	26 July 1685
The Earl of Thanet's Regiment of Horse	
Thomas Tufton, 6th Earl of Thanet	27 July 1685
Robert Werden	24 October 1685
The Earl of Arran's Regiment of Horse	
James Hamilton, 1st Earl of Arran	28 July 1685
Charles Hamilton, 2nd Earl of Selkirk	20 November 1688
Charles Godfrey	31 December 1688
The Earl of Shrewsbury's Regiment of Horse	
Charles Talbot, 12th Earl of Shrewsbury	29 July 1685
Marmaduke Langdale, 2nd Lord Langdale	22 January 1687
Richard Hamilton	15 February 1687
John Coy	31 December 1688
Princess Anne of Denmark's Regiment of Horse	
Robert Leke, 3rd Earl of Scarsdale	30 July 1685
Charles Beauclerk, 1st Duke of St Albans	1 December 1687
The Queen Dowager's Regiment of Horse	
Richard Lumley, Viscount Lumley	31 July 1685
Sir John Talbot	29 January 1687
Sir George Hewett	31 December 1688
The Marquis de Miremont's Regiment of Horse	
Armand de Bourbon, Marquis de Miremont[1]	22 September 1688
The Lord Brandon's Regiment of Horse	
Charles Gerard, Lord Brandon	1 October 1688
Henry Slingsby's Regiment of Horse	
Henry Slingsby	4 October 1688
George Holman's Regiment of Horse	
George Holman	10 October 1688
The Earl of Salisbury's Regiment of Horse	
James Cecil, 18th Earl of Salisbury	5 November 1688

	Date of Commission
The Royal Regiment of Dragoons	
John Churchill	19 November 1683
Edward Hyde, 3rd Earl of Clarendon	1 August 1685
Robert Clifford	24 November 1688
Edward Hyde, 3rd Earl of Clarendon (reappointed)	31 December 1688
Princess Anne of Denmark's Regiment of Dragoons	
John Berkeley, 4th Viscount Fitzhardinge	17 July 1685
Thomas Maxwell	24 November 1688
John Berkeley, 4th Viscount Fitzhardinge (reappointed)	31 December 1688
The Queen Consort's Regiment of Dragoons	
Charles Seymour, 6th Duke of Somerset	2 August 1685
Alexander Cannon	2 August 1687
Richard Leveson	31 December 1688
The First Regiment of His Majesty's Foot Guards	
Henry Fitzroy, 1st Duke of Grafton	14 December 1681
Sir Edward Henry Lee, 1st Earl Lichfield	30 November 1688
Henry Fitzroy, 1st Duke of Grafton (reappointed)	31 December 1688
The Second Regiment of His Majesty's Foot Guards	
William Craven, 1st Earl Craven	6 January 1670
The Royal Regiment of Foot	
Lord George Douglas, 1st Earl of Dumbarton	21 October 1655[II]
Frederick Herman Schomberg, Duke of Schomberg	31 December 1688
The Queen Dowager's Regiment of Foot	
Percy Kirke (senior)	19 April 1682
The Holland Regiment of Foot	
John Sheffield, 3rd Earl Mulgrave	26 January 1684
Sir Theophilus Oglethorpe	23 October 1685
Charles Churchill	31 December 1688
Prince George of Denmark's Regiment of Foot	
Sir Charles Littleton	15 February 1668
The Queen Consort's Regiment of Foot	
Sir Charles Trelawney	23 April 1682
Sir Charles Orby	1 December 1688
Sir Charles Trelawney (reappointed)	31 December 1688
The Royal Regiment of Fuzileers	
George Legge, 1st Lord Dartmouth	11 June 1685
Princess Anne of Denmark's Regiment of Foot	
Robert Shirley, 1st Earl Ferrers	19 June 1685
James Fitzjames, 1st Duke of Berwick	1 November 1686
John Beaumont	31 December 1688

	Date of Commission
Henry Cornwall's Regiment of Foot	
Henry Cornwall	19 June 1685
Oliver Nicholas	20 November 1688
John Cunningham	31 December 1688
The Earl of Bath's Regiment of Foot	
John Granville, 1st Earl of Bath	20 June 1685
Sir Charles Carney	8 December 1688
John Granville, 1st Earl of Bath (reappointed)	31 December 1688
The Duke of Beaufort's Regiment of Foot	
Henry Somerset, 1st Duke of Beaufort	20 June 1685
Charles Somerset, Marquis of Worcester[III]	26 October 1685
William Herbert, 2nd Marquis of Powis	8 May 1687
Sir John Hanmer Bt.	31 December 1688
The Duke of Norfolk's Regiment of Foot	
Henry Howard, 7th Duke of Norfolk	20 June 1685
Sir Edward Henry Lee Bt., 1st Earl of Lichfield	14 June 1686
Sir Robert Carey, 6th Lord Hunsdon	30 November 1688
Hon. Henry Wharton	31 December 1688
The Earl of Huntingdon's Regiment of Foot	
Theophilus Hastings, 7th Earl of Huntingdon	22 June 1685
Ferdinando Hastings[IV]	31 December 1688
Sir Edward Hales' Regiment of Foot	
Sir Edward Hales, Bt.	22 June 1685
William Beveridge	31 December 1688
Sir William Clifton's Regiment of Foot	
Sir William Clifton Bt.	22 June 1685
Arthur Herbert, 1st Earl of Torrington	12 May 1686
Hon. Sackville Tufton	12 April 1687
Sir James Leslie	31 December 1688
John Hales' Regiment of Foot	
John Hales	10 March 1688
Henry Gage's Regiment of Foot	
Henry Gage	27 September 1688
Solomon Richards' Regiment of Foot	
Solomon Richards	27 September 1688
The Duke of Newcastle's Regiment of Foot	
Henry Cavendish, 2nd Duke of Newcastle	29 September 1688
Archibald Douglas' Regiment of Foot	
Archibald Douglas	9 October 1688
Robert Hodges	31 December 1688

	Date of Commission
Bevil Skelton's Regiment of Foot	
Bevil Skelton	9 October 1688
John Carne's Regiment of Foot	
John Carne	13 October 1688
Earl of Stafford's Regiment of Foot	
Henry Stafford-Howard, 10th Earl of Stafford	8 November 1688
Regiments on the Scottish Establishment	
The Troop of Horse Guards	
George Livingstone, 4th Earl of Linlithgow	1 May 1684
Archibald Campbell, 1st Duke of Argyll	31 December 1688
The Royal Regiment Scots of Horse	
John Graham of Claverhouse, 1st Viscount Dundee	24 December 1682
The Royal Regiment Scots of Dragoons	
Thomas Dalzell	25 November 1681
Charles Murray, 1st Earl of Dunmore	6 November 1685
Sir Thomas Livingstone Bt., 1st Viscount Teviot	31 December 1688
The Scots Regiment of Foot Guards	
Hon. James Douglas	31 December 1688
The Scots Fuzileers Regiment of Foot	
Charles Erskine, 5th Earl Mar	23 September 1678
Thomas Buchan	29 July 1686
John Wachop's Regiment of Foot	
John Wachop	11 March 1688
Regiments on the Irish Establishment	
The Troop of Horse Guards (disbanded June 1685)	
Anthony Hungerford	1684
The Troop of Horse Grenadiers (disbanded June 1688)	
John Salkield	1 March 1686
The Duke of Ormonde's Regiment of Horse	
James Butler, 1st Duke of Ormonde	1684
Theodore Russell	Between 1 February and 21 June 1687
The Earl of Tyrconnell's Regiment of Horse	
Richard Talbot, 1st Earl of Tyrconnell	January 1685
The Earl of Ossery's Regiment of Horse	
James Butler, Earl of Ossery	1684
Vere Essex Cromwell, 4th Earl of Ardglass	29 January 1686
Piers Butler, 3rd Viscount Galmoy	1687
John Berkeley's Regiment of Dragoons	
John Berkeley, 3rd Baron Berkeley of Stratton	17 July 1685

	Date of Commission
Richard Hamilton	before 31 July 1685
John Butler	September 1687
The Irish Regiment of Foot Guards	
Richard Butler, Earl of Arran	Before 1672
James Butler, Earl of Ossory	29 January 1686
William Dorrington	1686
The Duke of Ormonde's Regiment of Foot[V]	
James Butler, 1st Duke of Ormonde	1684
Justin MacCarthy	January 1685
The Earl of Granard's Regiment of Foot	
Arthur Forbes, 1st Earl of Granard	1 April 1684
Arthur Forbes, 2nd Earl of Granard	1 March 1686
Sir John Edgeworth	1 March 1689
Viscount Mountjoy's Regiment of Foot	
Sir William Stewart, 1st Viscount Mountjoy	28 April 1684
Sir Thomas Newcomen's Regiment of Foot	
Sir Thomas Newcomen Kt[VI]	1684
[Thomas or Robert?] Ramsay	1688
Sir William King's Regiment of Foot	
Sir William King	1684
John Russell	1685
Anthony Hamilton	January 1687
Thomas Fairfax's Regiment of Foot	
Thomas Fairfax	1684
Donogh MacCarthy, 4th Earl of Clancarty	December 1687
Sir Charles Feilding's Independent Company of Foot	
Sir Charles Feilding	
Roger McElligott's Regiment of Foot	
Roger McElligott	12 March 1688

Notes

I   Miremont was the Earl of Feversham's nephew.

II   Officially Dumbarton was not colonel of this regiment during the period early 1684 to August 1685 because his Roman Catholicism excluded him from the position. The vacancy was never filled, however, and James 'backdated' his recommissioning to cover the gap.

III   Lord Worcester was the son and heir of the Duke of Beaufort. It appears that at the same time as he was appointed to this colonelcy he resigned command of his independent troop of horse in favour of his brother Lord Arthur Somerset.

IV   Cousin to the Earl.

V   Although Justin MacCarthy had been colonel of this regiment since January, the state of the army at Charles II's death still shows the Duke of Ormonde as the colonel; cf. Dalton, *Irish Army Lists 1661–1685*, pp. 149–150.

VI   This officer should be differentiated from Sir Thomas Newcomen Bt, who was also a field officer in the Irish Army during this period.

Appendix III

The Post 1688 Descent of the Regiments of James II's Army

James II Regiment	1815 Successor	1985 Successor
The King's Royal Regiment of Horse Guards	1st Life Guards	The Life Guards
The Royal Regiment of Horse	Royal Horse Guards	The Blues and Royals
The Queen Consort's Regiment of Horse	1st King's Dragoon Guards	1st Queen's Dragoon Guards
Earl of Peterborough's Regiment of Horse	2nd Queen's Dragoon Guards	1st Queen's Dragoon Guards
Earl of Plymouth's Regiment of Horse	3rd Prince of Wales' Dragoon Guards	Royal Scots Dragoon Guards (Carabiniers and Greys)
Earl of Dover's Regiment of Horse	Disbanded June 1686[I]	
Earl of Thanet's Regiment of Horse	Disbanded 31 January 1689[II]	
Earl of Arran's Regiment of Horse	4th Royal Irish Dragoon Guards	4th/7th Royal Dragoon Guards
Earl of Shrewsbury's Regiment of Horse	5th (Princess Charlotte of Wales') Dragoon Guards	5th Royal Inniskilling Dragoon Guards
Princess Anne of Denmark's Regiment of Horse	Disbanded Summer 1692[III]	
The Queen Dowager's Regiment of Horse	6th Regiment of Dragoon Guards	Royal Scots Dragoon Guards (Carabiniers and Greys)
Marquis de Miremont's Regiment of Horse	Disbanded 3 January 1689[IV]	
Lord Brandon's Regiment of Horse	Disbanded 3 January 1688[V]	
Henry Slingsby's Regiment of Horse	Disbanded 3 January 1689[VI]	
George Holman's Regiment of Horse	Disbanded 7 January 1689[VII]	
Earl of Salisbury's Regiment of Horse	Disbanded 7 January 1689[VIII]	
The Royal Regiment of Dragons	1st (Royal) Dragoons	The Blues and Royals
Princess Anne of Denmark's Regiment of Dragoons	4th or Queen's Own Dragoons	Queen's Own Irish Hussars
The Queen Consort's Regiment of Dragoons	3rd (King's Own) Dragoons	Queen's Own Hussars

THE ARMY OF JAMES II, 1685–1688

James II Regiment	1815 Successor	1985 Successor
1st Royal Regiment of Foot Guards	First Regiment of Foot Guards	The Grenadier Guards
2nd Royal Regiment of Foot Guards	2nd or Coldstream Regiment of Foot Guards	The Coldstream Guards
The Royal Regiment of Foot	1st Regiment of Foot or The Royal Scots	The Royal Scots (The Royal Regiment)
The Queen Dowager's Regiment of Foot	The Queen's Own Royal Regiment of Foot	The Queen's Regiment
Prince George of Denmark's Regiment of Foot	Reduced into the 2nd Royal Regiment of Foot Guards in Spring 1689[IX]	
The Holland Regiment of Foot	3rd (The Buffs) Foot	The Queen's Regiment
The Queen Consort's Regiment of Foot	4th or King's Own Regiment	The King's Own Royal Border Regiment
The Royal Regiment of Fuzileers	7th (Royal Fusiliers) Foot	The Royal Regiment of Fusiliers
Princess Anne of Denmark's Regiment of Foot	8th (The King's Regiment) Foot	The King's Regiment
Henry Cornwall's Regiment of Foot	9th (East Norfolk) Foot	Royal Anglian Regiment
Earl of Bath's Regiment of Foot	10th (North Lincolnshire) Foot	Royal Anglian Regiment
Duke of Beaufort's Regiment of Foot	11th (North Devonshire) Foot	Devonshire and Dorset Regiment
Duke of Norfolk's Regiment of Foot	12th (East Suffolk) Foot	Royal Anglian Regiment
Earl of Huntingdon's Regiment of Foot	13th (1st Somersetshire) Foot	The Light Infantry
Sir Edward Hale's Regiment of Foot	14th (Buckinghamshire) Foot	Prince of Wales' Own Regiment of Yorkshire
Sir William Clifton's Regiment of Foot	15th (York, East Riding) Foot	Prince of Wales' Own Regiment of Yorkshire
John Hales' Regiment of Foot		
Henry Gage's Regiment of Foot	Disbanded January 1689[X]	
Solomon Richards' Regiment of Foot	17th (Leicestershire) Foot	Royal Anglian Regiment
Duke of Newcastle's Regiment of Foot	Disbanded January 1689[XI]	
Archibald Douglas' Regiment of Foot	16th (Bedfordshire) Foot	Royal Anglian Regiment
Bevil Skelton's Regiment of Foot		
John Carne's Regiment of Foot	Disbanded January 1689[XII]	
Earl of Stafford's Regiment of Foot	Disbanded before 19 December 1688	
On the Scottish Establishment		
The Troop of Horse Guards	1st Life Guards	The Life Guards
The Royal Regiment of Scots Horse	Disbanded early 1689	
The Royal Regiment of Scots Dragoons	2nd Royal North British Dragoons (Scots Greys)	Royal Scots Dragoon Guards (Carabiniers and Greys)
The Scots Regiment of Foot Guards	3rd Regiment of Foot Guards	The Scots Guards
The Scots Fuzileers Regiment of Foot	21st (Royal North British) Fusiliers	Royal Highland Fusiliers
John Wachop's Regiment of Foot	Disbanded Autumn 1717	

James II Regiment	1815 Successor	1985 Successor
On the Irish Establishment		
The Troop of Horse Guards	Joined the Jacobites in 1689	
The Duke of Ormonde's Regiment of Horse	Joined the Jacobites in 1689	
The Earl of Tyrconnell's Regiment of Horse	Joined the Jacobites in 1689	
The Earl of Ossery's Regiment of Horse	Joined the Jacobites in 1689	
John Berkeley's Regiment of Dragoons[XIII]	Disbanded in England 6th January 1689	
The Irish Regiment of Foot Guards[XIV]	Disbanded in England January 1689[XV]	
The Duke of Ormond's Regiment of Foot	87e Régiment d'Infanterie de Ligne (of the French Army)	87e Régiment d'Infanterie
The Earl of Granard's Regiment of Foot	18th (Royal Irish) Regiment of Foot	Disbanded on 31 July 1922 at the partition of Ireland
The Duke of Ormond's Regiment of Foot	Disbanded on 31 July 1922 at the partition of Ireland	
Viscount Mountjoy's Regiment of Foot	Joined the Jacobites in 1689[XVI]	
Sir Thomas Newcomen's Regiment of Foot	Joined the Jacobites in 1689	
Sir William King's Regiment of Foot	Disbanded in England 7 January 1689	
Thomas Fairfax's Regiment of Foot	Joined the Jacobites in 1689	
Roger McElligott's Regiment of Foot	Disbanded in England 8 January 1689[XVII]	

Notes

Where dates are given for the disbandment of regiments it should be noted that these were the regiments that had come to England in 1688. The majority of the remaining regiments rallied to the cause of James in exile and served the King during the Irish campaigns of 1689–1692. Some, most noticeably the Foot Guards (who had sent only a 'battalion' to England), then followed James into exile in France and eventually entered the French Army as part of the 'Irish Brigade'.

I   When Dover was appointed to command the newly raised 4th Troop of Horse Guards.

II   Montagu Army Accounts, British Library Add MS 10123, f. 3. Some secondary accounts give the disbandment of this regiment as winter 1690/1691.

III   After having been virtually destroyed covering the retreat of the army after the Battle of Steenkirk.

IV   Montagu Army Accounts, British Library Add MS 10123, f. 3. The warrant for the disbandment is dated 31 December 1688 and states 'you are to dismiss and disband the Commission Officers and Quarter-Masters of the said Regiment and to dispose of the Private Troopers … and their Horses as the Lord Churchill shall direct', PRO WO5/5 f. 9. A further warrant of the same date adds 'upon disbanding the Commission Officers of the Marquiss de Miremont's Regt of Horse to cause the Colonel's and Lieut Colonel's Troops to be incorporated into the Regiment late under the Command of Sr John Fenwick; the two next oldest Troops in the Earl of Selkirk's Regiment, And the Two youngest Troops in the Regiment late of Major General Hamilton.' PRO WO5/5 f. 35.

V   Montagu Army Accounts, British Library Add MS 10123, f. 3. The disbandment warrant is dated 31

December 1688 and is in PRO WO5/5, ff. 8–9. A second warrant dated the same day directs that 'upon disbanding the Commission Officers of the Lord Brandon's Regiment of Horse you are to cause the Colonel's and Lieut colonel's Troops to be Incorporated into the Regiment late under the Command of the Earl of Peterborow; the two next eldest Troops in the Regt commanded by Coll Langston, And the two youngest Troops in the Regt late of Sr John Talbot', PRO WO5/5 f. 35.

VI   Montagu Army Accounts, British Library Add MS 10123, f. 3. The warrant for the disbandment is dated 1 January 1689, PRO WO5/5, f. 10. An undated order, but presumably of the same date, adds 'upon the Disbanding the Regiment of Horse commanded by Coll Henry Slingsby, Fifty Troopers of the said Regiment with their Horses be Encorporated into the Regiment of Horse, whereof Henry Earl of Peterborow was late Colonel, and that the other Troopers of that regiment with their Horses be Disposed of into such other Regiments as you shall think fitt.' PRO WO5/5 f. 36, the copy warrant unfortunately does not state to whom it was addressed.

VII   Montagu Army Accounts, British Library Add MS 10123, f. 3. The warrant for the disbandment is dated 1 January 1689, PRO WO5/5, f. 10.

VIII   Montagu Army Accounts, British Library Add MS 10123, f. 3. The warrant for the disbandment is dated 1 January 1689, PRO WO5/5, f .10.

IX   'Our W and P is that the sevll Private Soldiers and Non-Commission Officers of Prince George Hereditary Prince of Denmark's Regt of foot, now in Gravesend be forthwith put on board the Ships bound for Holland, and incorporated as they are hereby incorporated in the Coldstream Regiment of our ffoot Guards. Given at our Court at Whitehall the 19th day of March 1688/9 … to Our Rt T. and W. Councellor John Lord Churchill Lieutenant Genll of Our Forces'. National Archives WO5/5 f. 108.

X   The warrant for the disbandment is dated 31 December 1688. PRO WO5/5, ff. 9–10.

XI   *Ibid.* The warrant for the disbandment is dated 31 December 1688. PRO WO5/5, ff. 9–10.

XII   *Ibid.*

XIII   Although raised in England this regiment was transferred to the Irish Establishment in September 1685. It returned to England as part of the Irish Army during the Prince of Orange's invasion.

XIV   This regiment was raised in England in April 1662 for service in Ireland.

XV   The regiment was reformed in Ireland for service with the Jacobite army from companies and elements left there.

XVI   About half of this regiment rallied to William III and retired into Londonderry to join the Williamites.

XVII   'Montagu Army Accounts', British Library Add MS 10123, f. 3v.

Appendix IV

The Independent Troops of Horse raised in 1685

The following list is taken almost solely from Charles Dalton's *English Army Lists and Commission Registers 1661–1714*, volume 2, pp. 14–18. Dalton also lists the lieutenants and cornets for each troop but for brevity I have listed only the captains here, readers wanting the full list are recommended to Dalton's original work.

After Sedgemoor the majority of these troops were used to raise the seven new regiments of horse. Troops for which no date of disbandment is given can be found listed in Chapter 3. The sole exceptions to this are the two troops of the Earl of Newburgh and the Duke of Albemarle for which neither formal disbandment nor incorporation information has been found, it is therefore possible that neither of these two troops were actually formed. All commissions were signed at Whitehall.

Commission dated 15 June 1685
Lieutenant Colonel Bernard Howard of Norfolk

Commissions dated 18 June 1685
Sir Edmund Andros; William Baggot; Sir Maurice Berkeley, Viscount Fitzhardinge (disbanded 25 July 1685[1]); Henry Bertie; Richard Bertie; Francis Brudenell, Lord Brudenell; Thomas Bruce, Lord Bruce; Robert Cornwall; Bryan, Lord Viscount Cullen; Robert Fielding[2] (disbanded 25 July 1685[3]); James Griffin; Thomas Herbert, 8th Earl of Pembroke and 5th Earl of Montgomery (disbanded 25 July 1685[4]); Jonathon Lloyd (disbanded 4 August 1685[5]); Richard Lumley, Viscount Lumley;[6] Francis Spalding; Robert Sutton, Lord Lexington; Sir John Talbot; Sir William Villiers, Bt; Lyonel Walden; Thomas Windsor, 1st Earl of Plymouth

Commissions dated 19 June 1685
Robert Byerley; Sir Symon Leach[7] (disbanded 25 July 1685[8])

---

1 National Archives, Kew, WO5/1, f. 182/3.
2 Mustered at Warwick.
3 PRO WO5/1 f. 182/3.
4 National Archives, Kew WO5/1, f. 182/3.
5 National Archives, WO5/1, f. 218.
6 See also Lumley's commission below under the date of 27 June.
7 Mustered at Exeter.
8 National Archives WO5/1, f. 182/3.

THE ARMY OF JAMES II, 1685–1688

Commissions dated 20 June 1685

Allan Bellingham[9] (disbanded 25 July 1685[10]); Robert Bertie, Lord Willoughby de Eresby; Sir Edward Carterett; Edmund Chafin; Hugh, 2nd Viscount Cholmondeley; Sir Thomas Fairfax Bt;[11] Jonathon Fetherstonhalgh; Thomas Harrington; Henry Hevingham; Henry Jermyn, 1st Baron Dover; Robert Leke, 3rd Earl of Scarsdale, Charles Livingston, 2nd Earl of Newburgh;[12] Jonathan Lovring[13] (disbanded 25 July 1685[14]); Sir Thomas Mauleverer; D'Oyley Michel; Charles Montague, 4th Earl of Manchester; William Ogle; William Paston, 2nd Earl of Yarmouth; Roger Pope; Henry Savile, Lord Eland; Robert Smith; Charles Somerset, Marquis of Worcester; Charles Talbot, 12th Earl of Shrewsbury; Sir Thomas Taylor, 2nd Bt[15] (disbanded 25 July 1685[16]); Sir Charles Tufton; Thomas Tufton, 6th Earl of Thanet; Sir Edward Villiers[17] (disbanded 25 July 1685[18]); Sir Michael Wentworth (disbanded 25 July 1685[19]); Henry Yelverton, Lord de Grey of Ruthyn.

Commissions dated 22 June 1685

Ambrose Browne; Archibald Clincard; Sir Thomas Grosvenor, 3rd Bt.

Commissions dated 25 June 1685

Claudius Hamilton, 4th Earl of Abercorn; Sir John Reresby[20] (disbanded 25 July 1685[21])

Commissions dated 26 June 1685

Baldwin Leighton[22] (disbanded 25 July 1685[23]); Richard Lumley, Viscount Lumley.[24]

Commissions dated 27 June 1685

John O'Neille[25] (disbanded 25 July 1685[26])

---

9   Mustered at Kendal.
10 National Archives, Kew, WO5/1, f.182/3.
11 Grandson of the first commander of the New Model Army.
12 Mustered at Cirencester. This troop may never have been formed, but it is also possible that command had been handed to one of the two captains whose troops were disbanded but for which commissions cannot be traced, Captains Slingsby and Walker, see below.
13 Mustered at Cheltenham.
14 National Archives, Kew, WO5/1, f. 182/3.
15 Mustered at Rochester and Chatham.
16 National Archives, Kew, PRO WO5/1, f. 182/3.
17 Mustered at Hatfield.
18 National Archives, Kew. WO5/1, f. 182/3.
19 National Archives, Kew, WO5/1, f. 182/3.
20 Mustered at York.
21 National Archives, Kew, WO5/1, f. 182/3.
22 Mustered at Shrewsbury.
23 National Archives, Kew, WO5/1, f.182/3.
24 This is, to say the least, odd. According to Dalton, *English*, vol. 2, pp. 14–18, Lumley received two commissions as a captain of horse, one dated 18 June and the other dated 27 June. The lieutenant in the former case is not mentioned but the two cornets are different. It is therefore not impossible that Lumley did indeed raise two troops. Both would have gone into his regiment of horse although which actually composed the bulk of the colonel's troop is impossible to say. It is also possible that something happened to prevent the raising of the first troop and only the second was raised.
25 Mustered at Hertford.
26 National Archives, Kew. WO5/1, f. 182/3.

Commission dated 4 July 1685
Christopher Monk, 2nd Duke of Albermarle[27]

The King also issued commissions for the raising of volunteer troops of horse but after Sedgemoor these simply stood down, if indeed they had ever actually assembled. For completeness the known captains are:[28]

The Earl of Abingdon (2 Troops)[29] 26 June 1685
Lord Thomas Howard   1 July 1685
Colonel James Porter   1 July 1685
Sir Bourchier Wray   2 July 1685 (disbanded 25 July 1685[30])
William Constable   3 July 1685

On 18 July 1685[31] orders were given for the disbandment of a number of troops and companies, which include two troops not listed elsewhere. These were the troops of horse of Sir Thomas Slingsby, and James Walker.

It should be noted that when James ordered the reduction of all troops to 50 troopers on 16 July 1685 the warrant was individually sent to each captain.[32] Albermarle, Abingdon, Howard, Porter, and Constable do not appear on this list suggesting that at the time of the warrant either their troops had already disappeared or that they were never actually raised.

---

27 Davies, 'Letters on the Administration of James II's Army'. Letter from Secretary at War William Blaythwayt. From the date, and the fact that Albermarle was captain and colonel of the 1st Troop of the Royal Regiment of Horse Guards, this may have been a 'volunteer' troop rather than one of the independent troops. The fact that Albermarle was at the same time commissioned to raise a troop of dragoons argues against this idea, however it does appear likely that he never actually formed these troops, a hypothesis supported by his being omitted from the King's circular letter of 16 July.

28 Dalton, *English*, vol. 2, p. 16.

29 Two blank commissions for captains of horse were sent to the Earl dated 20 June 1685.

30 National Archives, Kew, WO5/1, ff. 182–3.

31 *Ibid.*, ff. 170–3.

32 *Ibid.*, ff. 167–170, lists all these officers and thus is effectively a list of all units then in the army.

Appendix V

The Independent Companies of Foot Raised in 1685

The independent companies commissioned in June 1685 were all intended to strengthen the garrisons in England.

Captain	Date of Commission	Garrison
Richard Arundell, 1st Baron Arundell of Trerice[I]	22 June	Pendennis Castle
Roger Kirkby[II]	24 June	Chester
Sir Thomas Slingsby[III]	24 June	Scarborough Castle
Lionel Copley	25 June	Hull
Sir Thomas Haggerston[IV]	26 June	Berwick
Charles Hildyard[V]	26 June	Berwick
George Weld[VI]	26 June	Berwick

Notes

I   Incorporated into The Earl of Bath's Regiment of Foot on 17 March 1686.

II   Incorporated into Sir William Clifton' Regiment of Foot on 18 July 1685 (National Archives, Kew, WO5/1 ff. 170–173).

III   Disbanded 18 July 1685 (*Ibid.*, f. 171).

IV   Absorbed into the Queen Consort's Regiment of Foot, early 1687?

V   Disbanded 18 July 1685 (*Ibid*).

VI   Incorporated into Sir Edward Hales' Regiment of Foot on 27 July 1685.

Appendix VI

The Independent Troops of Horse Raised in 1688

As with the 1685 lists, this is taken almost entirely from Charles Dalton's *English Army Lists and Commission Registers 1661–1714*, p. 179. Again Dalton also lists the lieutenants and cornets for each troop, which are omitted here for brevity.

Some of these troops were probably incorporated into the new regiments of 1688, however troops whose incorporation or formal disbandment cannot be identified are indicated with an asterisk.

Captain	Date of Commission
Edward Widdrington*	30 September 1688
Charles Lord Baltimore[1]*	10 October 1688
Sir Jonathon Gifford, 2nd Bt*	11 October 1688
Sir Jonathon Yates, 2nd Bt*	11 October 1688
Sir William Holford*	18 October 1688
Sir Thomas Burton, 3rd Bt	19 October 1688
	disbanded 4 January 1689[2]
Thomas Eccleston*	20 October 1688
Thomas, 4th Viscount Fitzwilliam*	20 October 1688
Sir Gilbert Gerard, 1st Bt*	25 October 1688
Sir Louis Palmer, 3rd Bt*	21 November 1688
Stephen Tempest*	27 November 1688
Earl of Salisbury*	27 October 1688[3]

Possibly many of these troops had barely begun to be raised before the crisis was over and James had fled, hence why there is no evidence of a formal disbandment order.

---

1 Dalton comments that this nobleman's name should have been 'John'. See Dalton, *English*, vol. 2, p. 179.
2 'Montagu Army Accounts', British Library Add MS 10123, f.3. When the troop was given full pay from 3 November 1688.
3 National Archives, Kew, WO5/3, f. 315.

Appendix VII

The Independent Companies of Foot Raised in 1688

Thirty-one new independent companies of foot were ordered to be raised in 1688,[1] although Dalton lists 32 commissions because the initial 31 included only one company from Chelsea Hospital, and actually two were raised. A number of these newly raised companies appear to have gone into the standing regiments to increase their strength. The rest of the companies were probably intended to be later merged into additional regiments and although this was not done during James's reign, in 1689 William III created Colonel Francis Luttrell's Regiment of Foot from these independent companies, although all with different captains from those under which they were raised.

The list below is, again, mainly compiled from Charles Dalton's *English Army Lists and Commission Registers 1661–1714*, pp. 180–181. As is customary Dalton lists both lieutenants and ensigns, but for brevity only captains are given here.

Commission signed 27 September 1688
Richard Smith. One of the two companies formed from the pensioners of Chelsea Royal Hospital. The company received formal marching orders on 4 November 1688,[2] so, coupled with the fact that it had received arms on 2 October, it must have been complete or by that stage.

Commissions signed 29 September 1688
Richard Anthony; Samuel Arnold; Henry Davies;[3] Robert London; Thomas Neale.

Commissions signed 30 September 1688
Ulrick Bourke; Charles Collier; James Courtney; Henry Crofton; Maurice Flynn; William Gibbon;[4] Jonathon Mair; Jonathon Leeds; Spencer Littleton; James Merrick; Francis Watson; John Withrington; Edward Wolf.

---

1 National Archives, Kew, SP 44/165, 104.
2 National Archives, Kew, WO5/3, f. 321.
3 Mentioned in marching orders on 23 October 1688. National Archives, Kew, WO5/3, f. 290.
4 *Ibid.*, f. 291.

Commissions signed 1 October 1688
Thomas Bowles; Henry Bruning; Edward Branghall (struck off the army list on 31 December 1688); George Cony;[5] Benjamin Laney; Thomas Motley; Henry Pounds; Antonio Power.

Commissions signed 6 October 1688
William Low; Matthew Smyth (merged into the Duke of Norfolk's Regiment in March 1689).

Commission signed on 6 October 1688
Edward Picking. The second of the two companies formed from the pensioners of Chelsea Royal Hospital. The company received formal marching orders on 5 November 1688.[6] As with Smith's Company it had received arms on 2 October and must have been complete by the time it received its marching orders.

Commission signed 8 October 1688
Elias Beake; Francis Ingoldsby.

---

5   Mentioned in marching orders on 23 October and 5 November 1688. National Archives, Kew, WO5/3, ff. 290, 321.
6   National Archives, Kew, WO5/3, f. 321.

Appendix VIII

The Army Mustered on Hounslow Heath, June 1686

A LIST *of* KING JAMES *Army on Hounslow Heath as they lay encamped, with the Names of all the General and Field Officers. Colour of their Cloaths, Number of Men, and Manner of Encamping, &c. June 30th, 1686*[1]

HIS MAJESTY, Generalissimo

Earl of Craven }	Lord Churchill }	
Earl of Feversham } Lieutenant Generals	Col Worthen } Major Generals	
Earl of Dunbarton }	Col Mackey }	
Sir John Phenwick }	Col Orbee } Adjutant Generals	
Sir John Lannerc } Brigadier Generals	Col Ramely }	
Col. Sackville }	Col Maxwell } Quarterm'r General	
Col. Kirke }	Lord Ranelagh Paymaster General	
	Captain Sheales Commissary General	
	Lord Dartmouth Gen. of Ordnance	

HORSE ON THE RIGHT					
Regiments	Field Officers	Colour of Cloaths	Troops or Comp'nies	Men Each	Total Men
1 Earl of Oxford	E. of Oxford Col. Sir Fra. Compton, L. Col. ------ Litleton, Maj.	Blue lin'd with red	9	50	450
2 Major Gen. Worthen's	Maj. Gen. Worthen, Col. Barni. Howard, L. Col. ------ Morgan, Maj.	Red lin'd with red	6	40	240
3 Queen Dowager's	Lord Lumley, Col. ------ Vernon, L. Col. ------ Cunningham, Maj.	Red lin'd with green	6	40	240
4 Earl of Shrewsbury's	E. of Shrewsbury, Col. ------ Coy, L. Col. John Skelton, Maj.	Red lin'd with buff	6	40	240

---

1   From a contemporary newssheet reprinted in *The Antiquarian Repository*, Vol. 1 (London: Frances Grove & Thomas Astle, 1807), pp. 229–232. The original article contains a 'commentary', which is an excellent example of a Whig anti-James II diatribe.

Regiments	Field Officers	Colour of Cloaths	Troops or Comp'nies	Men Each	Total Men
5 Earl of Peterborough's	Earl of Peterborough, Col. Sir John Talbot, L. Col. ------ Chiltam, Maj.	Red lin'd with red	6	40	240
FOOT					
1 The 1st battalion, Col. Stradling Commandant 2 The King's 3d battalion, Capt. Reresby Com	D. of Grafton, Col. William Eaton L. Col. Knevit Hastings, Maj.	Red lin'd with blue, blue breeches and stockings	7, incl. one of grenadiers 6	80 80	560 480
3 Earl of Craven's lst battallion, Major Hewit Col Commandant	E. of Craven, Col. Col. Sackville, L. Col. ------ Hewit, Maj.	Red lin'd with blue, blue breeches and white stockings	6 half grenadiers	80	520
4 lst battallion of Scotch Guards, Maj. Murray Commandant	Sir James Douglas, Col. ------ Wondrum, L. Col Sir Charles Murray, Maj.	Red lin'd with white, white breeches and stockings	7	80	560
5 Prince George's	Sir Chas. Littleton, Col. ------ Nicholson, L. Col. ------ Baggot, Maj.	Red lin'd with yellow, grey breeches and stockings	12	50	600
6 Colonel Oglethorp's	Sir Theo. Oglethorp, Col Lord Hunsdon, L. Col ------ Starling, Maj.	Red lin'd with ash, ash colour'd breeches and stockings	12	50	600
7 Earl Huntington's	E. of Huntington, Col. Ferd. Hastings, L. Col ------ Morgan, Maj.	Red lin'd with yellow, yellow breeches, grey stockings	10	50	500
8 Earl of Litchfield's	E. of Litchfield, Col. ------ Salisbury, L.Col. ------ Trapps, Maj.	Red , lin'd with white, blue breeches and stockings	10	50	500
9 Marquis of Worcester's	M. of Worcester, Col. Sir John Hanmore, L. C. Carr, Ml	Red lin' d with tawny tawny breeches, and stockings	10	50	500
10 Earl of Bath's	E. of Bath, Col. Sir Nich. Slanning L. Col. Sir Cha. Carney, Maj.	Blue lin'd with red, red breeches and stockings	10	50	500
11 Colonel Kirk's	Charles Kirk, Col. ------ Kirk, L. Col. ------ Lesley, Maj.	Red lin'd with green, green breeches and white stockings	10	50	500
12 Earl of Dunbarton's	E. of Dunbarton, Col. ------ Douglas, L. Col. ------ Douglas, Maj.	Red lin'd with white, grey breeches and stockings	11, incl. one of grenadiers	50	550
HORSE ON THE LEFT					
1 Earl of Plimouth's	Earl of Plimouth, Col. ------ Sunderland, L. Col. ------ Worthen, Maj.	Red lin'd with green	6	40	240

Regiments	Field Officers	Colour of Cloaths	Troops or Comp'nies	Men Each	Total Men
2 Earl of Scarsdale's	Earl of Scarsdale, Col. ------ Langton, L. Col. ------ Norton, Maj.	Red lin'd with yellow	6	40	240
3 Earl of Arran's	E. of Arran, Col. ------ Needby, L. Col ------ Parker, Maj.	Red lin'd with white with white silk sashes	6	40	240
4 The Queen's	Sir John Lannere, Col. ------ Legg L. Col Sir William Board, Maj.	Red lin'd with yellow	6	40	240
DRAGOONS					
1 The King's	Lord Cornbury, Col. L. Col. Maj.		6	40	240
2 Princess of Denmark's	Charles Bartlett, Col. L. Col. ------ Halley, Maj.		6	40	240
3 The Queen's	D. of Somerset, Col. L. Col. Maj.		6	40	240
The Fusiliers	Lord Dartmouth, Col. ------ Saintclare, L. Col. ------ Soper, Maj.	Red lin'd with yellow, grey breeches and stockings	12, incl. one of miners	50	600
			Gunners Mattrosses	55 28	84
					10,144
Note: only private centinels are reckoned					

THEIR MANNER OF ENCAMPING

The Horse, Foot, and Dragoons are encamped in a direct line, the intervals between each Regiment of Horse about 50 paces, the interval between the Foot 70 paces, the intervals between the Horse of the Left and the Dragoons (because of the ground) is near half a mile. -The Lieutenants' and Ensigns' Tents in the Rear of their respective Companies in a direct Line, 17 paces from the Soldiers' hutts or tents; the Captains' tents 12 paces behind the Lieutenants'; the Colonels' tents behind the Captains', 10 paces; the Lieutenant Colonel on the right of the Colonel, and the Major on the left in a direct line.

Sir John Phenwick (as eldest Brigadier) his tent in the rear of the center of the Horse on the right, 20 paces behind the Colonels' tents. Sir John Lannerc (as 2d) in the rear of the left Regiment of Horse on the left. Colonel Sackville (as 3d) in the rear of the interval between Lord Craven's Regiment and the Scotch Guards. Colonel Kirk's (as 4th) in the rear of the interval between his own and the Earl of Bath's Regiment, all four in a direct line.

The King's Quarters is in the rear of the left of the Horse on the left, in an inclosed field, in which quarter are the following tents, viz.

The King's Tent and Chappell
> The General's Quarters is behind the King's, in which are these Earl
> of Feversham's tents, viz Col. Worthen's, Lord Ranelagh, Col. Orbe

Lord Churchill's
Adjutant Generall's
Quarter Master Generall's
Sir Charles Murray's
Earl of Dunbarton's

The Fuziliers are encamped in the rear of the Line, a good distance behind the interval between the Earl of Craven's Regiment and the Scotch Guards, and in several parties about the Store Carriages – The guns are planted about 100 pace, before the line, before the interval between the Scotch Guards and Prince George's Regiment, guarded by a party of Fuziliers, each gun having 2 gunners and a matrosse to attend it. –– The Queen's Scaffold was about 150 paces to the right of the guns, something more advanced from the Line. –– The Suttlery Booth, are about 200 paces in the rear of the Line.

Note, That besides the Forces above mentioned there were three Troops of the Horse Guards and Grenadiers this day.

Appendix IX

Establishment of the Scots Army that marched into England in 1688[1]

Regiment	Quarters in England	Strength
Troop of Horse Guards	Westminster, Tower Hamlets & Minories	132
Royal Regiment of Scots Horse	Westminster, Tower Hamlets & Minories	352
Royal Regiment of Scots Dragoons	Southwark, Lambeth, and Rotherhithe	357
Scots Regiment of Foot Guards	Precincts of Holborn	1,251
Royal Regiment of Scots Fuzileers	Spitalfields and Tower Hamlets	744
Colonel Wachop's Regiment of Foot	Clerkenwell and Adjacents	927

---

1   Dalton, *English*, vol. 2, p. 410.

Appendix X

Deserters Notices From *The London Gazette*, 1685–1688

The London Gazette first appeared as *The Oxford Gazette* (the Court then being at Oxford, where it had fled to avoid the plague) with a date of *Nov. 7 to Thursday November 16 1665*. Thereafter it appeared twice weekly, usually on Monday and Thursday, and from issue 24, *From Thursday, February 1. to Monday, February 5. 1665*, it became *The London Gazette*. It is still published today, but it is now simply *The Gazette* although it still carries official Court information, government and legal announcements, etc.

Numb. 214 Monday to Thursday 2–5 Dec 1667, contained for the first time a notice for a missing servant and offered a reward for information or his return. *London Gazette Numb 1312, From Thursday June 13 to Monday June 17 1678* for the first time contained a notice for a deserter from the army:

> One John Williams, a Welchman, of about 30 years of age, of a middle stature, his head being usually shaved, a scar on his forehead, small hollow grey eyes, one of his teeth on the upper side of his head being broke, or out before, Run away from his Colours, the 8th instant, with Fifty pounds of Capt. Francis Villers's. Whoever gives notice of him to my Lord Grandisons in Petty-France, Westminster, or to Colonel Villers in Dukes-street near St. James's, shall have 40s Reward.

Thereafter such notices became commonplace if irregular and are an invaluable source of information on the army's rank and file for the period before the sort of details recorded in them were kept by the regiments as a matter of course.

The notices reprinted here cover the period from Charles II's death, on 6 February 1685, to 10 December 1688, when James fled Whitehall; original spelling, punctuation and font style has been retained throughout. There are just over 100 individuals covered in these four years, or around two per month on average – as a comparison there were over 50 further desertions in the six months after James' fall from power, roughly 10 per month.

These have all been extracted from the near-complete collection of *The London Gazette* from issue 1 onwards in the British Library (King's Library, shelf marked 97.h.1 onwards). Original spelling and font style has been retained throughout and I have given the full date and reference for each entry allowing for easy follow-up and cross-referencing.

Note: one particular term may cause some confusion with modern readers. Several notices below refer to the subject as 'a black man'; this is the 17th century term for a man of a dark swarthy complexion – hence Charles II was described as 'a black man' on the wanted notices issued by Parliament when he was being hunted after the Battle of Worcester in 1651.[1] It does not refer to, and the term is not used for, someone of African descent. There are a very few examples in later deserters notices, as also for missing servants, for men of African origin and the term used to describe them is universally either 'a Negro' or 'a Negroid man'.

London Gazette **Numb 2024, From Thursday April 9 to Sunday April 13 1685**
George Hawkes and Thomas Johnson, Soldiers at Sheerness, are run away from their Colors, being both in Yellow Coats and Red Breeches, with Swords and Shoulder-Belts, aged between 30 and 40, and much of a size, and very light brown Hair, they had with them a very remarkable ruff white Spaniel with a hurt upon his Forehead lately bitten. Whoever shall give notice of them so as that they be secured, to Captain Crawford at Sheerness, or to Mr. Beavoir at the Silver Ball in the Pall-Mall, shall have a Guinea reward for each.

London Gazette **Numb 2092, From Monday December 7 to Thursday December 10 1685**
Run away from Lieutenant Colonel Douglas the 7th Instant, a Frenchman, of low stature, aged about 28, of ruddy a Complexion, sharp nose, and brown eyes, speaks broken English and Dutch, wears a light Wig, tyed up, a grey Coat lin'd with black, and over it a brown Cloath Coat the sleeves fac'd with blew Plush; he stole about 300 l., in Gold, amongst which was several five Guinea pieces, and several pieces of broad Gold, and a Bavarian piece of about two pound value. Whoever apprehends him and gives to Mr. Knowles at the three Squirrils in Kings Street Westminster, shall have twenty Guineas Reward.

London Gazette **Numb 2106, From Thursday January 21 to Monday January 25 1685**
Charles Platter (of Bristol) a thick middle siz'd Man, ruddy and full faced, with short brown hair. John Brown, an Irish Man, middle siz'd, well set, with long curl'd hair, inclining to a sandy colour. Thomas Cobb, an Irish Man, tall, thin faced, slender, with dark brown hair long and lank, lately Run away out of Capt. Cornwallis's Company of Grenadiers in the Holland Regiment (quartered now in Southwark) every one of them with a new Red Coat lin'd with a buff colour'd lining, surtout sleeves, cross Pockets with three scolops, large plain round pewter Buttons, Breeches of the same colour as the Coat lining, and with His Majesties Arms. Whoever gives notice of any of these three Deserters to any of Capt. Cornwallis's Serjeants at the Green Dragon in Blackman-street, near St. George's Church in Southwark, so that they may be Apprehended, shall have for every of them a Guinea Reward.

London Gazette **Numb 2107, From Monday January 25 to Thursday January 28 1685**
Philip John and Edward John (belonging to Capt. Peyton's Company in the Holland Regiment) deserted their Colours the 19th instant. The first is about 21 or 22 years of age, not very tall, but of a middle stature, brown hair, not long, a little curl'd, hath a druggit Coat, lined with a whitish Silk. The latter is about 19 or 20 years of age, not so tall as the other, but of a thick, well proportioned Body, a ruddy round Face, lank short flaxen hair, sanguine Complexion, a little down-lookt, hath a blackish Coat, the Sleeves fac'd with Red, neither of them speaks good English, being Jersey men, whose Native Language is French. Whoever gives notice of them at Capt. Peyton's Quarters at the Queens-head near the Falcon on Bankside, Southwark, shall have a Guinea reward for each.

London Gazette **Numb 2127, From Monday April 5 to Thursday April 8 1686**
Edward Love, a middle-aged Man, with Pockholes in his Face, brown hair, about 30 years old. Edward Woodcock, a tall raw-boned Man, down lookt, light lank hair, down visage, about 25 years. James Davis, a tall Man, short black hair, about 25 years. Lacells Barton, a thick set Man, about 29 years, Run away out of Captain

---

1 There are numerous other known examples to demonstrate this usage for a swarthy caucasian, including Dick Turpin on many of his wanted posters!

Pope's Company in the Regiment of Foot Guards, called, The Coldstreamers, commanded by the Earl of Craven. Whoever gives Notice of any of them to Captain Pope at his house in Sherard-street near Piccadilly, shall have 10s for each Man.

London Gazette **Numb 2128, From Thursday April 8 to Monday April 12 1686**
John Johnson, and Maurice Murrah, tall, well-set, likely Fellows, with healthful Complexions, their own Hair of a dark brown, with sad-coloured Cloaths, Run away from Sir Hugh Middleton's Troop of Dragoons, in the Regiment commanded by Colonel Berkeley, quartered at Leverpoole. Whoever gives notice of them to the said Quarter, or to Sir Hugh Middleton's Lodgings at Mr Hutchinson's a Sadler, in the middle of the Pall-Mall, shall have a Guinea Reward.

William Leech, a Corporal, a tall Man, of a ruddy Complexion, lisps in his Speech, about 32 years old; and Walter Douglas, likewise a tall man, aged about 37 years, Run away out of Capt. Macarty's Company quartered at Hull. Whoever gives Notice of them, or either of them, so as that they may be apprehended, shall have a Guinea Reward.

London Gazette **Numb 2138, From Thursday May 13 to Monday May 17 1686**
Walter Wadling (being about the age of 22 or 23) of a middle stature, long dark brown bushy hair, a little pock-fretten in his Face, of a swarthy Complexion, having a sad coloured Coat, black Hair-buttons. Likewise Philip Home, about the same age and stature, stooping in the shoulders, having light lank short hair, with a thin pale Face, a gray close Coat, a pair of red Breeches, a strip's Neckcloth, both of Capt. Godolphin's Company in the Earl of bath's Regiment. Run from their Colours at Guildford in Surrey, the 14th Instant. Whoever gives Notice of both, or either of them, to Francis Bluet at Mr. Emps's house at Charing-cross, shall have Two Guinea's Reward for each of them.

London Gazette **Numb 2123, From Monday July 12 to Thursday July 15 1686**
John Manning, of middle stature, about 23 years old, brown hair, sallow complexion, having both his arms under Cure, Ran away from Capt. George Churchill's Troop of Dragoons, in a light coloured stuff Suit, lined with black, and black Buttons, with an Iron gray Gelding about 6 years old, 14 hands and a half high, a shorn mane, and whitish round mark about his further hip, and a croop Saddle and Bridle, having cheated the Landlord at the George in Heston of Seven Guinea's. Whoever shall secure the said person, or the Horse, and give notice thereof to the Lord Cornbury at his House in Jermain-street, or any of the Officers of his Regiment at the Camp, shall have a Guinea Reward.

London Gazette **Numb 2158, From Thursday July 22 to Monday July 26 1686**
One Robert Minors, serjeant to Capt. Richard Kidley in Colonel Cornwall's Regiment, deserted his Colours, and took away with him, besides his own, four new Coats lin'd with Orange-colour; He is a very short black Man, aged about 33, a swarthy Complexion, pretty full-faced with gray eyes. Whoever gives notice of him to Mr. John Adams at Sadlers-Hall Court in Cheapside, shall be well rewarded.

London Gazette **Numb 2159, From Monday July 26 to Thursday July 29 1686**
Run away out of Lieutenant Colonel Halting's Company in the Earl of Huntingdon's Regiment, William Reyner, a Welshman, having upon his Left Foot 6 Toes, and on his Left Hand two Fingers growing together, and the Little Toe on his Left Foot always sticks out of his Shoe; He is pretty tall, black hair, lean-visag'd, about 30 years old. Whoever gives Notice of the said William Reyner at Lieutenant Colonel Halting's House in Downing-street, Westminster, shall have a Guinea Reward.

London Gazette **Numb 2162, From Thursday August 5 to Monday August 9 1686**
William Faton, a Soldier in Capt. Seymour's Company, in His Majesties First Regiment of Foot-Guards, near 30 years of age, having lately had the Small-pox, a thin middle sized Man, run away from his Colours, and stole a grey Cloth suit. Whoever gives notice of him, shall have a Guinea reward from the said Captain, at the Foot-Guard at Whitehal.

London Gazette **Numb 2168, From Thursday August 26 to Monday August 30 1686**
Benjamin Ridley, aged about 30 years, a middle sized man, well set, with short light brown hair, by Trade a Blacksmith, being a soldier in Captain Throckmorton's Company in the First Regiment of Foot-Guards, Run from his Colours about 14 days since. Whoever gives Notice of him so that he be apprehended, to Serjeant Thomas Howard at his House in Mercers-street near long-Acre, shall have a Guinea Reward.

London Gazette **Numb 2171, From Monday September 6 to Thursday September 9 1686**
Plimouth, Septemb. 2. On Tuesday last a Soldier of Col. Trelawney's Regiment, being condemned to be hanged for running from his Colours, was executed here.

London Gazette **Numb 2174, From Thursday September 16 to Monday September 20 1686**
Charles Whitwood, middle sized, round vizaged, with short lank hair, having a gray Coat, the Sleeves faced with black Velvet, blue Breeches, and blue Stockings. Run away from his Colours the 11th instant, in His Majesties First Regiment of Guards. Whoever gives Notice of him to Captain Sandys at his lodgings in Downing-street, Westminster, shall be rewarded.

Whereas Joseph Loe, a middle-sized Man, full, pale-faced, thin dark brown hair with a small voice, Shoemaker. George Hornsy, a tall, thin Man, long visag'd, a Hawk-Nose, a squeaking voice, long brown curl'd hair, a Seaman. William Harris, an indifferent tall Man, a thin fresh-colour'd face, dark curl's hair, with some few gray hairs, about 40 years of age, Shoemaker, Stephen Frankes, a short broad Man, broad fac'd, full of Pockholes, black curling hair, with an impediment in his speech almost to stuttering, Shoemaker, Jonathon Seaborn, servant to Lieutenant Thornhill, a sizeable Man, large legs, with some Pockholes in his face, inclining to ruddy, with a large scar thwart the forepart of his Head, wears a Periwig, a Shropshire Man, Barber. All soldiers in Colonel Herbert's Regiment, and in Captain William Stow's Company, have deserted their Colours. Whoever shall give Notice of them, or any of them, so as they may be apprehended, to Mr. Thomas Pelling at the Cock and Crown near Kingsgate in High-Holborn, shall have a very considerable Reward.

London Gazette **Numb 2179, From Monday October 4 to Thursday October 7 1686**
Robert Kirkman, a black thick short man, broad Shouldered, a Sawyer by Trade; and John Macdonough, a pretty tall handsome fellow, of ruddy Complexion, and reddish Hair, having run away from their Colours in Captain Maccarty's Company in the Earl of Huntingdon's Regiment. Whoever gives Notice of them, or either of them, to Dr. Davis at Mr. Cumley's House in Norfolke-streeet in the Strand, shall be well Rewarded.

London Gazette **Numb 2187, From Monday November 1 to Thursday November 4 1686**
William Harrison, born at Lowerton near Redford in Nottinghamshire, hath deserted his Colours from Sir Edward Hale's Regiment; he is a tall well set Man, brown curl'd Hair. Whoever gives Notice of him, so that he may be apprehended, to Capt. Aylmer at his Quarters at the Falcon Inn on the Bank-side, Southwark, shall have 20.s Reward.

London Gazette **Numb 2193, From Thursday November 22 to Monday November 25 1686**
An Highland Scotchman, named John Maccfarling, speaks bad English, a middle-sized Man, short black hair, about 30 years old, sometimes served in Capt. Bell's Company in the Earl of Maars Regiment in Scotland, Run away from his Colour on the 17th Instant, in Lieutenant-Colonel Barklay's Company in Sir Edw Hale's Regiment,

taking with him a Red Coat, Sword and Belt, besides several things of his Comerades and landlords. Whoever gives Notice of him (at his Officers Quarters in Southwark) so as he be Apprehended, shall have a Guinea Reward, and reasonable Charges.

London Gazette **Numb 2195, From Monday November 29 to Thursday December 2 1686**
Two young Men, John Doning, and James Edwards, the former of middle stature, the latter a little Taller; in Red Coats lin'd with Yellow, being Soldiers in His Royal Highness Prince George, Hereditary Prince of Denmark, his Regiment of Foot, commanded by Sir Charles Littleton, deserted their Colours at Sheerness not long since; Whoever apprehends them and gives notice of it to Mr. Richard Beavoir, at the Silver Ball in the Pall-Mall, or to Capt. George Rooke at Sheerness, shall have Two Guinea's Reward for each man, and their charges born. Also Tso. [sic] Hawthorne, a Soldier in Capt. Wray's Company in the said Regiment, and Garison, deserted his Colours about the same time; he is by Trade a Tanner, a well-proportion'd Man, in a grey close bodied Coat, fac'd with Plush of the same colour, wants one joint of his Thumb on his left Hand, aged about 32 years. Whoever apprehends him, and gives Notice to the said Mr. Beavoire, or his Capt. Wray, shall have 2 Guinea's Reward, and their Charges born.

London Gazette **Numb 2199, From Monday December 13 to Thursday December 16 1686**
Nathaniel Keindge, a broad sett Man of middle stature, pale Complexion, by trade a Shoemaker. William Bishop, a Man of the same size, ruddy Complexion, and black Hair. John Cartmall, a middle-siz'd Man, fair Complexion, and sad coloured Hair. John Ward, a slender young Man, of a ruddy Complexion, about the same stature with the other, in a light coloured Periwig; being all four of them Soldiers in Sir Martin Beckman's Company, in His Majesties Royal Regiment of Fewseleers, Commanded by the Right Honourable the Lord Dartmouth, lately Run away from their Colours. Whoever can secure any of them, and give Notice thereof to Sir Martin Beckman, or either of his Lieutenants, or to Mr. Shekelton Adjutant of the said Regiment, at the Tower of London shall have 5 Guinea's.

Run away the 6th Instant one William Colvert, Soldier in Major Stuart's Company in His Majesties First Regiment of Foot Guards; he is a tall lean Man, with short black bushy Hair, disfigured with the Small Pox; he was in a red Coat, blue Stockins, a black hat laced with Gold Lace. Whoever gives notice of him to Major Stewart aforesaid, shall be well Rewarded.

London Gazette **Numb 2202, From Thursday December 23 to Monday December 27 1686**
Robert Williams, a Welch-Man, Born at or near Little-Church in Derbyshire, speaks bad English, light Hair, about 25 years of Age, Run away from his Colours out of Capt. Thomas Weld's Company, in the Regiment of Sir Edward Hales, and Robbed his Quarters of one Silver Tobacco Box, William Spering engraven on it; a little Trunk, and several parcels of his Landlord's wearing Apparel. Whoever apprehends the said Person,, or gives such Notice (that he may be Taken) to the Officer that Commands in Chief at his Quarters in Southwark, shall receive 2 Guinea's Reward.

London Gazette **Numb 2207, From Monday January 10 to Thursday January 13 1686**
Thomas Lovell and Charles Lovell, middle-sized men about 26 or 27 years of age, lank hair'd; one with a long swarthy visage, and the other ruddy complexion'd, Run away out of Capt. Reresby's Company in His Majesties first Regiment of Foot guards, with their Arms and Cloaths, and stole the King's Bedding out of the Savoy. Whoever gives Notice of the said Persons to Capt. Reresby in Dukes Court near St Martins Church, or to the Guard at Whitehall, shall be well rewarded.

London Gazette **Numb 2217, From Monday February 14 to Thursday February 17 1686**
Thomas Lenton, a lofty Man, about 25 years of age, lank brown hair, somewhat disfigured with the Small pox. George Nicholls a Man of a middle stature, with black bushy hair, round and full-flavoured, with a pitt in his left Cheek, about 20 years old, Deserted out of Capt. Dowcett's Company in the Earl of Lichfield's Regiment of

Foot. Whoever secures them, and gives Notice thereof to captain Dowcett in Windsor, or Mr. William Tuttle an Apothecary at the Golden Acorn in the Strand over against the New Exchange, shall be well rewarded.

London Gazette **Numb 2221, From Monday February 28 to Thursday March 3 1686**
The 27th past, Run away from his Colours, one John Hill a Soldier in the Earl of Litchfield's Regiment, in Captain Wharton's Company at Tilbury Fort; he had a Red Coat lin'd with white, and a black Peruque; and is a thin spare Man about 25 years of age. Whoever gives Notice of him to Captain Wharton at his Lodgings in Green street near Leicester Fields, or to Lieutenant Seppens at Tilbury Fort, shall have a good reward, and all his Charges.

London Gazette **Numb 2224, From Thursday March 10 to Monday March 14 1686**
Run away out of Sir Francis Edward's Company in Colonel Cornwall's Regiment at Portsmouth, Jonathon Matthews a proper well set Man, having brown strait hair, a Shoemaker by Trade, born at Wrexham, and about 30 years of age. Richard Burras a pretty tall young Man, something slender, having dark brown hair, born at Shrewsbury, a Sheerman by Trade, and about 20 years of age. Peter Phithion, alias Pithyn, a handsum well-proportion'd young Man, having lank light brown hair, a Taylor by Trade, born in Cheshire, and about 22 years of age. Whoever secures any of them, and gives Notice to William Bissel Esq; Agent of the said Regiment at his House next door to the Queens-head in Sharewel-street, near the Hay-market in London, or to Mr. William Fosbrooke at the Mitre in Shrewsbury, shall have 10s. Reward.

London Gazette **Numb 2228, From Thursday March 24 to Monday March 28 1687**
A well-set middle-size Man, named John Barnes, about 27 years of age, a full redish face, full of Pockholes, sandy-coloured hair, a Cheshire man, by Profession a Pavier, Ran away from his Colours, the 22nd Instant, out of Major Soper's Company in the Right honourable the Lord Dartmouth's Regiment of Fusiliers, in a Red coat lined with Yellow, with brass Buttons, but has been seen since in a grey cloth Livery Coat lined with blue and pewter Buttons; he carried away from a Gentleman 5 l in money. If any can give notice of him (so as he may be secured) unto the said Major Soper, or to Mr. George Macy in the Tower of London, shall have a Guinea Reward.

London Gazette **Numb 2234, From Thursday April 14 to Monday April 18 1687**
London, April 15. William Grant, Soldier in Captain Parson's Company in His Majesties First Regiment of Guards, and Richard Crane Soldier in Sir Edward Hales's Regiment, having at the Sessions held at the Old Baily, been Convicted of Felony for Deserting their Colours, and accordingly sentenced to be Hanged; the first was Executed on Wednesday last in Covent-Garden, and the other this day on Tower-Hill.

London Gazette **Numb 2239, From Monday May 2 to Thursday May 5 1687**
Thomas Hurst Soldier in Captain Robert Wythe's Troops of dragoons, Quartered at Birmingham in Warwickshire, Run away from his Colours the First Instant, and stole a bright bay Gelding about 12 hands high, with two white Rings round his Ears, and a little star in his Forehead, and things of a considerable value. He is a short thick Fellow, with some Freckles in his Face, his hair short, and of a light colour, and commonly wore a light coloured Coat. Whoever can discover him, and are desired to secure both Man and Horse, and give Notice to the said Captain Wythe at his Quarters aforesaid, or at the Two Blue Flower-Pots in Panton street, shall have 40s. Reward.

London Gazette **Numb 2144, From Monday May 16 to Thursday May 19 1687**
Wheras Clement Clarke a Trooper in the Regiment Commanded by the Right Honourable the Earl of Peterborow, was for divers Misdemeanours lately cashiered; came afterwards to an Inn in Abbington, and by force and violence breaking open the Stable door, took away a Horse belonging to the Regiment. These are to give notice, that whoever discovers the said Clarke (for whose apprehension the Lord chief Justice of England has already given out his Warrant) to any of His Majesties Justices of the Peace, so as that he may be apprehended, shall have 5 l. reward, with their Charges, to be paid by the Agent of the said Regiment.

London Gazette **Numb 2244, From Thursday May 19 to Monday May 23 1687**
Plymouth May 18. William Deale, a Soldier in Capt. Thomas St John's Company in the Queen Dowagers Regiment Commanded by Col. Kirke, having been Tried and Convicted at Reeding, for Running away from his Colours, and having afterwards received Sentence of death at the King's-Bench Bar, he was brought to this place where the said Regiment is Quartered, and was executed here on Monday last.

Thomas Walby, a middle sized Man, with brown Hair, by Trade a Shooemaker, Evan Jones, a lusty Man, and whitely coloured, lately sick, Soldiers in Sir Martin Beckman's Company in his Majesties Royal Regiment of Fusiliers, Commanded by the Right Honourable the Lord Dartmouth, Run lately from their Colours. Whoever can give Notice of either of these Deserters at His Majesties Jewel House in the Tower of London, or to Mr. Shakelton Adjutant to the same Regiment in Garison there, shall have a Guinea Reward, if apprehended.

London Gazette **Numb 2248, From Thursday June 2 to Monday June 6 1687**
Francis Orser, Born in the Parish of Aberlandertoft, in the County of Camberland, Run away the 28th past, from his Master Capt. Rook, with a sum of money; He is a short squat Fellow with a Fillamote Livery, lin'd with Blue, the Sleeves, and the hind part of the Coat lac'd with a Silver Galoom. Whoever gives Notice of him to the said Capt. Rook in the Prince's Regiment, Encamp'd on Hounsloe-Heath, or to Mr. Selby, at the White Posts in Rider-street, so as he may be apprehended, shall have two Guinea's Reward.

On Friday last Run away from Col. Cornwalls own Company at Kingston, John Burges, by Profession a Gardiner, a very tall well proportion'd Man, with long black greasie Hair hanging over his Face, which is a little pock-broken; he went away in a Red Coat lin'd with Orange colour, grey Breeches, white Stockins, but has been seen in London in a sad colour Coat. Whoever shall give Notice of him (so that he may be apprehended) to the Commandant of the said Regiment on Hounslow-Heath, or to the Agent of the said Regiment, at his House in Sherwood-street, near the upper end of the Hay-market, shall have five pounds Reward.

London Gazette **Numb 2250, From Thursday June 9 to Monday June 13 1687**
On Monday last, John Barry, aged about 28 years, a tall black Man, with a long strait Body'd stuff Coat, of a darkish brown colour, and a black Hat. Also Joseph Francis about 30 years old, a tall lean Man, with curled short hair, his Eyes of the least size, and sharp visag'd; he has a red Coat lin'd with yellow, and an old yellow Coat under it: Run from their Colours at Brentford, from Capt. Crawford's Company, in his Royal Highness Prince George of Denmark's Regiment of Foot, Commanded b y Sir Charles Littleton. Whoever gives Notice of them, or either of them, to Mr. Beauvoir at the Silver Ball in the Pall-Mall, or to Lieutenant Symonds of the said Regiment, at the Camp; so that they be apprehended, shall have two Guineas reward for each.

London Gazette **Numb 2257, From Monday July 4 to Thursday July 7 1687**
One John Glover, a middle-sized Man, about 23 years of age. Joshuah Bamforth, about 22 years of age. The first had lank brown hair: the other is a tall black Man: they both deserted their Colours from Captain George Ailmer's Company, in Sir Edward Hales Regiment. Whoever shall apprehend both, or either of them, shall have five pounds Reward for each.

London Gazette **Numb 2258, From Thursday July 7 to Monday July 11 1687**
One John Lowthion, a middle-sized man, fresh coloured, light brown Hair, about 21 years of Age, deserted his Colours from Captain John Stanhop's Company, in Colonel Sackville Tutton's Regiment of Foot. Whoever apprehends him, and gives Notice to his Captain aforesaid, shall have 2 Guinea's Reward.

London Gazette **Numb 2263, From Monday July 25 to Thursday July 28 1687**
One John Seabrook, a tall lusty Fellow, above 40 years of Age, short brown curled Hair, with a flat Nose, by Trade a Butcher; formerly residing at Mile-End near London; Run away lately out of the Company of Grenadiers in Colonel Tufton's Regiment, from the Camp, with a red Coat lined with red, white stockings, and a Grenadiers Cap edged with white with the King's Cypher, he is in Company with a Woman who pretends to be his Wife. Whoever can secure him, and give Notice to Mr. Ascott, Agent to the said Regiment, at his Lodging at a Simstresses house in Sidney-street by Leicester Fields, shall have a Guinea Reward.

London Gazette **Numb 2267, From Monday August 8 to Thursday August 11 1687**
On Friday the 5th Instant, one John Humpreys a middle-sized Man about 20 years old, with lank brown Hair, stammereth in his Speech, Run away from his Colours and took with him a Buff Belt and Sword and a Bay Gelding about 15 hands high, paceth most, and a little heated in its fore Feet. Whoever gives Notice of him to Gilbert Thomas Esq; at the Golden Hart in Great Russel street, Bloomsbury, or at the Cock and Pie over against my Lord Craven's gate in Drury-Lane, shall have 2 Guineas Reward.

One George Wallace a slender Faced Man, long blackish Hair, a Glover by Trade, Run from his Colours on the 5th Instant, from Capt. Tho. Douglas's Company in Col. Buchan's Regiment of Foot. Whoever gives notice of him, to Mr. William Lillie, Apothecary in Bedford-street Covent Garden, shall have 3 Guineas Reward.

London Gazette **Numb 2271, From Monday August 22 to August 25 1687**
On the 16th Instant John Croot, about 30 years of age, pretty tall, well sett, full Faced, with a long Nose, short yellow curling Hair, large red Whiskers, an old blew Coat lined with red, with red and white Loops, red Breeches, and red Stockins, an old white Hat, Run from his Colours out of Capt. John Granville's Company of Grenadiers. Whoever gives notice of him to Mr Richard Beauvoir at the Silver Ball in the Pall-Mall, or to Lieutenant Elliot in Tilbury Fort, shall have two Guineas Reward.

London Gazette **Numb 2284, From Thursday October 6 to Monday October 10 1687**
Samuel Eyton a Soldier in Capt. St Anges Company in the Right Honourable the Lord Dartmouth's Regiment of Fusiliers within the Garison of the Tower, slender in Body, long thin visag'd, in a dark colour'd cloth serge Coat with long Pockets, went away the 4th Instant from the said Garison with 7 l. in money, besides a parcel of Linen belonging to Mr. Richard Sturgeon. Whoever gives Notice of the said person to Mr. Richard Sturgeon at the Office of Ordnance in the Tower , shall be very well rewarded.

London Gazette **Numb 2289, From Monday October 24 to Thursday October 27 1687**
Robert Mason, aged about 56 a thick set Man of a middle Stature, a very fresh Complexion, grey Hairs and a Beard, wearing a Red Coat lin'd with Green, missin from the Company of Lieutenant-colonel Salusbury, in the Earl of Litchfield's Regiment. Whoever brings him to Ensign Bowe's Quarters at Mr. Murray's at the Dog in Barnaby street, Southwark, or to Mr Tophall's at the Golden Anchor over against the New Exchange, shall have 2 Guinea's Reward.

Whereas David Slocomb, a Man of middle Stature, strait brown hair, who rambled up and down in the first camp 1686, and afterwards went to London, clothed with a yellow Coat, and a Granadiers Cap; since which, his friends cannot hear of him, but are informed that he is dead; if any Person make positive Proof where he is, dead or living, to Mr. Robins in Freeman's-yard, Cornhill, or to Captain Bacon at Harpford near Taunton in Somersetshire, shall have 2 Guinea's.

London Gazette **Numb 2290, From Thursday October 27 to Monday October 31 1687**
Robert Smith, a tall Man, round favoured, with pockholes in his Face, cropt brown hair, aged about 24. Christopher Stark, a thick set fellow, middle stature, black lank hair, round visag'd, aged about 22, Deserted, the 23rd Instant, from Capt. Thomas Dowcett's company in the Right Honourable the Earl of Litchfield's Regiment of Foot now in Southwark. Whoever gives Notice of both, or either of the said Persons, at the Sign of King Henry the Eighth, or the Talbot in Southwark, shall receive two Guinea's Reward.

Richard Nicholson, a middle-sized man, aged about 26, light yellowish colour'd hair, a scar from his Nose to the left side of his Cheek, went away from his Quarters at reading, Berks, from Capt. George Hasting's Troop. Whoever can apprehend the said Person, and give Notice to Mrs Thruckton in Durham-yard, shall have two Guinea's reward.

London Gazette **Numb 2294, From Thursday November 10 to Monday November 14 1687**
George Dorden, Centinel in Capt. Richard Brewer's Company of the Honourable Sir Edward Hale's Regiment, Ran from his Colours at Salisbury. He is a long ill shaped Fellow, aged about 26, has dark brown, lank thin hair. Whoever gives Notice of him to Mr. West at the Elephant and Castle in Salisbury Court, Fleet-street, shall have a Guinea Reward.

London Gazette **Numb 2298, From Thursday November 24 to Monday November 28 1687**
Andrew Poultny, a Soldier in Sir Hugh Myddleton's Troop in the Princess Anne of Denmark's Regiment of Horse, aged about 36, yellowish short hair, pale fac'd, of a midling stature, Run from his Colours, on Wednesday 23d Instant, with a Red Coat lined with Yellow, Holster Caps with the Princesses Cypher, a Red Cloak fac'd with Red, and a Case of Pistols on the Kings; on a daple grey Gelding about 15 hands high, with the hair off one of his Legs. Whoever secures Man or Horse, shall have two Guinea's Reward paid them by Mr. Hardy Agent of the said Regiment, at the Earl of Scarsdale's in Dukes street, Westminster.

London Gazette **Numb 2307, From Monday December 26 to Thursday December 29 1687**
Thomas Cory, a Soldier in Major Nott's Company, in Colonel Tufton's Regiment, of middle stature, aged 22 thick lip'd, goes awker'd with his Legs, a brown bob Periwig, a sad coloured cloth Coat lined with Red, Run from his Colours at North Yarmouth on the 18th Instant, and took with him a Sorrel Nag of adjutant Bromes, all his Linen, and divers other things. The said nag is about 14 hands, new bob'd, a malender on one leg, rough coated and untrim'd, about 7 years old, trots all. Whoever secures the said man or horse and gives Notice to Mr. Richards at the Queens Head in North Yarmouth, or to Mr. Aiskell Agent to the said Regiment, in Sidney street, Leicester-fields, shall be well Rewarded.

London Gazette **Numb 2317, From Monday January 30 to February 2 1687**
One Charles Lucas in a Red Coat lin'd with Yellow, well sett, middle stature, a mold on one side of his Face, about 28 years of age, Soldier in Capt. George Rook's Company in his Royal Highness Prince George of Denmark's Regiment of Foot, after committing a Robbery at Maidstone, deserted his colours the 15th Instant. Whoever causes him to be apprehended, upon Notice given to Mr. Deavoir at the Silver Ball in the Pall-Mall, or to the said Capt. Rooke at his Quarters in Maidstone, shall have two Guinea's reward, and reasonable charges.

London Gazette **Numb 2320, From Thursday February 9 to Monday February 13 1687**
Run away the 30th last past, from Captain Wharton's Company, in the Right Honourable the Earl of Litchfield's Regiment of Foot, James Lock, an Irish Man, of a middle stature, aged about 20, thin visag'd, fair lank hair, a brown coloured Coat. Whoever gives Notice of him to Captain Wharton at the White Hart Inn in Southwark, shall have two Guinea's Reward.

London Gazette **Numb 2328, From Thursday March 8 to Monday March 12 1687**
One Zechariah Pickford, a Soldier in Captain John Port's Company, a Scowrer by Trade, lately living in a Paved Alley near St. James's House, is gone away with a Cantoon grey Cloth Bed, and severall other Goods; he is mark'd with the small Pox, grizled light brown Hair, a down look, and long Nose, wearing lightish coloured Frieze Coat, red Wastecoat with black Buttons. Whoever gives Notice of him to Mr. Rowland Pearce a Silk Dyer in St. Alban's-street near St. James' Market, shall have 2 Guinea's Reward, or can give intelligence where the said Bed is, shall have one Guinea Reward, besides what Monies it is sold or pawn'd for.

London Gazette Numb **2341, From Monday April 23 to Thursday April 26 1688**
Peter Reynolds, about 25 years of Age, of an indifferent stature, small featur'd, wearing his own short lank brown Hair, in a grey coat lin'd with black. And Tho. Watkins, about 23 years of Age, ruddy Complexion, fair spoken, wearing his own black Hair inclined to curl, by Trade a Shoe-maker; run away from Captain Booth's Company, in the Regiment of the Honourable Colonel Cornwall. Whoever can give notice of either of them to Captain boot at Carlisle, or to Mr. Roger Syzer at the Pay-Office at the Horse guards over-against Whitehall, shall have a Guinea Reward for each, and reasonable charges.

London Gazette **Numb 2343, From Monday April 30 to Thursday May 3 1688**
Stephen Gellor, a Man of middle stature, with a light brown Periwig, a Fleming born. Who for a short time served as a Corporal in the Troop of Horse commanded by the Honourable Bernard Howard of Norfolk, and was commanded by him not to leave his Quarters till another Corporal was sent to take his place, Cloaths, &c. went away from thence on or about the 14th past by Day break unknown to any Officer of the said troop, and took with him all the Kings Arms except his Carbine, and such Cloaths and Horse Accoutrements as Corporals use upon Duty, and a Grey Gelding about 15 hands high. Whoever gives Notice of him, so as that he, or what he carried away with him, may be secured, to the Officer commanding the said Troop, at his Quarters at Coventry, shall be very well Rewarded.

London Gazette **Numb 2351, From Monday May 28 to Thursday May 31 1688**
Henry Greenwood, a tall thin Man, with lank brown Hair, and Richard Sheaf, a short thick Man with brown Hair, both of Colchester. Run away from Capt. Studds Company, in the Honourable Col. Hales's Regiment of Foot, from their Quarters at Teddington. Whoever shall seize the said Persons, so as they shall be secured, shall have a Guinea for each of them, with their Charges; upon giving notice thereof to the said captain Studd, at his Quarters at Teddinton, near Kingston upon Thames, or to Mr. Daniel Studd at Colchester.

London Gazette **Numb 2364, From Thursday July 12 to Monday July 16 1688**
Philip Rogers of a middle size, dark brown lank Hair, a swarthy Complexion, full Face and shoulders; and John Malters, of middle size, sandy Hair, indifferent long, of a whitely Complexion, and thin Fac'd; Both Soldiers in Lieutenant Colonel Bellasis's Company in his Majesties Second Regiment of Foot guards, Commanded by the Earl of craven, and are run from their Colours. Whoever gives notice of them at the Tile yard at Whitehall, shall have a Guinea.

On James Pringle, tall, raw bon'd, swarthy Complexion, lank brown Hair, aged 28 born neir Leath in Scotland, Run from his Colours out of the Company of Sir Geo. Barkeley in Sir Edward Hales's Regiment at Plimouth. His Coat Red Lined with red. Whoever secures him, or causes him to be secured, and gives Notice to Mr. William Wallis in Sherwood street near the Golden square, shall receive two Guinea's.

London Gazette **Numb 2371, From Monday August 6 to Thursday August 9 1688**
Lately Run away from Capt. Cranford's Company in his Royal Highness Prince George of Denmark's Regiment of Foot with all their Cloathing, Red Coats lined with Yellow, dark grey Breeches, white Stockings, Hats laced

with a broad gold coloured Lace, &c. John Reeves, a Kentish man, near Sandwich middle sized, lank brown hair, freckled, aged about 24. John Taylor a Kentish man near Ashford, a proper slender Fellow, dark brown hair, about 27. Sam. Cowling a Yorkshire man, a squat bow-legged squinting Fellow, almost blind of one Eye, about 30. And Will. Ross a Scots man, much Pock-broken, lank brown hair, aged about 35. and has commonly a sore leg. Whoever secures any of them and gives Notice to Mr. Richard Beauvoir Esq; at the Silver ball in the Pall-Mall, or to Capt. Cranford at Sheerness Fort, or his Lieutenant at Rochester, shall have 2 Guineas Reward for each man.

London Gazette **Numb 2372, From Thursday August 9 to Monday August 13 1688**
Lately Run away from Capt. Crauford's Company, in his Royal Highness Prince George of Denmark's Regiment of Foot with all their Cloathing, Red Coats lined with Yellow, dark grey Breeches, white Stockings, Hats laced with a broad Gold coloured Lace, &c. James Forbus, a Scots-Man, a very lusty young Fellow, much freckled, and reddish lank hair. Alex MacCleland, a Scots-Man, about 20, a little clear fresh coloured Man, bright well curling Hair. Tho. Sample, a Scots-Man, by Trade a Taylor, a proper well shap'd Man, much freckled, black curling Hair, and aged about 25. Whoever secures any of them, upon Notice give to Mr. Richard Beauvoir Esq; at the Silver ball in the Pall-Mall, or to Capt. Crauford at Sheerness Fort, or his Lieutenant at Rochester, shall have 2 Guinea's Reward for each.

London Gazette **Numb 2376, From Thursday August 23 to Monday August 27 1688**
Lately Run away from Capt. Crauford's Company, in his Royal Highness Prince George of Denmark's Regiment of Foot with all their Cloathing, Red Coats lined with Yellow, dark grey Breeches, white Stockings, Hats laced with a broad Gold coloured Lace, &c. Tho. Carmichal, a Scots-Man, about 22, middle siz'd, very clear complexion'd, whittish Hair, and squints very much. Andrew Christy, a Scots-Man, about 28, a lusty proper Fellow, with very short light coloured Hair. James Anderson, a Scots-Man, about 20, a slender Fellow, much freckled, with nasty lank reddish Hair. John Merry, a Yorkshire man, middle siz'd, much pock-broken and freckled, aged about 30. Whoever secures any of them, upon Notice give to Mr. Richard Beauvoir Esq; at the Silver ball in the Pall-Mall, or to Capt. Crauford at Sheerness Fort, or his Lieutenant at Rochester, shall have 2 Guinea's Reward for each.

London Gazette **Numb 2379, From Monday September 3 to Thursday September 6 1688**
Run lately from Captain George Rooke's Company in his Royal Highness Prince George of Denmark's Regiment of Foot, Walter Finley, a Scotch man, in a Frock, a tall well proportion'd man, some Freckles in his Face, about 30 years old; and Robert Burnet, a Scotch man, in a Red Coat lined with yellow, middle sized, fair hair and Complexion, about 26 years old. Whoever secures both or either of them, and gives notice thereof to Mr. Richard Beauvoir at the Silver ball in the Pall-mall, shall have 2 Guineas Reward for each, and Charges.

London Gazette **Numb 2385, From Monday September 24 to Thursday September 27 1688**
Whereas Robert Louther, a thick short man, aged near 60, of a ruddy Complexion, ran lately from Sir Charles Hamilton's Troop in the Lord Galmoy's Regiment of Horse in Ireland, with a light grey Coat with brass buttons, and lined with red, a black Hat laced with a Galoom a Buff Shoulder-belt, and the King's Arms, carabin, Pistols, and Sword, and a squat light grey Horse, about 15 hands; he is supposed to be come from England or Scotland. Whoever secures him with his Horse, Arms, and Accoutrements, and gives notice to Mr. Tho. Palmer, Agent of the said Regiment at Dublin, or to Mr. Hugh Rod, Mercer in the City of Hereford, shall have 5 Guineas Reward, with reasonable Charges.

London Gazette **Numb 2388, From Thursday October 4 to Monday October 8 1688**
Robert Edwards, Corporal of Horse belonging to Captain Doughty, a fat portly Man, about 6 foot high, with a brown Mole and a Scar near the right side of his Mouth, in a brown Cloth Coat, and a blue Wastecoat with Silver fringe down before and at his Sleeves, full faced, thick Legs, brown short Hair, and sometimes wears a brown Wig, aged about 34, hath been absent from his Colours since the first of this Instant, with a considerable Sum of

the King's Money in his Custody. Whoever secures him and gives Notice to his said Captain at his House in York Buildings, or to Mr. Benj. Richards at the Custom House, shall have 20 l. Reward.

London Gazette **Numb 2390, From Thursday October 11 to Monday October 15 1688**
Robert Edwards, Corporal of Horse in Captain Doughty's Troop, a tall portly Man, about 6 Foot high, with a brown Mole and a Scar on the right side of his Mouth, having been absent from his Colours since the first-instant, with a considerable Sum of the King's Money in his Custody. These are to give Notice that if he doth forthwith repair to his Captain, he shall have reasonable time to adjust his Accompts, and for payment of what he shall be found Debtor; but if he does not whoever gives Notice of him, so that he be secured, to his said Captain at his House in York Buildings, or to Mr. Benjamin Richards at the Custom House, shall have a Reward of Twenty Pounds.

London Gazette **Numb 2393, From Monday October 22 to Thursday October 25 1688**
Robert Edwards, Corporal of Horse in Captain Doughty's Troop, a tall portly Man, about 6 Foot high, with a brown Mole and a Scar on the right side of his Mouth, having been absent from his Colours since the first-instant, with a considerable Sum of the King's Money in his Custody. These are to give Notice, That if he doth forthwith repair to his Captain, he shall have reasonable time to adjust his Accompts, and for payment of what he shall be found Debtor; but if he does not whoever gives Notice of him, so that he be secured, to his said Captain at his House in York Buildings, or to Mr. Benjamin Richards at the Custom House, shall have a Reward of Twenty Pounds.

London Gazette **Numb 2395, From Monday October 29 to Thursday November 1 1688**
One John D'Petepass run away from his Quarters the 28th of September, from Sir William Villers Troop, which is quartered at Riply in Surrey; he is a short fellow, wears a Perriwig, his Face all spotted with Gun-Powder; he took with him his Horse, which is a brown bay Gelding, no white about him, about 15 hands high. Whoever gives Notice of him to Sir William Villers in the Mews, shall have a Guinea Reward.

London Gazette **Numb 2402, From Monday November 19 to Thursday November 22 1688**
Henry Mason, a tall well-set Man, with dark brown hair, a large red Nose, a wide Mouth, talks much, a Bricklayer by Trade, ran away from his Colours in Sir James Phelyppes his Troop of Dragoons, in Her Royal Highness the Princess Anne of Denmarks Regiment, the ninth of this instant November at night. Whoever shall secure him, and give Notice of him at Sir James Phelyppes his House in Downing-street in Westminster, shall have Thirty Shillings Reward.

London Gazette **Numb 2407, From Monday December 3 to Thursday December 6 1688**
A Soldier in Captain Cornwall's Troop, being a well set Man, strong made, but short, light frizled Hair, about 30 years of Age; went away the first instant, at Night from the Golden-Lyon in St. John's street, London, and took with him a black Gelding, near 15 hands, his Main half shorn, brown Muzzle, a large Star in his Forehead, the Saddle blue Velvet, with Silver Twist, new Holster-Caps of the same, and several wearing Cloathes and Linnen with some Chirugeon's Instruments. Whoever gives Notice of him to Mr. Baily Poulterer at Charing-Cross, or at the Golden Lyon aforesaid, shall have 2 Guinea's Reward..

Appendix XI

The de Velde Drawing at the National Army Museum[1]

The Press Release from the National Army Museum, January 2004

'An important Old Master drawing by Dutch artist Willem van de Velde the Elder purchased by the *National Army Museum* is the first drawing in the museum's collection to go on permanent display in the public galleries.

The drawing, a contemporary pen and ink depiction of one of the earliest formal musterings of the British Army during the 1680s, is extremely fragile and would be damaged by continued exposure to light. A specially designed case has been constructed to enable the drawing to be displayed while protecting it from prolonged glare. Fibre optics bring out all the details and the depiction now seems to glow, while timed lighting and filters minimise the risk.

The drawing was purchased for £110,000 with grants of £42,500 from both the National Art Collections Fund (Art Fund) and the Heritage Lottery Fund (HLF).

The picture is beautifully detailed and conveys a strong sense of occasion and the sheer presence of the massed regiments of the King's infantry drawn up and paraded under their colours,' said Jenny Spencer-Smith, Head of Fine Art at the museum. 'It's of great historical significance as an eyewitness record of one of the earliest musterings of the British Army. It's also the only visual record of the reviews of the 1680s to remain in this country. We're delighted to have received support from the Art Fund and HLF in securing such an important Old Master drawing for the nation.'

---

[1] This appendix is based on a paper by the author originally published in *Arquebusier*, vol. XXVIII, No. 1, 2004.

Willem van de Velde the Elder and his Drawings of Hounslow Heath

Willem van de Velde the Elder (1611–1693) is best known as a maritime painter. Born into a naval family tradition, Willem was the son of a naval captain, and whilst one brother followed a career as a merchant skipper, another became a well-respected draughtsman and painter.[2] Willem himself spent part of his youth as a sailor before devoting himself to the drawing and painting of ships. His pictures, which are frequently grisailles, are detailed and faithfully accurate portrayals of ships and, as such, are greatly valued by naval historians – for a time Willem was even an official artist to the Dutch fleet. Nonetheless, in 1672, during the Third Dutch War when the Netherlands were at war with England, Willem and his family moved to London and entered the service of Charles II;[3] why he left his country at a critical moment in its fortunes remains a mystery.

In 1674 Charles II granted Willem the Elder and Willem the Younger an annual '*retaining fee*' of £100 each; the father 'for taking and making draughts of seafights' and the son '*for putting the said draughts into colours for our own particular use*'. The father and son partnership did not switch their allegiance to England completely however since both subsequently painted pictures of naval battles for the Dutch as well as the English market. Overall though it was Willem the Younger's influence which was to prove particularly powerful in England, where the later tradition of maritime painting has had its origins attributed to him.

Although Willem the Elder is best known as a maritime artist, he was present at least two of the annual Hounslow Heath camps that were instituted by James II, those of 1687 and 1689. Drawings of these two events, dated and titled, are in the collection of the *Museum Boijmans Van Beuningen* in Rotterdam. The 1687 ones are of particular interest, showing the 're-enactment' of the siege of Buda in great detail, from both inside and outside of the recreated fortifications.

Willem Van de Velde the Elder died at his house in Sackville Street, London, in December 1693 aged 82; he was buried at St James's Piccadilly on the 16th/26th of the same month. That he was still working right up to his death is evidenced by a signed drawing, which carries a date of 1693 in de Velde's own hand.[4]

Prior to its purchase by the *National Army Museum*, the drawing under consideration here appears to have been unknown and whilst the subject is obvious (the viewing platform, geography, etc. all conform with the site

---

2 Jan van de Velde (1593–1641). Jan's son, Jan Jansz van de Velde (1620–63) also followed the family tradition specialising in still life paintings.

3 Including his two artist sons Willem van de Velde the Younger (1633–1707), who was to outshine his father as a painter of maritime subjects, and Adriaen van de Velde (1636–1672) who specialised in more tranquil landscapes.

4 *Van de Velde Drawings: A Catalogue of drawings in the National Maritime Museum made by the Elder and the Younger Willem van de Velde* (Cambridge: Cambridge University Press for the trustees of the National Army Museum, 1958). My thanks to Jenny Spencer-Smith of the National Army Museum for this information.

The de Velde Drawing (part 2)

The de Velde Drawing (part 1)

© The National Army Museum

English 'battalion' of five or six companies. © The National Army Museum

and to the other 'Hounslow Drawings'), it carries neither title nor date. The drawing could therefore have been made at any of the Hounslow Camps from 1685 to 1689, although those of 1687 and 1688 would seem the most likely, since it can be confirmed that Willem the Elder was present on both occasions from the dates on the drawings in the *Museum Boijmans Van Beuningen* collection.

Dating the Drawing

The key to the dating of the drawing is that as well as the English battalions (identifiable by their colours of white with a hatched Cross of St George) and Scots battalions (identifiable by their dark hatched colours with a white saltire) there is a single, identifiably Irish battalion,[5] with white colours and a dark hatched saltire. Within this concept it is necessary first to understand that before March 1688 there were no regiments of the Irish Army establishment in England, thus precluding the 1687 camp as being the subject of this drawing. However between March 1688 and the end of 1689 Irish regiments were in England during the period of two of the annual Hounslow Heath camps and can be identified as actually being on Hounslow Heath itself on a third occasion. Which of these three times was the occasion for de Velde's drawing is, obviously, the key to the dating.

The three possible dates and units represented are:

1. **McElligott's Regiment, June 1688**

---

5   At the extreme right of the drawing.

On 12 March 1688 James commissioned Roger McElligott as colonel of a new regiment; to be raised for the Irish establishment from officers and men of Irish origins obeying the order for the recall of the Anglo–Scots Brigade in Dutch service.

The regiment was to be assembled and mustered in Chester and throughout the summer and autumn of 1688 the *Orders for the Marching and Moving of Forces*[6] gives a number of movement orders for small groups of 15–30 officers and men to go from London to the regiment's garrison in Chester. Additionally the same document contains fairly complete movement orders throughout mid and late June for all of the regiments ordered to attend the Hounslow Heath camp and McElligott's is not included in these.

The fact that the regiment, the only Irish regiment in England at the time, still had recruits being sent to it at Chester in June and July, together with its omission from *Orders for the Marching and Moving of Forces* to move to Hounslow, rules out the drawing as being of the June 1688 Hounslow Heath camp.

Some additional reinforcing evidence that McElligott's was not at Hounslow may be assumed from the fact that the regiment *was* ordered from Chester to Salisbury in late October.

(McElligott's was disbanded in January 1689, although the whereabouts of the regiment at the time of its disbandment have yet to come to light.)

2.   Granard's Regiment, October 1688

The Earl of Granard's Regiment was part of the Irish army ordered to England in September 1688 as part of James' preparations for war with the United Provinces. However, of the units brought over, only three were moved to London:[7] Butler's Dragoons, Granard's Foot and the Irish Foot Guards. The first of these, as dragoons, carried guidons not colours and the latter was an English regiment, having been raised in London in 1662, and thus carried English pattern colours utilising the Cross of St George; a tradition, incidentally, they continued when in French service after 1692. Thus, of the three, only Granard's carried colours displaying a red saltire.

On 23 November 1688 Granard's was on Hounslow Heath,[8] as was the Scots Guards, and a number of other units had been ordered to the capital (although not specifically to Hounslow). The evidence is that these latter units were simply 'garrisoned' within the confines of the city.

There is, however, no mention of any additional units being moved to Hounslow,[9] or of any review or establishment of any 'camp' in the form of previous arrangements. Thus it would seem unlikely that October/November 1688 could form the subject of de Velde's drawing, since this shows English regiments, as well as Scots and Irish and also shows a somewhat formal affair with a viewing stand, Yeomen of the Guard, etc. Furthermore there is no

---

6   National Archives, Kew, WO5/3.
7   *Ibid.*, f.279, warrant dated 19 October 1688.
8   National Archives, Kew, WO5/4, f. 14., warrant of that date, confirmed by several others over the next few days.
9   In either the National Archives, Kew WO5/3, or WO5/4.

Screens of shot to the sides and front of the pike. © The National Army Museum

evidence that James II was present on Hounslow Heath at this time and the portrayal of units like the Yeoman of the Guard dictate the presence of the sovereign in person.

3. Meath's Regiment, August 1689

Note: this is the regiment that had been Granard's (aka 'Fforbes') in 1688.[10] It was the only regiment to escape the wholesale disbandment of the Irish army in January 1689, and was the only Irish regiment in England throughout the period under consideration here, and thus the only regiment to carry colours displaying the Cross of St Patrick.

On 19 January 1689 the regiment was stripped of its Catholic officers and men, who were sent to the Isle of Wight,[11] the remainder of the regiment was sent to Stevenage, Buntingford, Baldock, Royston and Barkway.[12] Thereafter throughout 1689 Meath's followed the usual practice of moving constantly around the country and, after a number of movements, arrived in Shrewsbury in early July.[13] National Archives piece WO5/5, which covers the period up to 28 February 1690, thereafter has no further entries for Meath's (although it should be noted that the surviving records for 1689 are very incomplete when compared to those for 1686 and 1687).

---

10   It became Meath's on 1 May 1689.
11   National Archives, Kew, WO5/5, f. 40. All those concerned were to be disarmed before leaving the regiment.
12   *Ibid.*, f. 50, warrant dated 16 January.
13   *Ibid.*, f. 176, warrant dated 4 July directing Meath's to march from 'Ruthin, St Asaph and Holy Well' to Shrewsbury.

Meath's Regiment. © The
National Army Museum

On 11 August 1689 there was a major assemblage of regiments on Hounslow Heath for the 'Annual Camp'. Although there are a number of references to this camp in *Orders for the Marching and Moving of Forces*[14] these orders are not complete – for example there are no orders for the movement of any of the regiments of Foot Guards to Hounslow, although from another of de Velde's drawings we know that at least the First Regiment was at the camp.[15] Even regiments moving the relatively short distance from London to Hounslow are covered by 'Orders for Marching'.[16]

Meath's was not in the list of regiments that Schomberg mustered in the camp at Whitehaven on 11 August (coincidentally the same day as the opening of the annual Hounslow Camp),[17] and therefore could well have been at Hounslow on that day, although no documents so far conclusively prove it to have been so.

Conclusion

When Meath's left England for Ireland at the end of August there was not another Irish regiment in England for at least two years (I have not looked later than the end of 1691), so since I would definitely rule out both 1. and 2. above for the reasons given, we are left with the most likely being 3., that the de Velde drawing shows the camp of the 11th/12th August 1689, and that the regiment in question is that of the Earl of Meath – the later 18th Foot, 'The Royal Irish'.

---

14 *Ibid.*, WO5/5.

15 In Rotterdam there is a drawing with a titling, probably in de Velde's own hand, which reads 'The Arrival of the First Regiment of Foot Guards on Hounslow Heath, 11th August 1690'.

16 *Ibid.*, f. 215, a copy of a warrant dated 11 August ordering two unnamed regiments to march from the Tower to the Hounslow camp.

17 *Ibid.*, f. 214. According to *The London Gazette* these regiments sailed for Ireland on 12 August.

Military Aspects of the Drawing

An immediately noticeable aspect of the drawing is that the units shown by de Velde are not the 13 company regiments of the time but 'battalions' of five or six companies as shown by the number of colours carried by each body (see close-up of the English 'battalion', p. 185). This would make each of these battalions between 300 and 400 strong all ranks, an unusually small size for such units,[18] *but* interestingly the same size of battalion as James II sent west in 1685 to put down the rising by the Duke of Monmouth.[19]

Some further confirmation that this may have been the usual size for a battalion at this period can also be taken from a contemporary account of James II's army at the Hounslow Heath camp of 1686 which records:

The 1st Battalion [of the 1st Foot Guards] 7 Companies, one of them grenadiers

The King's 3d battalion [of the 1st Foot Guards] 6 Companies

Earl of Craven's 1st battalion [2nd Foot Guards] 6 Companies half grenadiers[20]

1st battalion of Scotch Guards 7 Companies'[21]

The formations that the battalions are in is also of interest. The pike are universally in the centre of each group flanked by the shot, *but* there appears to be an additional screen of shot several ranks deep across the front of the pike as well – somewhat reminiscent of the traditional 'Spanish Tercio formation' of the 16th and 17th centuries. It is, of course, difficult to be pedantic on these formations – that they are what de Velde actually saw seems certain but whether they are combat or marching formations is less certain. My hypothesis is that what is seen here are marching and manoeuvring formations rather than anything of use in combat. Thus I would surmise that the pikemen may be surrounded by the more flexible musketeers perhaps to protect them against surprise.

The English battalion in the centre of the drawing is undoubtedly in the traditional battlefield manoeuvre column with pike in the centre and shot front and back. A simple halt, and right or left turn of this formation puts it into the accepted combat formation of the time, pike in the centre flanked by shot – although here the shot will be maybe 10 ranks deep.

Although there are a number of mounted officers (although they could equally well be aides) around the battalions, it seems fairly obvious that

---

18 The English battalions that fought at the battle of the Dunes in 1658 were 500–600 strong and French battalions of that and later periods are calculated at about the same strength. Note: 'battalions' here refers to the combat formations, *not* the administrative ones.

19 cf. the order of battle of James II's army given in *The Army of James II: Uniforms and Organisation*, Stephen Ede-Borrett (Leeds, 1986), Appendix 5. In this case the First Foot Guards may perhaps be considered as two 'battalions', although it is, of course, equally possible that this is not coincidentally about half of each of the regular regiments.

20 That is, a half company of grenadiers, *not* half of the six companies being grenadiers.

21 All other regiments of foot are present in 10, 11, or 12 company strength. *A LIST of KING JAMES's Army on Hounslow Heath ... June 30th, 1686*. Printed in *The Antiquarian Repertory*, Volume 1: Francis Grose and Thomas Astle (compilers), London, 1807, pp. 229–232.

control is coming from the half-pike armed officers on foot, who are around the periphery of the bodies. It is possible, of course, that these individuals are in fact sergeants but that would beg the question as to where are the officers? Especially as one would expect to see these fairly prominently displaying their presence to their King and Captain General. These detached individuals also seem generally too relaxed to be mere sergeants – witness the two standing, apparently talking, at the right rear of what I hypothesise is Meath's, and a similar group at the left front of the extreme left-hand battalion. Also of great interest here is the officer at the right flank of Meath's pushing the private soldiers into their ranks by using his levelled half-pike, or maybe he is merely dressing the ranks.

The colours are, in all cases, situated in the front of the pike formation, exactly where contemporary military theorists said that they should be. It would be interesting to know what their actual position was when in combat, but with 12 feet or more of pike in front of them, a similar position even in action would not seem particularly unsafe.

Colour Plate Commentaries

Portraits

Plate P1

King James II in the Uniform of a General Officer *c*.1686. Godfrey Kneller, Oil on Canvas, National Army Museum London Collection, NAM, Reproduced With Permission.

This painting has already been discussed in outline in the main body of the text under 'General Officers'. As mentioned it is actually an anachronism to speak of a true 'general officer's uniform', since there were no regulations governing their dress, but James's appearance here is certainly indicative of how such men must have appeared, and probably many colonels would also have appeared similarly. There is evidence that generals and senior field officers vied with each other in the 'sparkishness' of their appearance.

Noteworthy in this portrait is the hue of the blue facings, this is the same as the blue of the sash of the Order of the Garter that the King wears and is distinctly lighter and brighter than the 'royal blue' of later periods but confirms the Duke of Tuscany's statement quoted above. The gold military scarf is unusual and whether this reflects common military use is unclear, although it is not dissimilar to the scarf worn by the Duke of Monmouth in Jan van Wyck's portrait in the National Gallery (painted *c*.1678), which is also gold without evidence of any 'colour'. As an aside it is worth mentioning that this latter portrait, again of a 'general officer' shows a broadly similar uniform, albeit that Monmouth's cuffs are white as opposed to the blue of the King's.

The background shown below the King's outstretched right arm probably represents one of the annual camps on Hounslow Heath and thus the painting was almost certainly executed in 1686 or 1687 (the Museum says '*c*.1686'), certainly the overall structure of this background is in line with the contemporary engravings of the Camp which appear to have been so popular.

The armour on the floor is purely a decorative addition and does not represent that in use by James, or his army.

Plate P2

Captain Francis Hawley of the First Royal Regiment of Foot Guards, 1685. Oil on Canvas, ©Private Collection, Reproduced With Permission.

This was first noted by C. Field in the *Journal of the Society for Army*

Historical Research,[1] and then later in great depth by William Carman in the same journal in 1985.[2] It is, therefore quite well known but the scarcity of its subject, a late-17th century company officer, justifies its inclusion.

Although the artist is unknown the portrait is inscribed in the lower right corner:

Coll. Fr. Hawley. 1685

Although this inscription must have been added later as in 1685 Hawley was only a captain. He had been commissioned as a captain in the Duke of Monmouth's Regiment of Foot on 1 May 1678 (the captain of grenadiers in the same Regiment was Thomas Hawley – a number of members of the family served in the army in the 17th and 18th centuries). On 14 July 1680 he transferred into the First Regiment of Foot Guards as a lieutenant under Captain George Bowes, and in November 1684 he was promoted captain of grenadiers in the same regiment, with which he served in the Monmouth Rebellion and was present at both Norton St Philip and Sedgemoor. On 17 July[3] Hawley was promoted major of the newly raised Princess Anne of Denmark's Regiment of Dragoons, becoming lieutenant colonel of the same regiment when it was recommissioned on 31st December 1688. Hawley was killed at Steenkirk on 29 July 1692 as lieutenant colonel commanding the regiment in the absence of its colonel, Lord Fitzhardinge. Since the inscription refers to Hawley as 'Coll.' It must have been added post-1688 ,although there is no doubt that it portrays Hawley as a captain of grenadiers under James II. Hawley left a widow and four children; Edward, his second son, was commissioned cornet in his late father's regiment on 1 August 1692 at the age of six! Hawley's eldest son, Henry, became an ensign in the regiment of foot of his father's half-brother Brigadier General Thomas Erle in January 1694 at the comparatively veteran age of nine. Hawley's widow, Judith née Hughes, received a gratuity of £40 from William III in late 1699 or early 1700, although whether this was repeated annually does not appear.

Many details of this portrait have already been discussed in the main body of the text, but it is worth noting the light blue belts, cuffs and even bayonet scabbard, all embroidered in gold. The fact that Hawley is carrying a plug bayonet suggests that he had been armed with a musket, or just possibly a carbine. Whether he was actually armed with grenades is somewhat contentious although not impossible. Interestingly there is no evidence that Hawley carries a sword. The lack of gorget is probably simply accounted for by his armament if a musket and (possibly) grenades – the use of both of which would have been impeded by the large gorget of the period.

1 C. Short, 'Uniform of a Grenadier Officer in the Army of JamesII', in *Journal of the Society for Army Historical Research*, Vol. X (1932), p. 55.
2 William Carman, 'Frances Hawley, First Regiment of Foot Guards 1685', in *Journal of the Society for Army Historical Research*, Vol. LXIII (1985).
3 William Mathews was commissioned as his replacement in the First Foot Guards on 26 July.

Alan Guy speculates that the 'action' which appears behind Hawley's left shoulder may refer to something from his service in Tangier,[4] but I would suggest that since the portrait seems to celebrate Hawley's service during the Monmouth Rebellion (after all, it has to have been painted between James' accession on 24th February 1685 and Hawley's transfer to Princess Anne of Denmark's Regiment of Dragoons on 17th July – or perhaps slightly later, if it indeed celebrates his actions during the Rebellion) this 'action' almost certainly represents either an unrecorded minor skirmish during the Rebellion or quite simply just a fantasy to enlighten the whole painting.

Plate P3

An Unknown Captain of The Earl of Bath's Regiment of Foot, c.1685/6. Oil on Canvas, Private Collection. ©Author's Photo

Unlike the well known portrait of Captain Francis Hawley of the Foot Guards discussed by William Carman in the *Journal of the Society for Army Historical Research* in 1985,[5] and in this work above, this portrait has generally passed unnoticed by historians, although it was discussed in the same journal in a short essay by the current author in 2010.[6] Because of its comparative obscurity I have taken this opportunity to give more details than perhaps otherwise necessary.

In direct contrast to the Hawley portrait both the sitter and artist of the portrait are currently unknown, although there appears to be a thin 'spidery' signature visible beneath the layers of dirt and varnish that the portrait has acquired over its life. This signature is just about visible on the illustration here, unfortunately it is illegible.[7] The heavy overlay of varnish is probably also responsible for the 'yellow' effect on the flesh tones as well as the overall darkness of the picture.

The painting is approximately 54 by 36 inches and has suffered some damage – there appears to be a repaired tear visible to the right of the sitter's shoulder and some further, unrepaired or at best poorly repaired, damage below his right cuff.[8]

The officer is portrayed within an 'oval' contrivance, composed of two drums at each of the lower corners, a cannon barrel along the bottom and drapery across the top and down the upper sides. The drums and cannon are obviously intended solely as a composition of this oval since they are not in scale either with the sitter or with each other. The drapery, however, is rather odd in that it goes across the top of the sitter's captain's half-pike, the tip of

---

4   *1688 Glorious Revolution : The Fall and Rise of the British Army 1660–1704* (London: National Army Museum, 1988), p. 48.

5   William Carman, 'Frances Hawley, First Regiment of Foot Guards 1685', in *Journal of the Society for Army Historical Research*, Vol. LXIII (1985).

6   Stephen Ede-Borrett, 'A Captain of the Earl of Bath's Regiment', in *Journal of the Society for Army Historical Research, Spring 2010* (2010).

7   It is to be hoped that eventually the painting might be cleaned and repaired, in which case the artist may well become known (if indeed this script is a signature) and further information might then become available.

8   All references to 'right' and 'left' are taken from the sitter's position not the viewer's, so as to prvent any confusion between the sitter's 'right hand' and the viewer's perception of the same.

which is just visible through it, suggesting that perhaps the full drapery was not part of the original composition. A secondary piece of evidence that this drapery may have been added later is the conflict in its perspective with that of the half-pike; whilst, as mentioned, the drapery is 'in front' of the half-pike, and thus obscures its point, in all other aspects it is well behind the sitter, a contradiction that does not sit well when the painting is examined in detail.

The putative signature mentioned above is on the upper skin of one of the drums in the left corner. It is possible that there is a device on the front of one or more of the drums that form the border, but this area is so dark that no details can be discerned.[9] By the officer's right hand is an idyllic rolling landscape, almost ubiquitous in portraits of this period. A low balustrade, just visible below the subject's right cuff, runs across the picture behind the sitter. The landscape contains no military detail of encampments or fortifications.

Although there is no attribution on the painting, nor any coat of arms or badge from which the officer can be identified, there are clues in the painting to the rank and regiment of the sitter.

The weapon in the officer's left hand is a simple half-pike, the weapon of an officer of a foot regiment. Whilst the length of a half pike could, from contemporary illustrations, be anywhere between six and nine feet, although around seven feet, as here, appears most common. The gorget is often stated to be the last piece of armour deriving from the medieval period, to remain in use, and whilst this statement is inaccurate (that honour must surely go to the helmet[10]), in this instance it is the gorget that indicates the officer's rank as well as giving some guidance as to the date of the picture.

As cited in the main body of the text, in September 1684 Charles II issued a Royal Warrant concerning the colour of "Corseletts" for officers of foot :-

For the better distinction of Our Severall Officers serving Us in Our Companies of Foot, Our will and pleasure is, That all Captains of Foot wear no other Corselett than of the Colour of Gold, all Lieutenants black Corseletts studded with Gold. And the Ensigns Corseletts of silver. And Wee do likewise think fitt, that all Lieutenants of Foot, Carry Pikes and not Partizans, which We do hereby Order to be Redelivered into the Office of Our Ordnance. And Wee do further direct that authentique Copies hereof be sent to Our severall Colonells of Foot and transmitted to the Governors of Our Forts and Garrisons, To the end that the Respective Officers of Our Forces may Govern themselves accordingly.

Given at Our Court at Winchester the First day of September 1684.[11]

Although the term 'corselett' most often meant a full cuirass, or 'back and breast' in contemporary parlance, in this warrant it referred to the gorget

---

9 As mentioned in the text it appears that Colonels often (or even customarily?) put their coat of arms and/or family heraldic badges on their regiment's drums, thus anything that could be seen on the drum's face would help confirm the conjecture of the sitter's unit.

10 The gorget has long since disappeared from the British Army, whilst the helmet has never fallen into disuse.

11 The National Archives, WO5/1, ff. 88–89.

worn at this period only by officers. Clearly the sitter in this painting must have held the rank of captain as shown by his gilded gorget.

The warrant was certainly observed during James II's reign and perhaps even into the early part of that of William III, although it had fallen into obsolescence by the late 1690s, and thus provides a guide to the dating of the painting. From this evidence the portrait was painted between 1684 and c.1695. The shape of the gorget itself, however, is of the old, fuller style favoured in the reigns of Charles II and James II and is significantly different to that shown by C. C. P. Lawson as dating from the reign of William III,[12] which suggests a date towards the earlier part of the above decade.

In turning to consideration of the captain's regiment perhaps the most significant and most apparent aspect is, of course, the blue coat in place of the more usual red one. Whilst a blue coat is perhaps unexpected, it is not as unusual as it would at first appear. Of the 15 regiments of foot on the English and Scots establishments at the end of 1685, 13 wore red coats, one wore yellow,[13] but only one wore blue – that of the Earl of Bath. Incidentally whilst a number of the new regiments of foot raised early in William III's reign adopted blue coats,[14] and there are also references to some officers of red-coated regiments taking to wearing blue coats as a 'compliment' to the new king, most of these quickly abandoned blue coats in favour of red; however Bath's is known to have continued wearing this colour clothing until c.1693/4, and it was almost certainly the last regiment to do so.

Clearly visible in the voluminous cuffs is the red facing colour with which, at this period, the entire coat would have been lined, and this colour also shows on the edges of the front opening and as a trimming on the pocket flaps which lie higher than expected immediately beneath the military scarf. The colour is also taken up on what can only be a waistcoat showing immediately below his laced cravat and it may be presumed that his breeches and stockings would have been of the same colour. These details coupled with the very early, indeed archaic, style of the gorget lend great weight to the attribution of the sitter to Bath's Regiment.

Also noteworthy on the coat is the unusual arrangement of 'double buttons' on the cuffs which seem to be simply ostentatious decoration and attributable to personal whim on the part of the officer himself or of the colonel.

---

12 C. C. P. Lawson, *A History of the Uniforms of the British Army*, volume 1, p. 23.

13 Prince George of Denmark's Regiment of Foot, the regiment that had been The Duke of York's regiment prior to his becoming James II. By the end of 1686 this regiment had adopted red coats.

14 See the notes on pp. 76–80 of Lawson's *History of the Uniforms of the British Army*, volume 1. Few, if any, of these regiments appear to have retained the blue coat beyond 1689–90, i.e. a single clothing issue.

Watercolours

The Army of James II. Watercolours by Mark Allen © Helion & Company 2017.

W1: The Regiments of Guards
1 & 2 Standards of the 1st and 3rd troops of Horse Guards

3 King's company colours, the First Regiment of Foot Guards

4 Major's company colours, the First Regiment of Foot Guards
The use of the pile wavy as major's device originated before the English Civil Wars, and is still in use on the colours of the Regiments of Foot Guards today.

5 First Captain's company colours, the First Regiment of Foot Guards
The method of differencing the Colours of the First Regiment of Foot Guards in 1685–1689 is essentially that in use during the English Civil Wars and after, known as the 'Venn System A'.[15] The appearance of the most junior company with 22 devices along the arms of the cross must have been a quite bizarre sight.
6 Lieutenant colonel's company colours, the Second Regiment of Foot Guards
7 Major's company colours, the Second Regiment of Foot Guards
8 1st Captain's colours, the Second Regiment of Foot Guards
9 Major's company colours, the Scots Regiment of Foot Guards
Unlike on English colours there was little use of the pile wavy as the major's device before the Restoration, although as with the other regiments of foot guards it is still in use today.
10 1st Captain's colours, the Scots Regiment of Foot Guards

A Pikeman, the First Regiment of Foot Guards
B Musketeer, the Second Regiment of Foot Guards
C–G The troops of horse guards with details of the troop colours for hatbands, ribbons, etc.

> *1st troop*: blue
> *2nd troop*: green. Under Charles II this troop had been the Queen's Troop; green was the livery colour of the House of Braganza and her regiments of both horse and foot (the Queen Dowager's under James II) had green facings and green standards and colours.
> *3rd troop*: yellow. Under Charles II this troop had been the Duke of York's, although yellow is a livery colour of the House of Stuart it seems to have been a favourite colour of James II who, as Duke of York, had also clothed his regiment of foot in yellow coats. The

---

15 See this author's studies and forthcoming work on *The Flags of the English Civil Wars* in this series.

regiment became Prince George of Denmark's in 1685 when James became king.

4th troop: the coats were red lined blue for all troops.

E Gentleman of the 1st troop

F Horse grenadier of the 1st troop

W2: The Regiments of Horse and Dragoons

1 Standard of the second Captain's Troop of the Royal Regiment of Horse

2 Standard of the Earl of Peterborough's Regiment of Horse

3 Standard of the Earl of Plymouth's Regiment of Horse

4 Standard of the Colonel's troop of the Earl of Thanet's Regiment of Horse

5 Standard of the Colonel's troop of the Earl of Shrewsbury's Regiment of Horse

6 Standard of the Queen Dowager's Regiment of Horse

7 Standard of Princess Anne of Denmark's Regiment of Horse

8 Guidon of the Senior Captain's troop of the Royal Regiment of Dragoons

9 Guidon of Princess Anne of Denmark's Regiment of Dragoons

A Trooper of Princess the Queen Consort's Regiment of Dragoons

B Trooper of the Queen Dowager's Regiment of Horse wearing the back and breast issued for campaign service. Note the belts worn crosswise, considered at this time as indicative of the regiments of horse over the regiments of dragoons, and the buff leather waistcoat just visible at the front of the coat. Troopers of the Earl of Plymouth's Regiment of Horse would have looked almost identical.

C Officer (suggested) of the Earl of Thanet's Regiment of Horse, again shown in back and breast as worn on campaign. The amount of lace worn may have been an indicator of rank as was the case in the Royal Regiment of Horse (see text).

W3: The Regiments of Foot

1 Colours of the Colonel's Company of the Royal Regt. of Foot

    1a Cords and Tassels for all companies of the Regt.

2 Lieutenant Colonel's Company Colours of the Royal Regt. of Foot

3 Major's company colours of the Royal Regt. of Foot

4 Colonel's company colours of the Queen Dowager's Regt. of Foot

5 Lieutenant colonel's company colours of the Queen Dowager's Regt. of Foot

6 First Captain's company colours of the Queen Dowager's Regiment of Foot

7 Colonel's company colours of Prince George of Denmark's Regt. of Foot

8 Colours of the lieutenant colonel's company of Prince George of Denmark's Regt. of Foot

9 Major's and First Captains' company colours of Prince George of Denmark's Regt. of Foot

10 Colonel's company colours of the Holland Regt. of Foot, by June 1686.

11 Lieutenant colonel's company colours of the Holland Regt. of Foot by June 1686

12 Colours the major's company of the Holland Regiment of Foot, by June 1686.

A Pikeman, the Earl of Huntingdon's Regiment of Foot. The colour of the scarf is speculative
B Grenadier of the Queen Dowager's Regiment of Foot
    b1 Another form of Grenadier cap in use in some regiments
C Ensign of the major's company of the Queen Dowager's Regiment of Foot with the company's colours. Note the 'self-lined' coat in place of the regimental green linings as used by some officers
D Musketeer of the Holland Regiment of Foot. The colouring of the powder bottles is speculative

W4: Colours of the Regiments of Foot

1 Colonel's company colours of the Queen Consort's Regt. of Foot, late 1685 issue
2 Lieutenant colonel's company colours of the Queen Consort's Regt. of Foot, late 1685 issue.
3 Colours of the major's company of the Queen Consort's Regt. of Foot, late 1685 issue
4 Colonel's company colours of the Royal Fuzileers Regt. of Foot
5 Lieutenant colonel's company colours of the Royal Fuzileers Regt. of Foot
6 Colonel's company colours of Princess Anne of Denmark's Regt. of Foot
7 Colours of the lieutenant colonel's company of Princess Anne of Denmark's Regt. of Foot
8 Major's company colours of Princess Anne of Denmark's Regt. of Foot
9 Colonel's company colours of Henry Cornwall's Regt. of Foot
10 Lieutenant colonel's company colours of Henry Cornwall's Regt. of Foot. This unique form of the Cross of St George is recorded on only one other English Colours – that of the Faringdon Ward company of the West Regiment of the London Trained Bands in 1588[16]
11 Colours of the lieutenant colonel's company of the Earl of Bath's Regt. of Foot
12 Captains' companies' colours of the Earl of Bath's Regt. of Foot
13 Colours of the lieutenant colonel's company of the Duke of Beaufort's Regt. of Foot
14 Colours of the captain's companies of the Duke of Beaufort's Regt. of Foot
15 Colours of the colonel's company of the Duke of Norfolk's Regt. of Foot
16 Colours of the captains' companies of the Duke of Norfolk's Regt. of Foot
17 Colours of the lieutenant colonel's company of Sir Edward Hales' Regt. of Foot
18 First Captain's company colours of Sir Edward Hales' Regt. of Foot
19 Colours of the major's company of the Scots Fuzileers Regiment of Foot
20 First Captain's company colours of the Scots Fuzileers Regiment of Foot

---

16 Stephen Ede-Borrett, 'English Ensignes in 1588', in *Arquebusier* XXIII/V, London 1989, pp. 20–25.

Reconstructions

With thanks to Alan Larsen

Musician

The musicians of the Royal Dragoons – drummers and 'hautbois' or 'hautboys' players – wore distinctive clothing befitting their responsibilities and status. There is however a dearth of information pertaining to their dress in 1685.

Our assumption is that, as with normal contemporary practice, they wore reversed colours – that is to say blue coats with red cuffs. That was definitely the case by 1708 as we know from correspondence of officers of the Royal Regiment of Dragoons published in the JSAHR. Yellow braid trim is logical, echoing the colours on the 'appointments' of saddle cloth and holster caps. Residual false 'hanging sleeves' are a standard feature and were the practice at least as early as the English Civil Wars, continuing on the sleeves of the musicians of the Household Cavalry today. Hence, whilst the reconstructed livery coat of our drummer is speculative, it does seem a reasonable deduction.

It is probable that, as a Royal Regiment, the musicians, on occasion, wore the very expensive very elaborate gold laced royal livery coats introduced in the reign of Charles II and which remain virtually unchanged to this day as the 'state coats' of the musicians of the Household Cavalry. These however would seem remarkably impractical clothing on campaign for dragoons, and perhaps even for the trumpeters of the Royal Regiment of Horse Guards?

Our drummer's instrument is slung by the 'drag ropes' on his back – a system that works surprisingly well on horseback. Another area of speculative reconstruction is how the drum itself was carried for playing. Earlier in the 17th century and at the time of the English Civil Wars, the drum had been carried on a wide silk sash that also acted as a badge of rank. By the end of the same century the drum was being carried on a shoulder sling across the body in what became the standard modern practice. Chronologically, in between those two systems, a wide-braided cloth neck yoke to take the weight of the drum was in use and this is the method I believe, was that used in 1680s England.

Drum sticks are carried in a trimmed cloth bag which is attached on the right hip to a matching blue and yellow sword belt.

[Drummer's accoutrements by Oireas Historical Services. Thanks to Simon Weir and 'Savannah'. Photo by Ben Luxmoore.]

Trooper

This grizzled veteran – quite possibly a survivor of the Tangier Horse (the regiment returned to England only in late 1684, when it became the Royal regiment of Dragoons) – smokes his pipe in a rare moment of peace during the 1685 campaign.

Of note is the carriage of the 'snaphaunce musquett strapt for dragoons' in one of the 'boots or socketts for ye muskets'.[17] The implementation of this system for re-enactment proved to be straightforward. The boot for the butt and the upper connecting strap around the barrel do hold everything firmly in place, even at the canter. It does take some little time however to unstrap the musket for use and it would seem logical that the weapon was simply carried across the dragoon's back ready for immediate use if combat was imminent.

A pistol butt is visible in the off side pistol holster. Whether a second pistol or a hammer hatchet [small axe] was carried on the saddle in 1685 is a moot point: the hatchet was certainly on issue by 1687[18]. If pistols [essentially a cavalry weapon] were carried in the Monmouth Rebellion by the Royal Dragoons then it was as a legacy of their previous service as cavalry in Tangier.

Of note are the 'housings' [saddle cloth] and holster covers. At a review on Putney Heath in 1684 these were recorded by Nathan Brooks as "embroidered with blue and yellow on red, with the Royal Cipher, holster caps the same, with the Royal Cipher."[19] This description seems pretty straightforward. However what are we to make of 'embroidered with blue and yellow'? We have chosen to interpret this as 'embroidered' meaning enhanced or trimmed for the following reason. In the Household Cavalry Museum is a remarkable and very rare survival – a Royal Dragoons other ranks saddle cloth from the 18th century – which matches, we believe, the 1684 description and is a continuation of the same pattern, albeit with a later pattern badge. The braiding on the edge is royal lace of blue on yellow stripes. Hence we have chosen to trim our reconstructed saddle cloth and holster covers accordingly, with the intertwined 'C' of Charles II's cypher – without an accompanying crown, as contemporary descriptions, including Brooks, specifically mention the addition of 'Royal Cypher and Crown' when that is used.

It is assumed that the four month delay between the death of Charles II and the beginning of Monmouth's Rebellion had not allowed time for the accoutrements of the regiment – housings, drum badges and flags – to have the cipher badge changed, at considerable expense it must be said, to the new King's 'JR'. Certainly the guidons carried by the regiment in the 1685 campaign [as recorded in the Windsor manuscripts] still carried the late King's cypher.

[With thanks to Shaun Fairlie and 'Savannah'. Accoutrements by Peter Bentham Hill. Photograph by Ben Luxmoore.]

---

17   The National Archives, Kew WO47/15 quoted in John Tincey's *Sedgemoor 1685: Marlborough's First Victory*, p. 22.

18   John Tincey, *The British Army 1660–1704* (London: Osprey, 1994).

19   Quoted in Lawson, *A History of the Uniforms of the British Army*.

Bibliography

Manuscript Sources

An Abstract of the Commissioned Officers of His Maties Army in Ireland. National Archives, Kew SP8/1, Part 2 ff. 97–102.

An Account of the Traynes of Artillery Issued out of His Majts Stores …. For the late Expedition against the Rebells in ye West…, Admiral Blake Museum, Bridgwater, Somerset.

Anon. *New Drawings of the Colours and Standards of the British Army: Tempore James II, &c. &c. &c.*, usually known as *The James II Colour Book*. Royal Library, Windsor, RCIN 1083409, 1686.

Buckley, Francis, *Notebook on Military Affairs 1680–1720*. Manuscript, National Army Museum London.

Colours of a Regiment of Foot under Lord Ferrers Colonel. British Library, Add MS 6832.

Cunnington, W. C., *The Military Encampments of James II*. Unpublished typescript dd 1964, Hounslow and District Historical Society, Ref : X.639/80.

Establishment of Guards, Garrisons and Land Forces From 1 January 1685. National Army Museum Mss 6807-143.

Explanation of the Changes which have occurred in the Establishments of the Garrisons from the Earliest War Office Record, Vol. I. National Archives, Kew WO25/3206.

Great Wardrobe Accounts, Royal Archives, Windsor Castle.

Hyde Papers 1664–1743, Vol. VI. British Library Add MS 15897.

Survey of Arms, Stores, Cannon, etc. (Inventory of the Ordnance Office), dated 17th September 1686. National Archives WO55/1730.

The King's Establishment for the Payment of his fforces and Garrisons…, National Archives, Kew SP 8/1 Part 2, ff. 257–259.

King William's Chest. National Archives, Kew.
> July 1670 to July 1688, SP 8/1
> June 15th 1686 to September 17th 1688, SP 8/4

Montagu Army Accounts. British Library Add MSS 10123.

Old Armour Issued out of The Tower. National Archives, Kew WO55/1656.

Orders for the Marching and Moving of Forces. National Archives, Kew.
> Volume I, 20th august 1683 to 31st August 1685, WO5/1
> Volume II, 31st August 1685 to 23rd July 1687, WO5/2
> Volume 3, 1st August 1687 to 6th November 1688, WO5/3
> Volume 4, 17th November 1688 to 10th December 1688, WO5/4
> Volume 5, 14th December 1688 to 28th February 1690, WO5/5

Roseweare, V. A., *Notes on the Hospital on Hounslow Heath During the Reign of James II*. Unpublished typescript, undated, in the Local Collection of Richmond Town Library

Scott, Christopher L., *Military Effectiveness of the West Country Militia at the Time of the Monmouth Rebellion*, unpublished PhD Thesis, Cranfield University 2011

State Papers, Domestic, Entry Books. National Archives, Kew
> Entry Book 164, SP 44/164
> Entry Book 165, SP 44/165

Sumner, Percy, *Notebook, 1665–1759*. Manuscript, National Army Museum London.

Published Sources

Anon, *The Prospect of the Royal Army Encamped on Hounslow Heath, London*. Undated but probably 1687 or 1688.

Anon, *Travels of Cosmo the Third, Grand Duke of Tuscany... etc.* (London, 1821)

Arni, Eric Gruber von, *Hospital Care and the British Standing Army, 1660–1714* (Aldershot: Ashgate, 2006)

Ashley, Maurice, *The Glorious Revolution of 1688* (London: Hodder & Stoughton, 1966)

Atkinson, C. T., 'Two Hundred and Fifty Years Ago', in *Journal of the Society for Army Historical Research*, Vol. XIV (1935)

Barnett, Correlli, *Britain And Her Army: A Military and Social History of the British Army, 1509–1970* (London: Allen Lane, 1970)

Barrington, *Michael Grahame of Claverhouse, Viscount Dundee* (London: Martin Secker, 1911)

Barthorp, Michael, *The Armies of Britain, 1485–1980* (London: National Army Museum, 1981)

Barthorp, Michael, *British Infantry Uniforms Since 1660* (Poole: Blandford Press, 1982)

Barthorp, Michael, *British Cavalry Uniforms Since 1660* (Blandford: Poole, 1984)

Beckett, J. C., 'The Irish Armed Forces, 1660–1685', in John Bossy, *Essays Presented to Michael Roberts* (Belfast: Blackstaff Press, 1976), pp. 41–53

Bill, John, *An Abridgement of English Military Discipline* (London, 1685)

Bill, John, *Rules and Articles for the Better Government of His Majesties Land Forces in Pay During this Present Rebellion* (London, 1685)

Blackmore, David, *Destructive and Formidable: British Infantry Firepower 1642–1675* (London: Frontline Books, 2014)

Brooks, Nathan, *A General and Complete List Military of Every Commission Officer of Horse and Foot now commanding in His Majesty's Land Forces of England*, London 1684. A copy of this publication is bound with British Museum Add MSS 10123 as ff. 29–40

Calendar of State Papers, Domestic Series, James II, Volume II, May 1 1684–February 5 1685 (London: HMSO, 1964)

Calendar of State Papers, Domestic Series, James II, Volume II, January 1686–May 1687 (London: HMSO, 1964)

Calendar of State Papers, Domestic Series, James II, Volume III, June 1687–February 1689 (London: HMSO, 1972)

Calendar of State Papers, Ireland, 1660–1662 (London: HMSO, 1905)

Callow, John, *James II: The Formative Years of a Fallen King* (Stroud: Sutton, 2000)

Callow, John, *James II: The Triumph and the Tragedy* (Kew: National Archives, 2005)

Cannon, Richard, *Historical Record of the Fourth, or the King's Own, Regiment of Foot* (London: Longman, Orme and Co., 1839)

Cannon, Richard, *Historical Record of the Fifth, or Princess Charlotte of Wales's Regiment of Dragoon Guards* (London: Longman, Orme, 1831)

Cannon, Richard, *Historical Record of the Sixth Regiment of Dragoon Guards, or the Carabineers* (London: Longman, 1839)

Cannon, Richard, *Historical Record of the Seventh Dragoon Guards* (London: Longman, Orme, 1839)

Cannon, Richard, *Historical Record of the Eleventh, or the North Devon, Regiment of Foot* (London: Parker, Furnivall and Parker, 1845)

Cannon, Richard, *Historical Records of the Third Light Dragoons* (London: Parker, Furnivall, & Parker, 1847)

Cannon, Richard, *Historical Records of the Tenth, or the North Lincolnshire, Regiment of Foot* (London: Parker, Furnivall and Parker, 1847)

Cannon, Richard, *Historical Records of the Twelfth, or the East Suffolk, Regiment of Foot* (London: Parker, Furnivall and Parker, 1848)

Cannon, Richard, *Historical Records of the Fifteenth, or the Yorkshire East Riding, Regiment of Foot* (London: Parker, Furnivall and Parker, 1848)

Cannon, Richard, *Historical Records of the Nineteenth, or the First Yorkshire North Riding, Regiment of Foot* (London: Parker, Furnivall and Parker, 1848)

Carman, William, *British Military Uniforms from Contemporary Pictures* (Feltham: Spring Books, 1967)

Carman, William, and Simkins, Richard, *Uniforms of the British Army: the Cavalry Regiments* (Exeter: Webb and Bower, 1982)

Carman, William, and Simkins, Richard, *Uniforms of the British Army: the Infantry Regiments* (Exeter: Webb and Bower, 1985)

Carman, William, 'Frances Hawley, First Regiment of Foot Guards 1685', in *Journal of the Society for Army Historical Research*, Vol. LXIII (1985)

Carman, William, 'The Train of Artillery in the Monmouth Rebellion', in Journal of the Society for Army Historical Research, volume LXVI (1988).

Chandler, David, *Sedgemoor 1685: An Account and Anthology* (London: A. Mott, 1985)

Childs, John, 'Monmouth and the Army in Flanders', in *Journal of the Society for Army Historical Research*, Vol. LII (1974)

Childs, John, *The Army of Charles II* (London: Routledge, 1976)

Childs, John, *The Army, James II and the Glorious Revolution* (Manchester: Manchester University Press, 1980)

Childs, John, *Nobles, Gentlemen and the Profession of Arms in Restoration Britain 1660–1688*, SAHR Special Publication No.13, London 1987

Childs, John, *The British Army of William III, 1689–1702* (Manchester: Manchester University Press, 1987)

Childs, John, *General Percy Kirke and the Later Stuart Army* (London & New York: Bloomsbury, 2014)

Clendenin, P. D., 'Two Early Pipers', in *Bulletin of the British Model Soldier Society*, December 1950 (London, 1950)

Croom, George, *The royal encampment of His Majesties forces on Hounslow Heath* (London, 1686)

Dalton, Charles, *English Army Lists and Commission Registers 1661–1714* (London: Francis Edwards, 1892–4)

Dalton, Charles, *Irish Army Lists 1661–1685* (London: private circulation, 1907)

Dalton, Charles, *The Scots Army, 1661–1688* (London: Eyre & Spottiswoode, 1909)

Davies, Godfrey (ed.), 'Letters on the Administration of James II's Army', in *Journal of the Society for Army Historical Research*, Vol. XXIV (London, 1946), pp. 69–84

Dawnay, Major N. P., *The Distinction of Rank of Regimental Officers 1684 to 1855*. Society for Army Historical Research Special Publication No. 7, London 1960

Dawnay, Nicholas, *The Standards, Guidons and Colours of the Household Division, 1660–1973* (Tunbridge Wells: Midas Books, 1975)

Earle, Peter, *The Life and Times of James II* (London: Weidenfeld and Nicolson, 1972)

Earle, Peter, *Monmouth's Rebels: the Road to Sedgemoor 1685* (London: Weidenfeld and Nicolson, 1977)

Ede-Borrett, Stephen, *The Army of James II: Uniforms and Organisation* (Leeds: Raider Games, 1986)

Ede-Borrett, Stephen, 'Drums for the Duke of Norfolk's Regiment', in *Journal of the Society for Army Historical Research*, Vol. LXIX (London, 1991), p. 137

Ede-Borrett, Stephen, 'The de Velde Drawing at the National Army Museum', in *Arquebusier: Journal of the Pike & Shot Society*, vol. VIII, No. 1 (Farnham, 2004), pp. 2–10

Ede-Borrett, Stephen, 'A Captain of the Earl of Bath's Regiment', in *Journal of the Society for Army Historical Research*, Vol. 88 (London, 2010), pp. 1–4

Evelyn, John, *Diary and Memoirs,* William Bray, ed. (London, 1818)

Field, C., 'Uniform of a Grenadier Officer in the Army of James II', in *Journal of the Society for Army Historical Research*, vol. X (2010) (London, 1935), pp. 64–65

Fortescue, J. W., *A History of the British Army* (London: Macmillan, 1910–1930, 13 vols.)

Fosten, Bryan, 'British Army Uniforms 1660–1900, 2nd & 3rd Foot Guards 1685', in *Airfix Magazine*, June 1974 (London, 1974)

Fosten, Don, '2nd Regiment of Foot, The Queen's Regiment, c.1686', in *Tradition Magazine Number Thirty-Four* (London, 1969)

Grose, Francis & Astle, Thomas (compilers), *The Antiquarian Repertory*, Volume 1 (London, 1807)

Guy, Alan and Spencer-Smith, Jenny (eds.), *1688 Glorious Revolution? The Fall and Rise of the British Army 1660–1704* (London: National Army Museum, 1988)

Haswell, Jock, *James II: Soldier and Sailor* (London: Hamilton, 1972)

Hodge, Alan, *The Battle of Sedgemoor; Souvenir Programme for the Sealed Knot Ltd's re-enactment of 1975.*

Lawson, Cecil C. P., *A History of the Uniforms of the British Army. Vol. 1, From the Beginnings to 1760* (London: Norman Military Publications, 1940)

Leslie, N. B., *The Succession of Colonels of the British Army from 1660 to the Present Day.* Society for Army Historical Research Special Number 11

London Gazette. Various Issues, London 1685 to 1688

Lyndon, Brian, 'Military Dress and Uniformity, 1680–1720', in *Journal of the Society for Army Historical Research*, Vol. LIV (London, 1976), pp. 108–120

MacKinnon, *Daniel, Origin and Services of the Coldstream Guards* (London: Richard Bentley, 1833)

Manning, Roger B., *An Apprenticeship in Arms: The Origins of the British Army 1585–1702* (Oxford: Oxford University Press, 2006)

Maxwell-Lyte, Sir H. C., *A History of Dunster and of the Families of Mohun and Luttrell* (London: St Catherine Press, 1909)

Miller, John, *James II : A Study in Kingship* (Hove: Wayland Publishers, 1979)

Milne, Samuel Milne, *The Standards and Colours of the Army From the Restoration to … 1881* (Leeds: Goodall and Suddick, 1893)

Murphy, John A., *Justin MacCarthy, Lord Mountcashel* (Cork: Cork University Press, 1959)

Murtagh, Diarmuid & Harman, 'The Irish Jacobite Army 1689–91', in *The War of The Kings: The Irish Sword Commemorative Issue*, Winter 1990 (Dublin, Eire, 1990), pp. 32–48

Oldmixon, John, *History of England during the Reigns of the House of Stuart* (London, 1730)

Parry, Sir Edward, *The Bloody Assize* (London: Benn, 1929)

Pollard, Tony, and Oliver, Neil, *Two Men in a Trench II: Uncovering the Secrets of British Battlefields*, (London: Michael Joseph, 2003)

Robinson, M. S., *Van de Velde Drawings: A Catalogue of drawings in the National Maritime Museum made by the Elder and the Younger Willem van de Velde* (Cambridge: Cambridge University Press for the trustees of the National Army Museum, 1958)

S., Captain J., *Fortification and Military Discipline In Two Parts* (London, 1688)

Sandford, Francis, *A List of the Several Commanders, on the Day of Their Majesties Coronation* (London, 1685)

Scott, Christopher, *The Armies & Uniforms of the Monmouth Rebellion* (Nottingham: Partizan Press, 2008)

Scott, Sir Sibbald, *The British Army: Its Origin, Progress and Equipment* (London: Cassell, 1880)

Scouller, R. E., *The Armies of Queen Anne* (Oxford: Clarendon Press, 1966)

Tincey, John (ed.), *Monmouth's Drill Book: An Abridgement of English Military Discipline* (Leigh on Sea: Partizan Press, 1986)

Tincey, John, *The British Army 1660–1704* (London: Osprey, 1994)

Tincey, John, *Ironsides: English Cavalry 1588-1688* (London: Osprey, 2002)

Tincey, John, *Sedgemoor, 1685: Marlborough's First Victory* (Barnsley: Pen & Sword Military, 2005)

Walton, Clifford, *History of the British Standing Army, A.D. 1660–1700* (London: Harrison, 1894)

Wheeler, Adam, *Iter Bellicosum*, in H. E. Malden (ed.), *Camden Miscellany*, Volume XII, (London: Royal Historical Society, 1910)

Whitworth, R. H. , '1685 – James II, The Army and the Huguenots', in *Journal of the Society for Army Historical Research*, Vol. LXIII (1985)

Winstock, Lewis, *Songs and Music of the Redcoats* (Harrisburg, Pa: publisher unidentified, 1970)

Winstock, Lewis, *Songs and Marches of the Roundheads and Cavaliers* (London: Leo Cooper, 1971)

The Troop

For over 20 years The Troop has provided high quality multi-period Cavalry reconstruction from the Roman period to the Great War. During that time, we have performed not only throughout the UK but also further afield at historic locations in Europe, the Crimea and Africa.

Underlying our work, is a love of history and of bringing to the public the stories of the riders and horses who comprised that most colourful and evocative of military forces – the Cavalry.

For more images and contact details please see www.thetroop.org.

Restoration period Kings Lifeguards at Festival of History Kelmarsh Hall 2014. Photo by and thanks to Stephen Moss @photosm